AGAINST AU

Since Mill's seminal work *On Liberty*, p........
theorists have accepted that we should respect the decisions oɪ ɪɪɪ..
vidual agents when those decisions affect no one other than themselves. Indeed, to respect autonomy is often understood to be the chief
way to bear witness to the intrinsic value of persons. In this book,
Sarah Conly rejects the idea of autonomy as inviolable. Drawing
on sources from behavioral economics and social psychology, she
argues that we are so often irrational in making our decisions that
our autonomous choices often undercut the achievement of our own
goals. Thus in many cases, it would advance our goals more effectively
if government were to prevent us from acting in accordance with our
decisions. Her argument challenges widely held views of moral
agency, democratic values, and the public/private distinction, and
will interest readers in ethics, political philosophy, political theory,
and philosophy of law.

SARAH CONLY is Assistant Professor of Philosophy at Bowdoin
College, Brunswick, Maine.

AGAINST AUTONOMY

Justifying coercive paternalism

BY SARAH CONLY

CAMBRIDGE
UNIVERSITY PRESS

CAMBRIDGE
UNIVERSITY PRESS

University Printing House, Cambridge CB2 8BS, United Kingdom

Published in the United States of America by Cambridge University Press, New York

Cambridge University Press is part of the University of Cambridge.

It furthers the University's mission by disseminating knowledge in the pursuit of education, learning and research at the highest international levels of excellence.

www.cambridge.org
Information on this title: www.cambridge.org/9781107649729

First published 2013
Third printing 2013
First paperback edition 2014

A catalogue record for this publication is available from the British Library

Library of Congress Cataloguing in Publication data
Conly, Sarah, author.
Against autonomy : justifying coercive paternalism / Sarah Conly.
pages cm
ISBN 978-1-107-02484-7 (Hardback)
1. Decision making – Political aspects. 2. Decision making – Philosophy.
3. Paternalism. 4. Autonomy (Philosophy) 5. Choice (Psychology) I. Title.
JA71.C575 2012
320.01–dc23

ISBN 978-1-107-02484-7 Hardback
ISBN 978-1-107-64972-9 Paperback

And certainly, the mistakes we male and female mortals make when we have our own way might fairly raise some wonder why we are so fond of it.

George Eliot, Middlemarch
(Dirigo Publishing, 1898), Part 1, chapter 9, page 74

Contents

Acknowledgements

I would like to thank the Harvard University Safra Center for Ethics for its support during my fellowship year, 2006/7, when I began the research for this book; and also the University of St. Andrews Centre for Ethics, Philosophy, and Public Affairs for its support during 2010. I am indebted to faculty and fellows at both institutions for their discussions of the issues discussed in this book. I would like to thank Bowdoin College for sabbatical support during 2010/11, without which this book could not have been written. In a more personal sense, I would like to thank Corey Brettschneider, Martha Nussbaum, and Charlotte Witt for their invaluable encouragement. I doubt that any of them agrees with the content of this book, but they were willing to help me despite that fact, and I appreciate it.

Introduction: The argument

We are too fat, we are too much in debt, and we save too little for the future. This is no news – it is something that Americans hear almost every day. The question is what can be done about it. The most common answer is that, first, we should exhort ourselves to be better: we should remind one another that eating too much of the wrong thing will make our lives shorter and more painful; should write admonitory op eds about how our failure to save will cost us individually and as a society; should, generally, tell ourselves things that by and large we already know. Second, we should simply exert more willpower to make ourselves do what we have been persuaded is right. The trouble with these two strategies, and generally with attempts to bring about change through education and persuasion, is that they aren't very effective. In this book I recommend that we turn to a better approach, which is simply to save people from themselves by making certain courses of action illegal. We should, for example, ban cigarettes; ban trans-fats; require restaurants to reduce portion sizes to less elephantine dimensions; increase required savings, and control how much debt individuals can run up.

This is not a popular view. It is said that to control people's choices in such ways fails to respect their autonomy, because we interfere with their ability to direct their lives according to their own reasoning. If some people choose poorly, that is unfortunate for them, but it is their own responsibility, and interfering, even with the most benevolent intent and the most beneficent effect, ignores that these are rational agents who have the right to make their own choices. I argue that, in fact, autonomy is not all that valuable; not valuable enough to offset what we lose by leaving people to their own autonomous choices. The truth is that we don't reason very well, and in many cases there is no justification for leaving us to struggle with our own inabilities and to suffer the consequences. Those who say we should respect autonomy by letting people hurt themselves irreparably do not, on my view, show as much respect for human value as they purport to. The common rationale for letting people choose poorly is that autonomy requires that people suffer the results of their own actions, for good or ill, but here respect becomes a justification for inhumanity: the principle that those who fail deserve to fail isn't one that is geared to support equality and mutual respect. What we need to do is to help one another avoid mistakes so that we may all end up where we want to be.

Writers since de Tocqueville have argued that the value we hold most dear is our liberty. In today's language, he might say we value our autonomy, our ability to order our lives according to our decisions. That we should respect autonomy is taken as obvious – it is taken to be the only way to manifest our belief that all people have intrinsic value. While we may interfere with people when they harm others – when they interfere with others' autonomy by imposing actions on them that they don't want – we are held, for the most part, to be morally bound to allow people to choose when it comes to determining how they themselves want to live. These claims, I hold, are false. Whether or not we actually care about autonomy as much as some political thinkers believe is open to question; however, if it is true that autonomy is what we hold most dear, it should not be, at least in the way that this is generally interpreted. In this book I argue that the ground for valuing liberty is the claim that we are pre-eminently rational agents, each of us well suited to determining what goes in our own life. There is ample evidence, however, from the fields of psychology and behavioral economics, that in many situations this is simply not true. The incidence of irrationality is much higher than our Enlightenment tradition has given us to believe, and keeps us from making the decisions we need to reach our goals. The ground for respecting autonomy is shaky.

However, psychologists and behavioral economists, while drawing attention to the nature of our cognitive deficits, have hesitated to draw conclusions from this that would radically alter the way we design government. It may be that they just don't see normative suggestions as their job; or, they may fear that such suggestions would justify governments that aren't democratic, that take the power of self-governance entirely away. Such a fear, though, is misguided. The existence of cognitive deficits does suggest a need for different sorts of legislation, but there is nothing in the existence of widely shared weaknesses in reasoning to suggest that one group should have power over others. These cognitive deficits are a general human phenomenon, not the peculiar property of one kind of person, so there is nothing to justify giving one group power over others on an autocratic basis. What we need is a democratically elected government, but one in which the government is allowed to pass legislation that protects citizens from themselves, just as we now allow legislation to protect us from others. I argue for the justifiability of coercive paternalism, for laws that force people to do what is good for them.

This book, thus, supports the use of coercion in what we normally think of as people's personal lives. This is something, I argue, that we are familiar with and which we often accept. If the person next to me is about to swallow a gulp of anti-freeze in the belief that it is an anti-freeze-colored sports drink, I will intervene. If I tell him it is anti-freeze, and he refuses to believe me, I will still intervene. If I have to grab his arm and pull it away from his mouth I will do that, even though his first reaction is likely to be one of indignation. The thesis of this book is that situations abound which are, in essence, the same. We should save people from doing things that are gravely bad for them when they do that only as a result of an error in thinking. Rather than suggest that individuals roam the planet interfering with each other's lives in a chaotic and inefficient fashion, however, I argue that the government should intervene in cases of obvious harm and should prevent certain actions from being taken. I argue for paternalistic laws, and more specifically, paternalism of the sort that forces people to act, or refrain from acting, according to their best interests.

Ideally, of course, the best way to save people from the results of error would simply be to inform them of their mistakes. When it comes to drinking anti-freeze, this might work: if we had time, we could convince the other person that it is really anti-freeze, not Gatorade, and the drinker would put the glass down. In other situations, though, the solution is not so simple. Not all cognitive errors can be mended by convincing people of the relevant facts. If we were perfectly rational then this might be effective, but part of the argument of this book is that we are not perfectly rational, and given this, the methods that would be effective for those clear-eyed, clear-thinking individuals we sometimes imagine ourselves to be won't actually work for us. Sometimes no amount of public education can get someone to realize, in a sufficiently vivid sense, the potential dangers of his course of behavior. If public education were effective, we would have no new smokers, but we do.

Some people will accept that education itself is often not sufficient to change people's behavior, but will argue that the best course of action is not coercion but a milder form of paternalism. We can provide incentives for not smoking, for example, by having better insurance rates for those who don't smoke, and provide disincentives by making cigarettes really expensive. There is no doubt that this has some effect. We see, though, that once again it doesn't have enough effect – the present rate of smoking among adults in the US is about 20 percent. That could be worse, but it could also be much better. Even though it's a good bet that the majority of those who smoke wish they didn't, incentivizing good actions, and discouraging bad ones, just isn't effective enough. Smokers typically wish they hadn't started, but the only way to have stopped them would be something we don't now embrace – coercive paternalism, where people are forced to do the right thing, or, in this case, prevented from doing the wrong one. Sometimes the only way to stop someone from making a terrible mistake is to intervene and prevent him from choosing freely.

As I say, this is an idea that is in some contexts very familiar. Letting the friend drink the anti-freeze on the grounds that, after all, it was his decision and it would be disrespectful to intervene with the judgment of a competent adult, strikes any sane person as a piece of gratuitous cruelty. It is not respectful of the value of humans to let one proceed in an error that will cost him his life. This case is easy, because we know the person in question suffers from simple ignorance – if we have time to convince him that the drink is anti-freeze, he would put it down. He wouldn't want it once he accepts the facts. Other cases are more complicated but also yield the conclusion that interference is justified. We accept the fact of prescription medicines, even though a person could presumably take the time to do research on whatever drug he contemplates taking. Prescriptions aren't required because the need for medication arises only in emergency situations where we have no time to apprise citizens of the facts. Rather, we seem to think that medicine is complicated and that most people don't have the expertise to decide on their own medication, even if, indeed, they read lots on the Internet about their own symptoms and the medicine they think may cure it. They can't really understand the facts they are presented with. Thus, we require that you meet with an expert and get his imprimatur before you have access to what you want.

These cases are relatively uncontroversial. The question is how, and whether, the reasoning that justifies our acceptance of paternalism in these cases can be extended to other situations where at present we do not accept paternalism, especially not in the form of government restrictions. The thrust of most thinkers on paternalism has been how to stop the extension of paternalism, how to find a cut-off line that clearly shows when paternalism is, and when it is not, acceptable, and furthermore a cut-off line that firmly keeps paternalism out of all but a very few decisions. Most people accept that it is implausible that we should do without paternalism entirely, but also fear a world in which too many of our actions are restricted on a paternalistic basis. Joel Feinberg, in his highly regarded *Harm to Self*, argued that paternalism is permissible when an action is involuntary, but not when it is voluntary, but describes involuntary actions in a way that makes many acts we normally would call voluntary, involuntary – including those where the actors are quite willing to perform the act in question but are perhaps not thinking very clearly. Others have argued that the dividing line should be between those who are mentally competent and those who are not, but once again this proves to be less than an entirely clear division – surely some of us who are generally competent have, at times, thought in just those ways that are typical of the incompetent. Others accept paternalism, whatever the state of the agent, if the harm that will come from his action is sufficiently great and sufficiently immediate – thus, we see widespread acceptance of seat belt laws, even for adults who are sober, rational, competent, and so on, because they so clearly prevent great harms in circumstances where there is no other way to stave off the damage that will otherwise ensue. Yet, it is not clear why other harms, equally severe but following less immediately on the dangerous act (like eventual cancer from the ingestion of carcinogens) shouldn't rate paternalistic intervention equally. And, it is hard to isolate what exact degree of harm is required to justify the paternalistic intervention – should it only be the prospect of death that allows us to intervene? Brain damage? Paralysis? Typically, those who allow paternalistic intervention in cases like seat belts or motorcycle helmets don't provide even a general theory of what the cut-off line should be, yet continue to think there should be a cut-off line that limits intervention to a very few cases.

There have been similar efforts, and similar difficulties, in differentiating between so-called "hard" paternalism and "soft" paternalism. This is actually a twofold distinction (or, attempt at a distinction). The terms "hard" and "soft" may differentiate between the methods used to induce paternalistic actions, where hard paternalism, like the one I promote here, advocates making some actions impossible, and soft paternalism merely recommends incentivizing certain preferable options, as discussed above. Or, the terms may be used to differentiate the content of the actions the paternalist promotes – the soft paternalist merely imposes what the agent would want if informed, while the hard paternalist may impose actions the agent would not want even if aware of the facts. Those who try to discover distinctions between the justification of more and less intrusive methods of interference, and those who try to distinguish between what an agent would want if informed versus what he would not want even if informed, generally have a hard time in delimiting which actions belong to one category and which to the other. If it is all right to disincentivize smoking by making it prohibitively expensive – thus effectively preventing people from smoking because they can't afford it – why is it wrong to simply make it illegal, when both have the same net effect? The former is thought of as a "soft" method, and thus relatively unobjectionable, and the latter as a "hard" method, and thus disrespectful of autonomy; but defending the permissibility of the first against the impermissibility of the second proves to be difficult.

The same is true for differentiating hard and soft forms of paternalism when this designates the difference between forcing people to do what they would want to do, if informed, and forcing them to do what they would not want to do, even if they were informed. The difference between being informed and not being informed proves hard to tie down, as we will see in Chapter 1. Are you informed if the bare facts are laid before you? Or do you not count as informed unless you somehow "appreciate" those facts? One justification for motorcycle helmet laws is that people would want helmets if they were properly informed about the danger of riding without them, yet many who choose not to use them are quite aware that it increases their risk of grave injury. The argument for nonetheless imposing their use is that such people just don't really appreciate the dangers – they don't fully grasp how likely an injury is, or don't vividly imagine what their life will be like following such an injury. They are in the colloquially familiar place where they "sort of know" the relevant facts. It's a familiar area because we live most of our lives there. What, then, counts as being informed? This is needed to justify a moral distinction between hard and soft paternalism in this second sense, and yet a neutral account of what it means to be informed is unavailable. A clear dividing line is hard to find.

I think it is hard to defend cut-off points in these cases because no such natural division exists. There is no identifiable point at which we go from being purely rational thinkers to completely irrational ones, or from acting entirely involuntarily to acting voluntarily. There is no clear distinction between disincentivizing an action and simply making it impossible to perform. There is no consensus on what it means to be informed, because there are differences of degree, rather than kind, between many states of being informed and many states of ignorance. Rather than trying to demarcate a (typically very small) area in which paternalism is permitted and a large area in which it is not, we should accept that we may often need help. In all these theories, a natural division between permissible and impermissible paternalism is hard to find – because, I will argue, no division exists other than that provided by a cost–benefit analysis. What makes paternalism permissible is not a function of the intrinsic features of the situations as much as how much some interventions costs us, both in terms of psychological burden and social ones. In some cases, paternalistic measures are worth the costs of intervention; in others, they are not, and that is the only determinant of acceptability. When they will give us more than they take away, we should recognize this and accept that it is justified to help people in these situations to avoid costly errors.

In short, paternalism is more often justified than we normally think. We know now that we are intractably irrational, and that this can't be rectified by simple care and introspection. We have already revised our view of human agency, following Marx, Freud, and the philosophical insights of feminism. What we see now, in light of contemporary psychology and behavioral economics, is that some further revision is necessary. This is not the end of the world, because it doesn't augur a general change in how we actually think in specific contexts. It recommends a recognition of the ways in which we actually think, and a response to that in the way we help one another through certain sorts of decisions. To the extent that there are disadvantages to paternalism, these lie in its side effects: the danger that there will be unintended drawbacks to its implementation. These dangers, though, while real, are typically overstated. All systems of law are capable of misuse if we are not careful about the circumstances of their administration and attentive to the content of specific regulations. Historically, we have discovered that the benefits are worth the costs, including the costs we must incur to apply laws effectively, and the costs that accrue on those occasions when we fail to take sufficient care in the justice and the efficacy of their implementation. The same is true of paternalistic laws: making good paternalistic laws is work, and when we fail this will do harm – but on the whole they will aid us far more than they hurt us.

OUTLINE OF CHAPTERS

In the chapter that follows I review the by now well-known evidence of our own irrationality in making decisions, and argue that the most plausible response to this new information is the greater acceptability of coercive paternalism. I look at the two most popular alternatives to coercive paternalism, which both leave us with our present level of personal liberty: liberalism, generally our present system, where we rely on education to improve people's decision making; and libertarian paternalism, where we leave people the liberties they now have but try to "nudge" or manipulate them in unconscious ways into making the decisions that are most beneficial. Liberalism is the view expressed by the practices we are most familiar with – it is typically expressed as a view that people should be left to make their own decisions unimpeded by interference. The role of government, to the extent it has one, is to try to guarantee freedom of action, to eliminate disinformation, and, in some cases, provide helpful information. Thus, we are allowed to smoke if we want, but cigarette companies should not be able to deceive us about the dangers of smoking, and the government will positively try to educate us about its dangers. This, I will argue, has been shown to be an ineffective way of helping people make good decisions – it's what has allowed the United States to be a nation of unhealthy and indebted citizens, despite the resources at its command.

An alternative, libertarian paternalism, has been effectively championed by Cass Sunstein and Richard Thaler, and I discuss their views and the problems that remain once libertarian paternalism has been deployed. Libertarian paternalists recognize our array of cognitive failings, and recommend that we try to affect people's behaviors not simply by rational argumentation, since that is too often ineffective, but by using their own biases to push them into making beneficial choices. Given that we have a tendency to accept the status quo, regardless of its merit, we should, for example, make sure that the status quo option is the best for us where that is possible. The argument of libertarian paternalists is that since they do not eliminate options – that is, people still have the freedom to choose badly – they respect autonomy; at the same time, given the nudges introduced into the choice situations, they are more likely to choose the beneficial outcome. I argue that insofar as libertarian paternalism is manipulative, it fails to capture the intuition that we should respect people's capacity to make rational choices; at the same time, it fails to give us the results that we want, because people can still have the options to pursue bad courses of action – they can still smoke, or run up intractable debt, or fail to save any money. It gives us, in a sense, the worst of both worlds.

Coercive paternalism, on the other hand, simply takes certain options away. This does not respect people's ability to choose well for themselves, since the coercive paternalist thinks that in many cases there is no such ability. On the other hand, it does result in beneficial outcomes. With coercive paternalism, for example, smoking would simply be illegal. Since so many choose poorly, that is, choose to smoke even when they are nudged in the opposite direction, the best thing to do is simply to take that option away. I argue that while coercive paternalism does posit a different view of human rationality than that upon which we normally like to congratulate ourselves, this is not disrespectful. It is not disrespectful to accurately estimate someone's abilities, and to respond to those appropriately. If anything, coercive paternalism manifests respect for the value of human lives by trying to help people live fruitful lives in which they are able to achieve their own ultimate goals.

In Chapters 2 and 3 I look at the argument that paternalism, however beneficial in particular instances, will inevitably have long-term psychological costs. In Chapter 2 I discuss John Stuart Mill's much respected argument that paternalistic legislation will inevitably undercut individuality. In *On Liberty* Mill famously argued that paternalistic laws would allow a monolithic and conservative society to impose its mores on everyone in that society, with the result that there would be no variation in human character or in human values. With this uniformity, we would decline, as a society, into enervated decadence, and as individuals would find ourselves unable to experience more than the most tepid satisfaction in anything.

I argue that Mill failed to adequately reckon with human psychology, as we now know it to be. While Mill thought that without an oppressive society to drum us into submission we would develop in genuine and distinctive ways, the truth is that we have a natural, even biological, tendency towards social conformity. We want to agree with other people, and we want to be like other people, even if other people do nothing to foist their values upon us. We may, in fact, need positive help to overcome our own tendencies to conform, and to fight our desire to accept the opinions of other people without regard for their truth. Furthermore, Mill overestimated the degree to which we would, if left to our own devices, actively and effectively pursue our own happiness. Mill assumes that if someone is unhappy, and free to change his ways, he will do what he needs to in order to improve his situation. He doesn't take into consideration a number of things: one, of course, is the poor instrumental reasoning discussed in Chapter 1. Further, he underestimates the power of inertia and the resistance people have to recognizing that a particular course of action that they are engaged in actually is making them worse off. Left to our own devices, free of pressure to do otherwise, we often continue to dig ourselves into a deeper and deeper pit, wondering the while why we haven't yet succeeded in getting out.

Since we do better at estimating efficacy when we are in a relatively objective position, government, insofar as those in it are not the ones who are at present tempted by the rewards of the poor decision, can intervene in ways that help us reach our own, individual goals better than we would do if left to our own devices. It can help to free us of the conformity of social opinion. One case in which government aids in the development of individuality is in education, where we are forced to learn critical skills, as well as facts that may be at variance with the beliefs of a closed, conservative community. Government legislation can, furthermore, shake us from our entrenched and destructive ways of living, changing traditions that are unhealthy and leading us to practices that make us better off even according to our own lights. Lastly, I argue that help of this sort will not, as has been suggested, result in infantilization, a disproportionate reliance on others to make our decisions for us that prevents us from developing our own critical skills. On the contrary, as Aristotle recognized, the more we make good decisions, even guided by others, the better we get at making good decisions. We will become better at choosing wisely with the help of paternalistic legislation.

In Chapter 3 I look at another possible area of psychological loss: the dangers of alienation and inauthenticity. Even if government legislation is intended to make us better in every way, it is possible that the accretion of even positive steps will leave us feeling the victims of too much control. It may not matter what the rules are, if simply having too many rules is bad for us. Some social critics fear that this is likely to result in either of two things: a sense of alienation, where we feel that we are no longer in control of our lives and resent that, becoming alienated from government and indeed all of society; or, perhaps worse, inauthenticity, where we enthusiastically accept government control only because we can no longer discern what we, individually, actually want. Both of these are bad, in their distinctive ways, and may furthermore result in what Mill feared – a loss of affect, an inability to feel anything very deeply.

I argue that while these are popularly imagined responses to totalitarianism, nothing in paternalism predicts totalitarianism. Paternalism is intended, by definition, to benefit those who are subject to it, and one relevant factor is obviously the psychological response to rules. The adoption of paternalism will require that we undertake a cost–benefit analysis as to whether or not it is worth interfering in people's behavior, and one major element of cost is the feelings of those who are imposed upon.

That said, it is obviously true that paternalistic regulation will regulate. Certain paths will be closed. However, this in itself does not threaten to produce either alienation or inauthenticity. For one thing, it is always the case that some paths are closed. We often can't pursue the careers we want, either because we haven't got the native ability or because of more accidental features, such as where we live or how much money we have for the requisite training. We can't always marry the person we want. Often we can't have the families we want. These are all serious issues, and yet we accept that we are constrained. Indeed, such acceptance is taken as a sign of maturity, rather than the first step towards inauthenticity. Circumstances, including social circumstances, always constrain our actions.

It is also true that in some cases being denied choices may be liberating. Some critics do not seem to realize that not all choices are equally valuable, and being released from choices we don't really want to be making is a relief. It is not that it is a relief because it frees us from the general necessity of having to make decisions, as some fear. Rather, government intervention allows us to focus our decision making on the decisions we actually care about. I don't want to assess all the food additives that are out there and then choose which are to be avoided. I'd rather someone else did that, thereby leaving me to use my decision-making talents on things in which I'm interested. I want to be healthy, of course, but that doesn't mean that I find all the decisions requisite to good health intrinsically rewarding. If someone else can decide what foodstuffs to make legal, what cars are unsafe, and so on, that leaves me free to pursue things I care about. In this sense, removing options leaves us free to pursue other options, and the psychological effect of this is good, rather than destructive. On the whole, then, paternalism has a beneficial psychological effect.

In Chapters 4 and 5 I look at the political dangers to be found in paternalistic systems. Many people argue that even if there is a *prima facie* case for paternalism, it is simply too dangerous a system. They fear that once we allow laws to regulate individual behavior without needing to justify those by showing that these behaviors harm third parties, all hell will break loose. In Chapter 4, "Misuse and Abuse: Perfectionism and Preferences," I examine the argument that paternalism allows those in control to impose values antithetical to those of private citizens. Some imagine a world in which paternalism is allowed as a totalitarian nightmare, where we are forced to live lives we hate because the paternalist believes they are somehow good for us. This might arise in either of two ways: first, the paternalist may correctly see what it is that we want but decide that our desires should not be respected because there is a different sort of life the paternalist believes to be more valuable. I argue, though, that the only reasonable form paternalism is one that helps people act according to their own values, rather than imposing foreign values upon them. I will argue that objective views about welfare – that regardless of what we ourselves want, some ways of living are better than others – are implausible in general, and that using them as a guide for governance is both implausible and impractical. Rather, paternalist regulations are designed to help us reach our own goals.

Secondly, even if the paternalist does want to promote the fulfilment of our own desires, this could prove problematic. It requires, first, that people actually have goals, and, second, that people who make regulations, who are themselves as subject to cognitive bias as the rest of the population, be able to ascertain what it is we want and make regulations that can successfully advance those. I argue that, despite some claims to the contrary, we do have some determinate ends – ends that are not variable with the biases that may influence our choices about means to our ends. Further, while those who do the choosing are indeed subject to bias, we know that we are better in some situations more than in others at avoiding error, and we have reason to believe that those making regulations for other people can avoid many of the errors we make when faced with a choice that affects us personally.

In Chapter 5, "Misuse and Abuse: Punishment and Privacy," I discuss two problems that may arise when we implement paternalist regulations, no matter how well conceived. First, we know that to be effective, regulations generally require sanctions. Since paternalist regulations will generally increase the number of sanctions we are subject to, it looks as if we inevitably will be punished for more things than we now are. Obviously, we don't like being punished, and particularly resent it when we have done something that doesn't hurt anyone else; indeed, if we have hurt ourselves then being punished on top of that seems cruel. Second, there is again a reasonable fear that paternalism, insofar as it tries to bring about improvements in our personal lives, will require an unacceptable invasion of our privacy.

These are both reasonable concerns. However, all good paternalistic policies include a consideration of costs as well as benefits. Even if a policy might, in different circumstances, be beneficial, it shouldn't be adopted if we are not in those circumstances. If a law would really drive people crazy, it's not worth having, even if it would be really beneficial if people didn't mind it so. One of the costs any paternalist needs to consider is the cost of sanctions themselves. One cost is institutional – enforcement – but another is the cost to the individual. If we are to be punished when we don't comply, punishment obviously imposes a psychological cost – people don't like it.

Given this, in many cases the best approach to achieving compliance will not be punishing individuals who fail to meet paternalistic regulations, but designing institutions that make failure difficult or impossible. For example, instead of punishing individuals who smoke, we can make cigarettes unavailable by not allowing their production. Obviously this still involves the threat of punishment – of companies that would try to produce cigarettes despite their illegality – but the burden of punishment is institutional rather than individual. This "impure paternalism," as Gerald Dworkin has called it, is in many cases both more effective in preventing a practice and less costly in its implementation.

That said, there will be attention paid to the behavior of individuals, and a second fear is that paternalism will result in an unacceptable loss of privacy. Not only is there less privacy in the sense of there being less control, overall, but more specifically there will be less informational privacy. If you are going to be prevented from running up excessive debt, this requires that someone, somewhere, knows how much debt you are running up. In a literal sense such things might be handled by computers rather than a conscious being, but the information would be out there, and subject to others' attention. More of your life will be kept track of than it be would under a libertarian system. If we take psychological burdens seriously, some will argue, this in itself will be so burdensome that paternalistic legislation will have trouble getting off the ground.

I think this is interesting. I think it is interesting because while many people worry about the costs of losing informational privacy, almost no one actually seems to feel this cost. While some people are under the impression that the twenty-first century is uniquely public, both in that the Internet allows information about you to be gathered without you knowing it and in the sense that many of us broadcast details about our personal lives to hundreds of Internet and Twitter "friends," the truth is that we evolved in circumstances where privacy was impossible. We are a social species. This may be why people are not generally concerned about the fact that so much is known about us, and why we are so eager to share our moods, sleep difficulties, likes and dislikes, schedules, and passing thoughts with people with whom we are barely acquainted. We do not like it, of course, if this information is used to our disadvantage. We are used to sharing health information with our doctor, but of course are justly resentful if our insurance company uses that information to expel us. Many of those who object, in theory, to the proliferation of personal information are really objecting to this, to the possibility of injury that such information may make possible.

This is a perfectly reasonable fear, but I argue that there is no reason to think that paternalistic intervention will make it worse. The increase of paternalistic laws does not entail, or even suggest, an increase in evil-doers who want to take advantage of the information that may be available. And, paternalist systems are perhaps uniquely able to protect us from the sorts of losses of privacy that occur when we ourselves place information in the public realm that makes us subject to harm – they can stop us form putting certain things out there.

It is possible that there are personal costs that accompany each loss of privacy, even if the specifics of such a loss are diminished as described. If so, these, of course, should be considered. In many cases, though, such costs will be transitory. At one point it may have seemed an outrage that the government should be allowed to know your income or how much your house was worth. Now, however, we take such things for granted. If the government's knowledge actually resulted in benefit to us, instead of higher taxation, I think we would not mind it at all. What we accept as a reasonable dividing line between the public and the private seems to depend on custom and on costs rather than on any intrinsic distinction between what may be known and what should not. The division is likely to change with some instances of paternalistic legislation, but neither the moral nor the psychological costs are prohibitive.

In Chapter 6 I look at possible applications of paternalistic laws. Many of those I discuss relate to health care. This is an obvious area for paternalistic intervention because it is one in which government interference can actually be effective, and because no one wants to be sick or facing premature death. Of course, it is arguable that while we may not want to end up sick, for example, we may want even less to give up our unhealthy foods. This is the sort of issue the paternalist always needs to face: what are people's values? What do they care about most? I will argue that once we have understood our cognitive failings, the argument that we prefer eating unhealthily to being fit is undercut. There is no reason to think that our present choices always correctly represent our values, especially given the subjective costs poor choices in these areas will normally have. I don't think that health care is the only area in which paternalistic policies are applicable, but because paternalistic regulations have been proposed and actually implemented here more than in other areas, they can serve as a model of how such regulations can work.

In Chapter 7 I address the lingering discomfort many people feel with paternalism, despite its efficacy. I argue that while paternalism is helpful in many areas, we need not fear its intrusion into every aspect of personal life. Both friends and foes of paternalism have suggested, for example, that it be might be used to try to bring about personal success in both love and work. Should we have arranged marriages, where knowledgeable psychologists select a mate more likely to suit you than the one you would choose yourself? After all, we all want to have happy marriages, and bad marriages are extremely painful. If they can be prevented, wouldn't this be an improvement? Should people be prevented from pursuing careers for which they have no talent, saving them from a life of frustration? I will argue that neither of these are plausible areas for paternalism: for one thing, we don't know enough about people to predict who will be successful at what. We don't know which two people are a good match – which is why we are confounded both at some romantic successes and some failures. We don't know who has talent for what career: remember the RKO assessment of Fred Astaire – "can't sing, can't act, balding, can dance a little" – and J. K. Rowling's twelve rejection slips. Furthermore, we don't know who may be happy pursuing a career at which they are not outstandingly successful, just for love of the activity. And of course, the costs to those who are held back from their marriage choice or dream job are great. I embrace the hope that there may be, in fact, other applications for paternalistic laws – but when and where these will occur will have to be consonant with a realistic psychological picture of human beings and not based on ideas of what might work if we were creatures different from what we actually are.

Lastly, I will return to our general assessment of paternalism. It is, to be sure, counterintuitive. Not all intuitions are equal, though, and it is the job of philosophy to evaluate which "intuitions" are simply reactions based on familiarity and unfamiliarity, and which rest on well-founded judgments. In the end, while the prospect of coercive paternalism is, initially, startling, I argue that it proves to be the policy that most coheres with our considered judgments.

CHAPTER I

Why value autonomy?

PATERNALISM

We do things that are bad for us – we take risks we soon regret, we thwart our own desires, we undercut our own fulfillment. Should we be stopped?

On the one hand, we value our liberty, and resent being told what to do. On the other, we often regret bitterly the choices that have diminished the quality of our lives, and wish we could do it over and choose better. In such cases, we may well wish we had been stopped, given the costs of our actions. The question I address here is whether society – typically in the form of government legislation – should step in, and make people do what is good for them. I will argue that, in many more cases than we now allow, it should; that preserving our liberty of action is not worth the costs of exercising choice. I argue, then, against autonomy. "Autonomy" is something of a portmanteau word, including many distinct concepts, and certainly there are ways the word is used that denote things which are unobjectionable. What I argue against is what Joel Feinberg has called "[t]he kernel of the idea of autonomy ... the right to make choices and decisions – what to put in my body, what contacts with my body to permit, where and how to move my body through public space, how to use my chattels and personal property, what personal information to disclose to others, what information to conceal, and more."[1] Whereas Feinberg argues that this ability to live according to the choices one has made is a core value that must be preserved, I will argue instead that it is something that has been overvalued. While in some cases autonomous action does no harm, in other cases it does, however "harm" is construed – as detrimental to happiness, detrimental to material survival, or even detrimental to the promotion of autonomous action. It is not worth our while to try to prevent all harmful action, of course, and so intervention is not always

---

[1] Joel Feinberg, *Harm to Self: The Moral Limits of the Criminal Law*, Oxford University Press, 1986, p. 54.

warranted. Other times, however, intervention is not only permissible but also obligatory, so that autonomous actions should be prevented.

We could, and I will argue we should, for example, make cigarettes illegal and generally reduce the number of unhealthy diet options. We could interfere in people's ability to amass debt, even though that may mean intervening in their decisions as to what sort of house to buy or whether to buy a house at all. The ways in which we should be constrained is something that can be discovered only through empirical analysis, but I will argue that there is no area of choice that is in principle off limits.[2] We need to limit people's freedom of action, their autonomy, in the interests of better living. Where such choices should be left to the chooser, and where intervention is permissible, will be a function of what is best described as a cost–benefit analysis, rather than a decision a priori that certain personal decisions should be sacrosanct.

I am arguing, then, for the permissibility of interference in personal lives, interference even in actions a person takes that will affect only himself. (Like most people, I also think we are right to interfere in actions a person takes that are unduly harmful to others; since this is relatively uncontroversial, I won't argue for that here, although I will make use of the fact that we accept interventions for the sake of third parties to argue that should accept them in order to prevent harms to the self.) This policy is known generally as paternalism. John Kleinig defines paternalism simply as any case where "X acts to diminish Y's freedom, to the end that Y's good may be secured."[3] Under this general rubric there are paternalists

---

[2] Here I am different from Peter de Marneffe, who, while ably defending paternalism from many unfounded criticisms, believes its use should be impermissible in regard to what he calls "basic" liberties ("Avoiding Paternalism," *Philosophy and Public Affairs* 34.1 [2006], 84). While I expect that we would decide that paternalistic intervention is not warranted in many of these same areas, that is not something we can rule out a priori. This will be discussed in greater length in Chapter 4.

[3] John Kleinig, *Paternalism* (Totowa, N. J.: Rowman & Allenheld, 1984), p. 18. A recent definition by Peter de Marneffe includes another condition, that the person who is affected by the policy would prefer that his choices not be so limited: "a government policy is paternalistic toward A if and only if (a) it limits A's choices by deterring A from choosing to perform an action or by making it more difficult for A to perform it; (b) A prefers A's own situation when A's choices are not limited in this way; (c) the government has this policy only because those in the relevant political process believe or once believed that this policy will benefit A in some way; and (d) this policy cannot be fully justified without counting its benefits to A in its favor." He also cites Richard Arneson and Gerald Dworkin as having believed a policy is only paternalistic if it is unwanted by the person to whom it applies. I am not unfriendly to this condition, properly understood. It doesn't seem paternalistic if a policy makes us do what we already want to do, although it might make such a policy redundant. As seen below, though, there is some ambiguity involved in determining what we want, since we may want conflicting things, including wanting both to achieve an end and to take a means that does not achieve that end. Peter de Marneffe, "Avoiding Paternalism," *Philosophy and Public Affairs* 34.1 (winter 2006), 68–94.

of many kinds, and they vary greatly in the extent to which and ways in which they are willing to constrain people's activities. What I will argue for is a specific and controversial position: that we may, and indeed are sometimes morally obligated to, force people to refrain from certain actions and to engage in others. I will call this strong position Coercive Paternalism, and will show that it is indeed more acceptable, in some cases, than softer forms of paternalism that may seek to guide rather than constrain.

We are all familiar with, and generally accept, coercive intervention in some contexts. Generally, we think there are two sorts of cases where it is permitted: first, where ignorance of the facts means that the person doesn't know what it is that he is choosing, and second, where the person is for some reason incompetent to make a rational choice. In the first area we have the easy and hypothetical case where you dash your companion's drink to the floor as she raises it to her mouth, believing that she is not aware that the nearby prankster has added cyanide to her beer. Even John Stuart Mill, the most significant opponent of paternalism ever to have written, agreed that we can stop someone from crossing a bridge he doesn't know to be broken.[4] A more complicated, but on the whole fairly easy case, is the whole practice of prescription medicine. I, the patient, may have searched the Internet assiduously to discover the causes of my symptoms, and may feel sure that I know what is wrong with me and what I need to treat it, but I am prevented from getting this medicine until I have seen a doctor and obtained a prescription. No matter how confident I am that I know what I need, those who make laws believe that people make mistakes – they may misdiagnose their ailment or take the medication the wrong way, or be unaware that there are new medications on the market with fewer side effects, or that this medicine is contraindicated for people with their family history, and so on. While this is occasionally frustrating, there hasn't been any groundswell movement to eliminate the necessity for a doctor's visit for certain medications – not only for addictive ones, whose use we may have special reasons to control, but for products ranging from anti-inflammatory creams to pills for hypertension. The idea seems to be that this isn't a judgment we can reliably make ourselves: the costs of a bad decision are great, expert knowledge is necessary and available, and we are thus, on the whole, better off having the decision taken out of our hands.

---

[4] John Stuart Mill, *On Liberty* (in *Utilitarianism and On Liberty*, Meridian British Philosophers Series, ed. Mary Warnock [New York: World Publishing, 1971]), ch. 5, p. 229.

The second general condition under which we typically allow coercive paternalism is that of incompetence. There are people we think aren't capable of dealing with the facts, even if they are informed of them. Their reasoning is impeded by any of a number of causes – youth, which may entail a whole host of factors that lead to poor decisions; mental retardation of a sufficient degree; psychosis; emotional duress such as debilitating fear, and so forth. Some people need help to get where they need to go, and even if it is help they don't want, we feel impelled to set them straight.[5]

The question is why we aren't willing to extend this acceptance of paternalistic interference into other areas. The standard response relies on the differentiation in the mental circumstances of those doing the choosing. When it comes to knowledge, we think that while some choices require knowledge that most people lack, many don't. We can't expect the average person to know much about medicine, but we can expect that average people know enough to be able to run their personal lives in the way that best suits them. Similarly for competence: most of us are thought to be capable – calm enough, rational enough, smart enough – to use facts appropriately to get us to our given ends. Naturally, there will be some legally competent adults whom we recognize as emotionally immature and not likely to change, or a little on the slow side and prone to make mistakes, but unless they are fit to be declared legally incompetent, they have met the basic threshold where respect for their decisions is due. If they don't make wise choices, it is not because they couldn't, but because they failed for some reason to exercise their abilities. In these and most areas of life, it is argued, we should honor a person's liberty of choice, and allow him to choose for himself.

A premise of this book is that these differences – between areas where one should bow to expertise, and where one's own comprehension is sufficient to assess a situation, and between the irrationality of the

---

[5] I will note here that more moderate antipaternalists also accept paternalism in some cases where the chooser may be neither ignorant nor incompetent: those where the dangers to the agent are very high and very proximate and very probable. Thus, some who generally oppose paternalism will allow it in cases such as motorcycle helmet laws (see Kleinig, *Paternalism*, ch. 4 and again pp. 109 ff.; and Feinberg, *Harm to Self*, chs. 20 and 21). They have some difficulty in arguing that paternalism is permissible in these cases but not more generally. I will suggest that the reason moderate antipaternalists allow paternalism when the costs of liberty of action are high and definite is really a function of a cost–benefit analysis. There is some cost to controlling people's actions, so when it doesn't matter, we don't think we should do it. But when it does matter enough, we think we should interfere. We are now seeing that there are more cases than we had thought where liberty of action results in sufficient disutility to justify paternalism.

incompetent and the rationality of the competent – are differences of degree, not of kind. It is true that there are times when we are sufficiently masters of the relevant facts that our opinion is as well founded as that of the expert, and it is true that there are ways in which our emotions are less likely to interfere with our reasoning than are those of children, where our misconceptions are not so great as those of the psychotic, and so forth. But we are still frail creatures, who too often get things wrong in ways that can hurt us profoundly. A second premise is that we need help, as patients need the physician to help keep them from relying on the wrong medication, and as the incompetent need parents and institutions to help them from doing what is self-destructive. The first claim, that we have common cognitive failures which are not a result of simple carelessness or bad character, has, at this point, been widely argued both by psychologists and behavioral economists, and has been widely accepted. The controversy is about how we should respond to this; whether and how we should help these flawed decision makers. Should we continue to allow ourselves our present liberty of choice? Should we introduce mild nudges, providing incentives to do what is right and disincentives for choosing wrongly, while allowing all options to remain open? Or, should we, as I argue here, simplify our decision making by simply taking certain options away?

COGNITIVE BIAS

We are all familiar with the results of poor reasoning. As I write, we are, we hope, beginning to recover from a financial crisis that resulted in a worldwide recession. While there were, no doubt, some people in finance who rationally foresaw that they were likely to bring about a crash but who didn't care as long as they themselves profited, there were clearly many others who just couldn't grasp the relevant facts. It is hardly surprising that one response has been to introduce new regulation – to rein in not only those who act out of greed but also those who simply miscalculate. Today's *New York Times* reads: "Paul Volker, the former Fed chairman, regrets his decades of silence as banks ran amok. Now he is doing what he can to push for tighter rules."[6] Of course, these government regulations are not primarily, or perhaps at all, paternalistic in motivation – the point is to save others who may be hurt by bank mismanagement, rather than those who make the bad decisions. Many actions that harm the performers of these actions also hurt others, and it is

---

[6] *New York Times,* on-line edition, July 10, 2010.

our tradition to manifest more concern for third parties than for the authors of the action, whom we tend to blame for their mistakes. The point here is simply that we are familiar with miscalculations, even by those who are experts and whose careers are at stake in getting the right decision. We accept, then, the idea that in some cases people, even experts in the field, need to be constrained by government, because they are prone to error.

We have tended to regard such failures as anomalies that result from the idiosyncratic problems of a small minority. However, in the last thirty years or so something of a cottage industry has been devoted to investigating such anecdotal evidence through scientific study, and the conclusion is that we are all prone to such errors in many more contexts than we had thought.[7] Behavioral economists and social psychologists demonstrate that failures to reason well are pervasive, as normal a part of psychology (if "normal" may be taken to be mean found in the average person) as any other. Research by Amos Tversky and Daniel Kahneman, in particular, has been presented in numerous academic papers,[8] and in 2008 the legal scholar Cass Sunstein and the economist Richard Thaler teamed up to present many of these and other similar findings in their well-received book, *Nudge*.[9]

Many of the cognitive biases they report relate the effect on our decision making of factors that even we, the decision maker, would consider irrelevant. We are, for example, unduly influenced by the particular description used in the presentation of our options (more likely to choose a medical procedure with a 20 percent chance of success than one described as having an 80 percent chance of failure); unduly prone to think that we ourselves are less likely than others to suffer misfortune,

[7] In addition to the works discussed below, representative titles include: Ori and Rom Brafman, *Sway: The Irresistible Pull of Irrational Behavior* (New York: Doubleday, 2008); Dan Ariely, *Predictably Irrational: The Hidden Forces that Shape our Decisions* (New York: Harper Perennial, 2010); Madeline L. Van Hecke, *Blind Spots. Why Smart People Do Dumb Things* (New York: Prometheus Books, 2007); Robert Burton, *On Being Certain: Believing You Are Right Even When You're Not* (New York: St. Martin's Griffin, 2008); Cordelia Fine, *A Mind of its Own: How Your Brain Distorts and Deceives* (New York: W. W. Norton, 2008); Joseph T. Hallinan, *Why We Make Mistakes* (New York: Broadway, 2010); J. D. Trout, *Why Empathy Matters* (Harmondsworth: Penguin, 2010).

[8] See, for example, Daniel Kahneman and Amos Tversky's "Prospect Theory: An Analysis of Decision Under Risks," "Advances in Prospect Theory: Cumulatve Representation of Uncertainty," "Loss Aversion in Riskless Choice: A Reference-Dependent Model," and "Rational Choice and the Framing of Decisions," all in *Choices, Values, and Frames* (Cambridge University Press, 2000).

[9] Richard H. Thaler and Cass R. Sunstein, *Nudge: Improving Decisions About Health, Wealth, and Happiness* (New Haven, Conn.: Yale University Press, 2008).

even of something entirely random, like lightning;[10] prone to miscalculate the value of a thing depending upon whether we do or don't yet own it;[11] prone to assuming things that have one superficial characteristic in common also have similarities throughout (commonly known as stereotyping).[12] Smoking, not surprisingly, seems to involve a number of errors in judgment: people use time discounting to undervalue how much the future matters; anchor the use of an irrelevant starting point to make comparisons, so that they judge that since the first ten cigarettes haven't hurt them then the next ten years' worth won't either; or employ wishful thinking, the tendency to reinterpret judgments to make what we are doing look OK, and to conclude that since they smoke, smoking can't really be harmful.[13]

It is hard, in these and other contexts, for us to think efficiently about what we need to do to achieve our ends. It was once thought that when the outcome of our decisions really mattered to us, we would somehow be more careful and avoid cognitive bias, but recent studies show this to be false. Almost of all of us want to be able to stop working eventually, and to be able to live decently when we do that. Despite this, what we see in people's actions is a failure to act on what is apparently a really strong preference. First of all, most of us, left to our own devices, don't actually save much money, if we save any at all. Since with every notification on how much you are due at retirement the Social Security Administration kindly reminds you that it won't be enough to live on, we have every reason to save where we can elsewhere. Here, the surprising results of various studies indicate that most people, given the choice, don't choose.

---

[10] David M. DeJoy, "The Optimism Bias and Traffic Accident Risk Perception," *Accident Analysis and Prevention* 21.4 (1989), 333–340; Neil D. Weinstein, "Optimistic Biases About Personal Risks," *Science* 246.4935 (December 8, 1989), 1232–1233; Dale Griffin and Amos Tversky, "The Weighing of Evidence and the Determinants of Confidence," in *Heuristics and Biases: The Psychology of Intuitive Judgment*, ed. Thomas Gilovich, Dale Griffin, and Daniel Kahneman (Cambridge University Press, 2002).

[11] Daniel Kahneman, J. L. Knetsch, and Richard Thaler, "Experimental Tests of the Endowment Effect and the Coase Theorem," *Journal of Political Economy* 98 (1990), 1325–1348.

[12] See Mahzarin Banaji and R. Bhasker, "Implicit Stereotypes and Memory: The Bounded Rationality of Social Beliefs," in *Memory, Brain, and Belief*, ed. Daniel Schacter and Elaine Scarry (Cambridge, Mass.: Harvard University Press, 2000), pp. 139–175; Nilanjana Dasgupta, Mahzarin R. Banaji, and Robert P. Abelson, "Group Entativity and Group Perception: Associations Between Physical Features and Psychological Judgment," *Journal of Personality and Psychology* 77 (1999), 991–1003; Mahzarin R. Banaji and Nilanjana Dasgupta, "The Consciousness of Social Beliefs: A Program of Research on Stereotyping and Prejudice," in *Metacognition: Cognitive and Social Dimensions*, ed. V. Y. Yzerbyt, G. Lories, and B. Dardenne (London: Sage, 1998), pp. 157–170.

[13] See Robert Goodin, "The Ethics of Smoking," *Ethics* 99.3 (1989), 574–624, for a detailed account of the cognitive biases typically involved in smoking.

It has been convincingly shown that the pension plan a group of employees has depends not so much on what would most efficiently advance their retirement goals, but largely on the "default option" they are offered.[14] If their company automatically enrolls them in a 401(k) retirement plan but allows them to opt out if they choose, they tend to accept the default. If, however, their company's default option is not to be enrolled, but they may easily accept enrollment by merely letting their company know, they tend not to enroll. The cost–benefit analysis clearly shows that the rational choice is to opt in, and yet we don't do it if it requires us to choose.

Why accept the default option, if it is obviously not best? Apparently the reason for this is simply procrastination.[15] That is, it is not that we assume the default option is the better option, or that we don't understand the difference between the two, or that we are worried that we might regret our choice. That is, it's not that we have anything against changing from the default option to the better choice – we just don't get around to it. Here, where it really matters, we accept the status quo. (And we may wonder, too, if bias has played a role in other significant financial decisions, as when we run up unpayable debts.)

These are just a few examples out of many; as I say, the research is extensive. We generally suffer from many flaws in instrumental reasoning that interfere with our ability to make effective and efficient choices. The number of biases cataloged is vast and the literature which demonstrates and discusses them is ever-growing. These tendencies to think along certain nonrational lines are pervasive, and, as one writer puts it, are "virtually as stable, durable, and universal as reflexes."[16]

SOLUTIONS

The question is what should be done in the face of this evidence. The answer I embrace is that we need external guidance – constraints on our actions through regulation, law, and institutional design. This, though,

---

[14] Brigitte Madrian and Dennis Shea, "The Power of Suggestion: Inertia in 401(k) Participation and Savings Behavior," *Quarterly Journal of Economics* 116.4 (2001), 1149–1187.

[15] Ted O'Donoghue and Matthew Rabin, "Procrastination in Preparing for Retirement," in *Behavioral Dimensions of Retirement Economics*, ed. Henry Aaron (Washington, DC: Brookings Institute, 1999). For a suggestion as to how to get our bias towards the default option to help us save, see Richard Thaler and Shlomo Benartzi, "Save More Tomorrow: Using Behavioral Economics to Increase Employee Savings," *Journal of Political Economy* 112 (February 2004), S164-S187.

[16] J. D. Trout, "Paternalism and Cognitive Biases," *Legal Philosophy* 24 (2005), 379. Trout concludes that all the evidence points to "a single moral – that the Enlightenment vision is profoundly mistaken."

is not popular. Ceding control to government is always dangerous. Our worst fears are those of a malicious and totalitarian government that uses its power to harm and oppress, something like Nazi Germany or Cambodia under the Khmer Rouge. Even if we remind ourselves that paternalistic measures must, by definition, be beneficent in intent, which the Nazis and the Khmer Rouge obviously were not, it is not much of a comfort. For one thing, we naturally fear that once such powers are in a benevolent and beneficent government's hands, a malicious totalitarian party may take over, using these powers to lead us to rack and ruin. And even if we can avoid this, we can easily think of a well-meaning government that makes bad decisions. (Think of Lois Lowry's sci-fi novel *The Giver*, where a benevolent government [somehow] does away with color because it allows for racial discrimination.)[17] Consider paternalism in actual parents: we don't want our mother or father to even buy our clothes, much less make decisions in more significant areas, although we entirely believe that they mean well. They have different values, and they don't understand what we want. Lastly, even in the most positive scenario, where benevolent, beneficent measures are taken which actually improve our lives, we imagine a feeling of frustration and indignation: what business have they to run our lives? When the law makes me do things I don't want, even if they turn out to be good for me, resentment is a natural response.

On the other hand, being addicted to cigarettes or obese, or bankrupt, or too poor to retire, much less to retire as we like, are frustrating, liberty-inhibiting conditions, too. The question is how we can avoid these and other debilitating circumstances that liberty of action brings us to, while simultaneously avoiding the psychological costs that constant surveillance and interference by big government are thought to bring. There are three primary possibilities: retaining our present liberty but providing better conditions for making choices, which is the classic liberal response; so-called libertarian paternalism, which suggests making bad choices more difficult and good choices more attractive, but which still allows the full range of options; and coercive paternalism, where we simply prevent some choices. I will argue that the first and second options aren't sufficiently effective in helping us achieve the lives we want; that the last option is not only more effective, but properly done, will not have the costs we fearfully envisage.

---

[17] *The Giver* (New York: Houghton Mifflin, 1993) won the Newbery Award in 1994, in part for its depiction of the dangers of paternalism.

Liberalism

Education

A standard liberal response to poor choice has been to educate the choosers about the dangers involved in some options – like putting warnings on cigarettes. Educating people about general tendencies to error proves more difficult. Ideally, realistic education on the vicissitudes of rationality would lead us to exercise caution in a way that prevents us from making self-destructive decisions. However, there are a number of problems with education as a solution. First, even with something as straightforward and specific as cigarettes, even a really thoroughgoing attempt at education has not been entirely successful. It's true that a smaller percentage of the population smokes now than did before it was discovered that smoking causes cancer. On the other hand, more than 20 percent of the American population does smoke, despite the millions of dollars spent in schools and the unmissable warnings on cigarette packages. These are not just old people lingering on from the days before anti-smoking education: 20 percent of high school students smoke, and although for a while the number of young smokers was declining, now it seems to be holding steady.[18] Educating people out of error is not easy, when errors arise in significant part from cognitive bias.

If teaching people the practical purport of one relatively simple fact (smoking is very dangerous) is hard, educating people more generally as to their own psychological frailty is more difficult still. For one thing, the only place we can force formal education on people without the coercive paternalism the liberal wants to avoid is public school. (Education of minors is an example of coercive paternalism, but when it comes to children we accept paternalism as both benevolent and efficient.) Teaching children about cognitive bias, and more to the point, trying to teach them ways to avoid it, is likely to prove much more difficult than convincing them that smoking is dangerous. Evidence of failures in rationality is much more complicated and unlikely to capture the imagination of children, who are, after all, constitutionally blithe when it comes to vague issues of prudence (or even vivid issues of prudence – as well as smoking, too many kids drink, drive drunk, and have unprotected sex). Adults might possibly be more interested, but we can't require that they learn a new area of psychology without the coercive paternalism the liberal

---

[18] From the Center for Disease Control, www.cdc.gov/tobacco/data_statistics/fact_sheet/youth_date/tobacco_use.

is trying to avoid. Public service announcements and the like, again, don't seem likely to attract a lot of attention.

Even if we paid attention, though, there is the question of what we could then do. Once we know we are prone to suffering from a given bias, how do we know *when* we are in fact doing that? How do we know when to doubt our own judgment, when we lack the judgment to do so? For one thing, the same mental shortcuts that have led us to so many bad decisions can also lead to good ones, so it would be undesirable, even if it were possible, to eliminate all these strategies. Saying to ourselves "I mustn't group things together on the basis of some similar characteristics lest I be prone to stereotyping" deprives us of a handy tool – since sometimes grouping like things together is appropriate. If Fred ate the red mushroom and immediately collapsed, frothing at the mouth and clutching his stomach, it seems like a good idea to say "stay away from all red mushrooms" rather than trying another to see if it is fatal. Saying "I will only group things together when appropriate" lands us back at the issue of how we know when such grouping is helpful and when it is leading us astray. Even if we could, we shouldn't leave some of these mental habits entirely behind.

Secondly, for those tendencies we might like to eliminate altogether – perhaps the influence of framing – the trick is to know when we are falling prey to them. Normally, when we are trying to be careful in assessing which of our beliefs can be trusted, we rely on a sense of certainty – this one I'm not really sure of, but about this one I feel absolutely convinced – but even the sense of certainty is not reliable: that we feel very certain of a conclusion is not caused exclusively (or even primarily) by its being based on a solid chain of argument. Instead, we feel more certain of the truth of propositions if we are more familiar with them, and if they are accepted by those around us.[19] While, again, this is a handy shortcut to assessing which of our beliefs are certain, it clearly doesn't give us a definitive differentiation between the false and the true. Our own experience tells us that self-criticism is not enough to show us if we are falling prey to error.[20] These biases "stubbornly resist efforts to control them by spontaneous acts of will."[21]

---

[19] See Burton, *On Being Certain* for an interesting discussion of the biological basis for the feeling of certainty.

[20] Nomy Arpaly, *Unprincipled Virtue: An Inquiry into Moral Agency* (Oxford University Press, 2003), has a convincing discussion as to how difficult it is to know what reasoning has brought one to a given conclusion, cognitive biases aside.

[21] Trout, "Paternalism and Cognitive Biases," pp. 407–408.

Experience

Of course, formal learning is not the only kind of learning. F. H. Buckley argues that, however foolish our decisions are to begin with, we will learn from our mistakes.[22] We don't need classes on general psychological tendencies since the application of such abstract knowledge may prove baffling. Rather, in given cases, we will learn what does and what doesn't work. Indeed, argue some, if we aren't given the opportunity to make our own mistakes, we will fail to accrue the self-reliance and critical expertise that adverse experience – that is, that making mistakes and suffering the ensuing results – gives us, and will be lesser people as a result.

This is an objection with some intuitive power, because of course we do sometimes learn from our mistakes. I've recently taken up Scrabble, and I have learned that if I give someone the chance to play on the triple word score they will do it, whereas at first I sort of hoped they would fail to notice and let me play it on my next turn. But there are also many cases where experience is not something we can rely on. For one thing, in many cases we learn too late. When you're diagnosed with lung cancer, it's too late to learn that your cognitive bias towards anchoring is something you shouldn't trust. When you are forced to retire and find that you don't have enough to live on, it's too late to learn that your tendency toward irrational time discounting has really done you harm. These things can't be fixed.

Furthermore, lots of people don't learn from their mistakes. Banks aren't eager to lend to people who've gone bankrupt on the grounds that now they've learned their lesson and will never be so foolish in future. Buying a lottery ticket every week doesn't teach people that it isn't a good use of their money. (Even saying it gives you "the chance to dream" depends on irrationality, since it wouldn't give rise to dreams of wealth if we really understood how unlikely it is to occur – why not dream of running across a million dollars in the street instead, about as likely and so much cheaper?) Procrastination doesn't work as a strategy to get things done (or to avoid having to do them eventually), but many intelligent, critically acute people continue to engage in it as if it were a really helpful strategy. Similarly, cognitive biases involving planning (specifically, the tendency to take on more than one can possibly accomplish) cause bad planning to occur over and over in the very same person.[23] Sometimes the failure of a

---

[22] F. H. Buckley, *Fair Governance* (Oxford University Press, 2009), p. 38.
[23] See the discussion of Daniel Kahneman and Amos Tversky, "Intuitive Prediction: Biases and Corrective Procedures," in *Judgment Under Uncertainty: Heuristics and Biases*, ed. Daniel Kahneman, Amos Tversky, and Paul Slovic (Cambridge University Press, 1979), pp. 414–421.

strategy to be successful leads us to choose a different strategy, and sometimes it doesn't, because we are not entirely rational when it comes to choosing means.

Some might argue that since we learn socially, at least others can take advantage of these failures and develop good habits even when it's too late for the actual victims. However, while this may happen sometimes, even this sort of learning is hampered by our difficulty in extrapolating from others' experience to our own. We know that 50 percent of marriages end in divorce, but which of us standing at the altar thinks our own marriage has only a 50:50 chance? There is a strong tendency for us not to learn from others' example, in part because of an overoptimistic belief that we are different from others. We suffer from what might be called the Lake Woebegone effect: we each think we are above average. Many studies in accident prevention have shown that most people consider themselves to be better-than-average drivers, and thus underestimate their likelihood of being harmed in an accident.[24] This overoptimism is not limited to areas of skill, where acquaintance with our own abilities might lead us to assume they are greater than those of others, about whom we know less. Individuals are similarly inclined to believe they are less likely than the average to suffer from misfortunes ranging from food poisoning to asthma, where the unfortunate consequence seems to be a function of luck rather than superior ability.[25] Given this, we are naturally less prone to take steps to secure our future well-being, even when we see other people coming to bad ends. And, our ability to recognize the likelihood of such dangers may not improve with greater expertise – knowing more need not make us better judges. Indeed, experts tend to exaggerate their own expertise and often make worse judgments than people who have no pretence of expertise. Nonexperts may rely on the statistically best bet, while experts often trust their own specialized knowledge to allow them to deviate from the guideline emerging from past studies – they think they can recognize an exception when they see it, whereas in fact they apparently can't. The result is that more knowledge leads to worse judgments, and experts do worse than nonexperts.[26]

---

[24] DeJoy, "Optimism Bias and Traffic Accident Risk Perception."

[25] Weinstein, "Optimistic Biases About Personal Risks."

[26] See Frederick Schauer, *Profiles, Probabilities, and Stereotypes* (Cambridge, Mass.: Belknap–Harvard University Press, 2003), pp. 92–101; See Trout's discussion of the susceptibility of scientists and other "highly educated people" to bias (*Why Empathy Matters*, p. 403). See also: Colin Camerer and Dan Llavallo, "Overconfidence and Excess Entry: An Experimental Approach," *American*

A lot of this may seem more like what we normally call weakness of the will than a cognitive flaw, and some of us tend to say that what such people need is simply to be more motivated to do the right thing. This may be why we so often blame the victims of bad thinking – we think they could just have tried harder and they would have avoided ending up in their predicament. To the extent that this is true, though, it is as a redescription rather than an explanation. We all know that strength of will is influenced by beliefs – even the most avid smoker would have the strength to refrain if he knew that this very cigarette would cause him to drop dead after the last puff. It is the difficulty in processing knowledge that involves incremental damage over a period of time that weakens resistance. As Aristotle argued, the weak person knows the truth in a sense, but only as the drunk man knows the verses of Empedocles.[27] The weak person lacks operative knowledge, and that is a cognitive failing that merely honing the strength of desires won't fix. It is not, after all, that we don't really want to be well off when we are old, or that we have a strong desire not to check a different box on the pension plan form. We have a mental failing, and not one that an effort of will can cure.

The problems we face are various, but all point to a difficulty in taking in facts that we really need to grasp in order to pursue our ends. No matter what direction we want to go in, we can't get there if we can't adequately assess the information we need in order to choose the best means to achieve our goals. Since it is our natural tendency to rely on our own judgment, all things being equal, we need something to change the balance so that all things aren't equal – we need outside interference. This won't substitute for judgment in most cases, but can help us in those areas where we are inclined to make poor decisions and where the costs of such bad decision making are very high and, often, irreparable. We need help.

Libertarian paternalism

An alternative to our present scenario has been articulated by Thaler and Sunstein in *Nudge*. They endorse what they call "libertarian paternalism." Their suggestion is that we help people do what is best for them by

Economic Review 89 (1999), 306–318; Leilani Greening and Carla C. Chandler, "Why it Can't Happen to Me: The Best Rate Matters, but Overestimating Skill Leads to Underestimating Risk," *Journal of Applied Social Psychology* 27 (1997), 760–780; and Ravi Mehta, Joandrea Hoegg, and Amitav Chakravarti, "Knowing Too Much: Expertise Induced False Recall Effects in Product Comparison," *Journal of Consumer Research* (2011).
[27] *Nicomachean Ethics*, Book VII, 1147b9–13.

making the right choice easier for those with cognitive biases. If it is a question of pension plans, we make the most advantageous plan (for the employee) the default option: if you do nothing, you end up with (what is at least generally) the best choice. If you need help choosing healthy food, we put the healthy fruit at eye level, and the deep-fried salted fat on the bottom shelf, since people are more likely to choose whatever is at eye level. We give you a nudge in the direction that is best for you. However, while we change the "choice architecture," we don't actually eliminate options. You can still get those BBQ-flavor pork rinds by bending over, and you can still opt for the pension plan that makes it most likely that you will end up dependent and poor. As they see it, this preserves your autonomy, and thus allows us to have our cake (beneficial consequences) and eat it too (as we respect liberty of choice).

There are two important things to notice about this, though. First, Libertarian Paternalism is manipulative. That is, it does not suggest that we engage in free and open discussion in order to rationally persuade you to change your ways. Sunstein and Thaler are not opposed to free and open discussion, but they don't think engaging you in rational argument is enough to get you to choose efficiently, because of the cognitive deficits they have described. The point of the nudge is to push you in ways that bypass your reasoning. That is, they use your cognitive biases, like the tendency to go with the default option, to bring about good effects. There is a sense in which they then fail to respect people's decision-making ability. The assumption is that because our decision-making ability is limited we need to use nonrational means to seduce people into doing what is good for them, and are trying to get people to act through the use of nonrational means. It is true that for libertarian paternalism all options remain open, which means that some people could, in fact, resist this nonrational persuasion and rely on their own cognitive abilities to decide what they want to do. The assumption is, though, that most people won't do this but instead will fall in the direction in which they are nudged.

I don't think this is morally wrong, since I agree that we need to help people get where they really want to go. However, insofar as it is supposed to render the position more palatable to the classic liberal, it fails. Rather than regarding people as generally capable of making good choices, we outmaneuver them by appealing to their irrationality, just in more fruitful ways. We concede that people can't generally make good decisions when left to their own devices, and this runs against the basic premise of liberalism, which is that we are basically rational, prudent creatures who may thus, and should thus, direct themselves autonomously.

Second, libertarian paternalism is less likely to achieve its goal, benefit to those who choose, than is the more intrusive system of coercive paternalism. More freedom to choose means more people will choose badly. It is true that since a libertarian paternalist system allows individuals the ability to act contrary to the nudge, those for whom the default option, and so forth, are not good choices could bypass the nudge to hit upon a choice more appropriate to their own particular case, and thus would benefit from the freedom this system allows. Libertarian paternalism might be the ideal choice if the manipulative nudges worked for those who would otherwise make foolish choices, while the remaining option to act differently allowed only those who are choosing the most rational means to their ends to deviate from the direction into which they are nudged. If this were true, people who would otherwise have procrastinated would have a good pension plan by default and would spend happier lives as a consequence, and those who really have a better idea as to what will best suit them could consciously opt out of the default pension and manage retirement savings in an alternative way that is most efficient for them. Those for whom pork rinds have no adverse health or aesthetic effects (or, whose ends really don't include or require good health or attractive appearance), and who enjoy them more than fruit, would make the slight extra mental and physical effort required to get the pork rinds. Those who are prone to heart disease and yet wish to live long lives would be nudged into getting the apple, thus achieving their goal of better health. We would each end up where we need to be.

However, when you allow people the option to choose contrary to the direction of the nudge, this freedom isn't preserved exclusively for those who are going to use it to do what is best for them. Some of those who ignore the nudge towards the fruit and go for the pork rinds will be wedging unhealthy, cholesterol-ridden bodies under the cafeteria table, because after years of such food they have a craving for fat and salt that no nudge will override, even while such a diet will give them shorter, more painful lives. Similarly, those who choose to smoke are really not likely to be those who have given it rational consideration and decided that it is truly worth it. Some people would refuse the pension plan because they have wild ideas about retirement (they want more to spend on lottery tickets) that will never yield the results they want. An irrational decision can be one accompanied by a very strong motivation. In other words, what libertarian paternalism does is not simply preserve the option of better choices for those who, for some reason, are different from the norm. It preserves options for those who have stronger motivations than others do, or for those who have stronger and crazier convictions than the norm. It preserves the option for error. The nudge will work for those whose motivation to the contrary isn't sufficiently strong, but some of us are too determinedly headed in the wrong direction to be prevented from taking our foolish actions by a simple nudge. The danger is, then, that libertarian paternalism may end up neither having its cake nor eating it – it doesn't really respect choice, in the sense of thinking that people should be left to their own devices in deciding what to do. And, while it would no doubt save many people from foolish actions by nudging them in a better direction, it will leave many others to suffer the consequences of their bad thinking. We may end up with neither of the valuable things libertarian paternalism hoped to promote.

Coercive paternalism

Liberalism respects our decision making abilities in a way, but in a way that is often not warranted. Thus, it leaves us "free" to be confounded by error and to end up in places we never wanted to be, and which may furthermore be situations that diminish the very agency liberalism wants to celebrate. We have seen that libertarian paternalism, on the other hand, while vaunted as the attractive alternative to traditional liberalism, does not respect our decision-making ability per se, in the sense of thinking of it as something that should not be circumvented through nonrational means. At the same time, it is less beneficial than it might be, since the option to err remains in place.

Coercive paternalism takes a different position. Rather than leaving us to sink or swim, as does liberalism, or engaging in mental manipulation, as does libertarian paternalism, the coercive paternalist will simply say some things are not allowed. I don't know that this is more respectful of people than manipulation is, but I don't see that it is less respectful. In either case, we are trying to control people on the grounds that their own decision making is not to be trusted. And, coercive paternalism is more likely to get us good results, because certain behaviors, like smoking, will be out of the question. I grant (and will discuss more in Chapter 6) that no prohibition on behavior is going to be 100 percent successful. There are always people who break laws. It's not clear how much people who are born after, say, a ban on cigarettes will want to smoke, as opposed to those who are now addicted to it, but presumably there will be some. The numbers, though, are surely likely to be much less than the present 20 percent of the population. So, instead of simply educating people about the dangers of smoking, as liberals do, or disincentivizing smoking by making it very expensive, I would recommend we get rid of cigarettes. Educating people simply isn't all that effective, because in some areas we are relatively ineducable. Raising taxes on cigarettes provides some incentive for some people to at least try to quit, but it also leaves a lot of people who start smoking anyway and can't quit, and who just spend a disproportionate amount of their income on a habit that will probably leave them in worse health and possibly shorten their life without bestowing compensating benefits. Coercive paternalism takes certain decisions out of our hands. It does this in order to help us do what we want to do, which is to lead longer and happier lives. We know that leaving people to fend for themselves is too often simply not successful in getting people to where they want to go. Instead of letting people languish in the misery caused by their own decisions, why not intervene, as we do with prescription drugs, as we do with seat belts, and help people out?

What exactly is the problem with coercion?

RESPECT

The initial answer is that to many, using coercion to stop people from doing what they have decided, however foolishly, that they want to do, seems somehow to devalue them, to degrade them; in short, to give them less than the respect they deserve. Stephen Darwall, for example, says that

> The objectionable character of paternalism of this sort is not that those who seek to benefit us against our wishes are likely to be wrong about what really benefits us … It is, rather, primarily a failure of respect, a failure to recognize the authority that persons have to demand, within certain limits, that they be allowed to make their own choices for themselves.[28]

What adequate respect consists in – indeed, what respect itself consists in – is a difficult question, to say the least, and much ink has been spilt in its pursuit. At the least, though, to respect something seems to mean to recognize that thing's value, and to act in a way that is consistent with that value. When it comes to persons, we are all agreed that all persons have unique value, by reason of their personhood, regardless of the particular kinds of lives they live. Beyond this consensus, though, there are many questions: whether the value of persons lies in their rationality ability or

---

[28] Stephen Darwall, "The Value of Autonomy and Autonomy of the Will," *Ethics* 116.2 (January 2006), 263–284, at 268.

their capacity for choice, or their capacity for moral thought, or some interrelationship of these; whether it is a function of their capacity for love, for sympathy, for sacrifice; whether it arises from their creativity and imagination, or even depends on their having been made in God's image, whatever that may mean. And, further, there is no very general agreement on what their valuable features, whatever they may be, call for in terms of behavior from others. Everyone seems to agree that certain behaviors are disrespectful: slavery, where one person is forever subordinated to the purposes of another, with no regard given to the way he himself wants to live his life, is a practice all parties agree is inconsistent with the respect due to a person, any person. For some, though, including Kant, the death penalty is a sign of respect, because it is an appropriate acknowledgement of the perpetrator's agency; for others, killing a human, whatever he may have done, is antithetical to respecting his value. For my purposes, fortunately, the defense of any particular articulation of the grounds for respect is unnecessary, and a defense of what this might mean in terms of the behavior we need to accord to others can, for the most part, be avoided. Instead, I will argue by analogy, from a practice we accept to the one I think we should accept.

We all agree that the government can stop people from doing some things that they want to do. Even when they are entirely aware of the consequences, it can stop your neighbors from bashing you over the head when your loud music irritates them, no matter how competent as agents they are. So, we prevent people from infringing your rights. Furthermore, we often stop others from doing something to you (such as raising money by agreeing to let other people beat you to a pulp), even if you consent to it. You may have given up your right in this case, but we think it is too harmful to you to be allowed. On the other hand, you are permitted to consent to be dropped into the dump tank at the fair to raise charity – what might otherwise be assault in this case is rendered permissible through your consent. The difference is the degree of harm you will suffer. Further, we sometimes require that others act positively for the sake of your welfare, rather than simply refraining from injuring you: we can make them pay taxes for uses you will benefit from but from which they won't. The fact that, when there is a conflict of interests, others may be required to do, or refrain from doing, something to you does not seem disrespectful. Why is it different when we require you to do, or refrain from doing, something when that is in your own interest? Some might say that in this case we prevent you from doing what you want to do, and in the other cases we only stop them from doing what you don't want, but that is simply not so. For one thing, as mentioned above, sometimes we will stop them from doing something to you that you want them to do, when we think it violates a right or causes a sufficiently great harm. For another, there is a sense in which paternalism in this case *does* help you do what you want to do. Admittedly, paternalistic action prevents you from doing something you want to do at that moment, but it does this for the sake of helping you obtain something you want more, something that your short-sighted action will make more difficult to achieve. So, the difference between the permissibility of third-person restrictions and first-person restrictions is not whether or not the action is one you want.

We might think, indeed, that imposing a cost on you for the sake of your long-term benefit would be less, not more, controversial than imposing a cost on someone else for your benefit. Judith Thomson discusses a relevant comparison in *The Realm of Rights.*[29] If you are unconscious, crushed by a tree, and the only way to save your life is to cut off your leg, we think it is permissible (and I would think even obligatory, if we have the medical wherewithal) to amputate your leg. On the other hand, if you are unconscious and the only way to save your life is to cut off the leg of another unconscious person, we are strongly inclined to think this is not permissible. In the first case, you will be compensated for the loss of your leg by having your life, but in the second case the other person gets no compensation for his loss. Imposing a cost is much more acceptable when the person on whom the cost is imposed will reap the overall benefit from that. Obviously, Thomson's case is not one of coercive paternalism: the presumptive amputee is unconscious, and we act in accordance with what we think he would want us to do if he were conscious. For most people, including Thomson, if the person is conscious and doesn't want the amputation, we have to respect his decision. The point of the comparison, as I use it here, is to show that often we are more willing to impose a cost on you, when you will benefit from that, than to impose a cost on others to benefit you. Yet, we do impose (some) costs on others to benefit you – we make them refrain from harming you when they want to, and so on. So, if we can justify restricting them, why can't we justify restricting you?

Of course, the immediate answer many people will give is that you simply have a right to determine what happens to you, as long as that does no harm to others. This, though, is an answer in need of an

---

[29] Judith Thomson, *The Realm of Rights* (Cambridge, Mass.: Harvard University Press, 1990), pp. 190 ff.

argument. Even if we accept that individuals have rights, and thus claims not to be harmed by others in certain ways, and to have (yet) others defend them in these claims, why would there be such a right here, where the point of the action is to help the person achieve what in the long run he wants, and what he would want now if he were not a flawed thinker? We recall that it is indeed permissible to prevent people from doing what they want where they don't know all the relevant facts, whether that is Mill's bridge case or prescription medicine. And, we bear in mind that even where people are normally competent, we prevent them from doing harm to others, because that interferes with others' doing what they want to do. Given this, it seems most consistent to say here that coercive intervention with an agent who is somewhere between the medical patient and the angry neighbor in competence, and who contemplates doing something that could irrevocably harm himself, should be at least prima facie permissible. Why, then, is this controversial? Much of this book will go to addressing this question, but at this point there are some preliminary points that may be made. While there are problematic issues concerning paternalism, they do not arise from disrespect per se.

Inequality

One difference between constraining your harmful action against another person, and constraining your harmful action against yourself, is that in paternalism there is a substitution of judgment: one party assumes that his judgment about what you need is superior to your own judgment as to what you need, to the point where, in coercive paternalism, he can force you to do what he thinks is best rather than what you think is best. This, in turn, is said to involve treating people unequally: one person's judgment about himself is held to be inferior to the other person's judgment about him.[30] This isn't what is going on when we force you to do something for the sake of someone else. If the government adjudicates a dispute between two parties, it can take both parties as equally competent to express what their own interests are. What they are not competent to assess is the other person's interests. So, I rightly argue that the loss of my house will be a great hardship for me. The town argues that not being able to use my property will be a great loss to the town that needs it for the new school access road. It is when I go on to assert that the town's loss of

---

[30] See, for example, Seana Shiffrin, "Paternalism, Unconscionability Doctrine, and Accommodation," *Philosophy and Public Affairs* 29.3 (2000), 213 ff.

the access road is less of a loss to them than my loss is to me that my judgment is doubted. Similarly, the town can accurately gauge the public interest in the access road, but isn't capable of forming a trustworthy comparison between that interest and mine. The objective third party, then, takes each party's report on what is in its interests and tries to do an objective comparison of the two. This is, obviously, an idealized picture, but it shows why forcing me to do something for the sake of someone else does not, per se, treat me as having poorer judgment than others have. Both of us are taken as good judges of our own interests.

Paternalism is different, because we doubt your competence in judging even your own interests, and further believe that someone else (in a given situation) is more competent to judge your interests than you are. Rather than regarding each of two conflicting parties as competent to judge what is best for himself, paternalist policies operate on the assumption that the person in the throes of making the decision about himself is less capable than those who have formulated the paternalistic policy on this issue. In relationships that are literally paternalistic – those between a parent and a child – this is regarded as relatively unproblematic. We think the parent's assumption of the superiority of his own judgment over his child's as to where that child's interests lie is well founded, and furthermore think that this inequality is temporary – the child will eventually gain the status of the adult. When one adult claims superiority of judgment over another adult, though, we wonder what could justify it, and furthermore fear that it consigns the "inferior" adult to his lower status for life, since we can no longer look to age as a liberating transition.

For this reason, on a political scale, accepting the legitimacy of this substitution of judgment is often taken to posit significant inequality among humans, inequality of a sort that could justify a class or caste system. The question frequently asked about paternalism is who will determine what rules there should be, and the fear is that there will be one class of persons, self-styled experts, who make the rules, and another class, the supposedly cognitively impaired, who obey them. This is undemocratic in a deep sense, dangerous in numerous ways, and for these reasons at least, morally unacceptable.

In fact, however, it is not an assumption of superiority, but of shared fallibility, that moves us to paternalism, and no assumption is made about the superiority of one group of people over another. While it is true that some pictures of paternalistic government have suggested that the more able will be in charge of the welfare of the less able, our present understanding of cognitive bias doesn't support the view that one group is entitled to that kind of authority over others. Not only does it not support a class division, it positively undercuts the grounds for such a division. There is no evidence of demarcation in education or IQ that distinguishes who is, and who is not, prone to the sorts of errors which can prevent us from reaching our goals.[31] This should hardly be surprising. We know, after all, that CEOs and government experts have made mind-boggling errors in their economic calculations, and presumably we are individually familiar with intelligent people who seem incapable of thinking straight in some instances of decision making. As was noted above, experts in their own fields who deviate from generally suggested guidelines because they think they can trust their own expert judgment are mistaken. It is not that knowing more can't be helpful in some cases – of course, the gardener who knows begonias won't thrive in the sun will make a better decision about their placement than the nongardener who places them wherever she thinks they will look prettiest. As discussed above, though, the occasions where paternalistic intervention is useful are those where the simple accretion of facts doesn't help us, because we don't handle the facts adequately. The sorts of errors the paternalistic intervention promoted here addresses are a function of circumstance rather than the kind of person doing the thinking. What we need, then, is for these sorts of decisions to be made under a different set of circumstances, not by a distinct class of people.

In *Nudge*, Sunstein and Thaler refer often to the doer and the planner: the planner is able to think about decisions where he is not subject to, for example, temptation – he decides on the day's food purchases while he is at home, not when he is standing hungrily in front of the bakery counter. The planner, then, is able to make better decisions because he is not in those circumstances that prompt errors of judgment. The doer and the planner, though, are the same person, just in different situations. What we need in creating paternalistic constraints is for people who are in the position of the planner – those not at that moment prey to the temptations which can lead any of us astray – to be making the rules that people in the position of doer must obey. Rules do not need to be made by a

---

[31] It is true that in the US, less-educated people smoke more than people who are more educated do, and some might take this to mean that less-educated people are, as a class, more prone to making irrational decisions (see Center for Disease Control, www.cdc.gov/tobacco/data_statistics). However, the same sources tell us that men also smoke more than women do, and that there are significantly different rates of smoking among different races, and no one suggests that these differences augur different degrees of rationality. We see no evidence that one group is generally more able to avoid cognitive bias than another.

superior bunch of thinkers, but by any and all of us when we are doing our superior thinking. In personal life, of course, a person may make such rules for himself, but sadly he cannot literally bind his "doing" self to obey the rule once in the grip of temptation. The advantage of legislation – and other institutional regulation – is that the rules are in fact binding. We no longer have to rely on our poor self-control when the opportunity to break our internal planner's rule arises.

This doesn't mean legislators won't make mistakes, of course, and such legislation, like all legislation, is best made under a democratically elected and accountable legislature under circumstances of transparency. As I discuss further below (in Chapter 4), even given the certainty of some bad legislation, on the whole we have found that having laws is better than not having them, at least as long as we have the possibility of changing those laws through democratic processes.[32] Too, an acceptance of the fact that we all suffer from cognitive biases might, indeed, lead to more humility in those political leaders who might otherwise think they themselves are immune to the errors they clearly see in others.[33]

Degradation

Even if we assume that we are equal in this regard, this will not satisfy everyone who thinks that paternalism is essentially disrespectful. Some people will argue that it is degrading to say of people that they are not fit to make all the decisions required for running their own lives, and if this is true of all people, rather than just some people, so much the worse. "What does have intrinsic value is not having choices but being recognized as the kind of creature who is capable of making choices. That capacity grounds our idea of what it is to be a person and a moral agent equally worthy of respect by all," says Gerald Dworkin.[34] While nothing in paternalism implies we can't make choices, Dworkin may be taken to mean that there is value in being able to make *good* choices about (all?) central areas of our lives, and this indeed is something the paternalist questions. Joel Feinberg says that when paternalism "is applied by another party to oneself it seems arrogant and demeaning."[35] Elizabeth Anderson has said paternalism

---

[32] See Chapter 4 below, "Misuse and Abuse," pp. 113–115.
[33] For more discussion general changes of attitude the acceptance of paternalism might bring, see Chapter 7 below.
[34] *The Theory and Practice of Autonomy* (Cambridge University Press, 1997), p. 80.
[35] Feinberg, *Harm to Self*, p. 22.

treats people as if they are "stupid,"[36] which she takes to be insulting.[37] Many writers suggest that paternalism involves some sort of degradation of the person who is treated paternalistically.

The question, though, is what degradation and insult consist in. One sort of insult occurs if someone says something, even something true, with the malicious intent of hurting me. So, an unkind passerby who yells "You are fat!" with the intent to make someone feel bad is insulting that person, even if he is fat, whereas a doctor who benevolently suggests that it's time to get some of the weight off does not. Clearly, though, constraints suggested by paternalists are not intended to hurt, either psychologically or materially, but to help. Second, as discussed earlier, someone may insult me if he underestimates my abilities. It seems to depend on the reason – if someone thinks I am incompetent to negotiate some business simply because of a mistake in identity (he thinks I'm the escaped mental patient because of our vivid resemblance), that doesn't seem insulting, just mistaken. If, on the other hand, someone refuses to acknowledge my abilities, perhaps because he assumes that someone of my race or sex simply cannot have them, he degrades me, because he refuses to acknowledge that someone with these characteristics can be as smart, as able, as valuable, as I am.[38] He refuses even to subject me to the appropriate scale of evaluation, because he refuses, on the basis of prejudice, to admit I might have these abilities, abilities I do have. He puts me down, trying to assign me to a category to which I don't belong and inferior to his own.

When someone accurately assesses my abilities, though, and finds me lacking in some respects, it is very hard for me to argue that I have been degraded, and thus disrespected. We regard it as insulting to treat humans like animals, but we don't regard it as insulting to treat Boston Terriers like animals, because they are animals. We regard it as insulting to act as if women aren't capable of balancing their checkbooks, because they can.

---

[36] Elizabeth Anderson, "What is Equality For?," *Ethics*, 109.2 (1999), 287–337, at 301–302.

[37] Peter de Marneffe thinks that if we show that errors in practical judgment are normal, then it follows that saying that a person has them does not imply that he is stupid. I think this needs more explanation. (See de Marneffe, "Avoiding Paternalism," 80.) Even if it would follow that he is not stupid relative to other humans, it might follow that he is stupid relative to some ideal (the way any given stupid Irish Setter may not be stupid for an Irish Setter, but may still be characterized as stupid relative to dogs in general or even to humans). So, here I try to explain why this ascription of stupidity does not, in the case of cognitively biased humanity, constitute an insult, even if it is correct to say we are stupid.

[38] In the case of prejudice, he degrades me in particular by associating my mental abilities with some irrelevant characteristic – skin color or reproductive capacity – rather than assessing me as an individual. One can degrade a person without such stereotyping, though, by simply refusing to acknowledge that they have the value they have.

We don't regard it as insulting to assume that the man on the street can't do quantum mechanics, because he can't (unless you're on a very special street). The paternalist believes that it is the facts that suggest a change in the status we accord people, a change from what we might have thought about ourselves to a more realistic acceptance of our inabilities. The suggestion here is simply that we should treat people in accordance with their real abilities and their real limitations. It may, of course, take away from someone's consequence, in the eyes of others or in his own eyes, if it is pointed out that he doesn't have a particular quality that he thought he had. However, it is more demeaning to pretend to have a quality that you don't than to admit to not having one you might like to have. The story of the Emperor's new clothes is illustrative – the Emperor wouldn't have suffered embarrassment before all the people of the kingdom if he had admitted that he couldn't see the "magic" clothes that the conmen tailors were trying to get him to accept. He would have saved all the money he paid for them, and would furthermore have avoided appearing naked and foolish before everyone in the land. What hurt him was pretending that he was one of the wise who were supposed to be able to see them. It was vanity that prevented him from admitting the truth, that allowed others to take advantage of him and made him look like a fool. Claiming to have a stature you don't is more disrespectful of self, and of one's real attributes, than is admitting to a lesser stature. It suggests that what you've got left when you eliminate the disputed property isn't worth much – but there is no reason to think this of people. We remain as we have been, as we have experienced ourselves, and have appreciated ourselves, and this is clearly valuable, whatever stature we may lose.

And what is the suggested loss of stature? Some critics argue that paternalism treats adults like children: Feinberg says that "[t]o treat an adult paternalistically is tantamount to treating that adult as one who is still normatively a child, as yet incapable of prudence," which he characterizes as an "implied insult."[39] But if this is anything more than a hyperbolic way of saying we don't like thinking of ourselves as imperfect, why think it is true? We know more than children do, and generally have more of a sense of what will work, and are better at making instrumental decisions. We are more prudent than children. We aren't perfectly prudent, but then no one ever thought we were perfectly prudent. So the argument here is that we are more imprudent than we had realized, and that given this, we need to help each other in ways we

[39] Feinberg, *Harm to Self*, p. 55.

hadn't realized we needed. Of course we can run a society in a way that children can't. (Practically speaking, of course, we also need to run society, since there is no one else to turn to, but we need not be afraid that paternalist arguments entail that we should share these responsibilities with our six-year-olds.) That the argument for paternalism does admit, and indeed insist, that our difference from children is quantitative, not qualitative, does not suggest that this is not a real distinction. Paternalists do not typically suggest that people are incapable of running society, of crafting good legislation, or ever making good decisions about their personal lives. There is empirical evidence to the contrary, and since what the paternalist is asking for here is that we include some psychological realism in planning our institutions, it would be foolish to assume that the paternalist will ignore our actual successes. We are what are, no less and no more. The justifiability of paternalism does suggest that we are not godlike beings, but that is because we are not godlike beings. Realism cannot be degrading, and treating people in accordance with their actual abilities is not insulting or disrespectful. Recognition of our actual status is all respect can call for.

IS THIS CONTROVERSIAL?

While many people find this position objectionable, there may nonetheless be a question as to whether this view says anything controversial. Even Mill, the most influential opponent of forcing other people to do what you think is good for them, admitted exceptions in terms of what may be called long-term desires: as mentioned above, in the broken bridge example, Mill said that if you see someone stepping on to a bridge that you know to be unsound, you can stop him. The most significant condition is that he does not know the bridge is broken. You further assume that he doesn't want to fall through the bridge, and see that there is no opportunity to apprise him of the bridge's condition.[40] Some take this to mean that even on Mill's account, we are allowed to engage in coercive paternalism when what we are forcing you to do is what you would want to do if you were adequately informed. Forcing you to act in accordance with what your informed desire would direct is sometimes called Soft Paternalism, and many people see its legitimacy as obvious and uncontroversial precisely because they don't think it violates autonomy. Some argue that soft paternalism isn't even paternalism, because for an

---

[40] Mill, *On Liberty*, ch. 5, p. 229.

action to be paternalistic, it has to be contrary to your desires. Joel Feinberg, for example, says:

> It is not as clear that "soft paternalism" is paternalistic at all, in any clear sense. Certainly its motivating spirit seems closer to the liberalism of Mill than to the protectiveness of hard paternalism. Soft paternalism holds that the state has the right to prevent self-regarding conduct … *when but only when* that conduct is substantially nonvoluntary … [T]he soft paternalist points out that the law's concern should not be with the wisdom, prudence, or dangerousness of B's choice, but rather with whether or not the choice is truly his. Its concern should be to help implement B's real choice not to protect B from harm as such.[41]

Feinberg goes on to argue that decisions that are made in ignorance of the facts, and which will result in harm to the self, should be considered nonvoluntary, so that state intervention is permitted (although, confusingly, an equally ignorant decision which will harm someone else can be considered voluntary, and thus blameworthy, if the ignorance is due to negligence).[42] The paternalism I promote here is not a paternalism about ultimate ends; that is, I do not argue that there are objectively good ends, or objectively rational ends, or ends objectively valuable in any way, which everyone should be made to pursue.[43] I am arguing for intervention in cases where people's choices of instrumental means are confused, in a way that means they will not achieve their ultimate ends. If my subjective end is happiness, and I think playing the lottery will promote that, not because the suspense gives me some evanescent pleasure, but because I really think I have a reasonable chance of winning, I am mistaken about my means. Of course, Feinberg's definition is not universally accepted: many argue that an action can be voluntary even if mistaken in some respects, and others simply define paternalism in light of its constraints on behavior in light of present desires, without qualifying those desires.[44] The point, though, is that if we constrain action only in order to get the person to do what he would want to do if he were fully informed and fully rational, this may seem unproblematic.[45]

If the position I am taking here is uncontroversial, I am quite willing to have it be so: we could proceed with crafting paternalistic legislation!

---

[41] Feinberg, *Harm to Self*, p. 12.   [42] Ibid., ch. 21, "Failures of Voluntariness."
[43] This will be discussed at greater length in Chapter 4 below.
[44] For a critical discussion of Feinberg's theory of what it takes for an act be voluntary, see Richard Arneson, "Mill Versus Paternalism," *Ethics* 90.4 (July 1980), 470–489.
[45] While Sunstein and Thaler, in *Nudge*, do not explicitly articulate what good is to be promoted through libertarian paternalism, they are plausibly interpreted to take informed desires as the end to be pursued. See Robert Sugden, "Why Incoherent Preferences do not Justify Paternalism," *Constitutional Political Economy* 19 (2008), 226–248.

This is not, however, obvious. What the discussion of cognitive bias shows us is that the difference between an informed and an uninformed person is complex.[46] Typically, people who smoke know the basic facts about smoking, including its dangers, its economic costs and its effect on their children; after all, it's hard not to. Still, about 20 percent of American adults smoke. What happens is that these facts fail to "take." People irrationally underestimate the dangers of smoking to themselves, even while admitting its general danger. So, do they know the dangers of smoking or not? A common and perhaps ultimately correct answer is "kinda." They satisfy the criterion of knowledge as Mill seems to imagine it in the bridge example; they know the facts. They fail to satisfy the criteria of rational choice, however, because of cognitive failures in applying these facts. The same ambiguities arise in other cases discussed in behavioral economics, where we know that policies that support 10 percent unemployment and 90 percent employment, respectively, are supporting the same thing, but yet we vote for the 90 percent employment plan and against the 10 percent unemployment plan. At the same time, these are people who do have the normal grasp on what percentages mean. There is a difference in ways of knowing. This ambiguity creates a difficulty when we try to assess whether the smoker's choice is voluntary, and thus whether the paternalist is overriding a voluntary act or, less controversially, an involuntary one: in one sense of voluntary, it is not voluntary. John Kleinig presents this distinction very clearly: if we require that for an action to be truly voluntary it meet the ideal circumstances of rationality and information, the biased action is not voluntary; if, on the other hand, we use the common standards for moral responsibility, where you are held responsible for actions that are performed under less than ideal conditions, because they are, in a common sense, voluntary, then the actions of the biased person would count as voluntary.[47]

CONCLUSION

Coercive paternalism, then, is a policy whereby people who, in one sense, may know the relevant facts and still choose an action – to smoke, or to take out a mortgage that requires 50 percent of their income – can be

---

[46] Some argue that Mill himself shows sensitivity to the fact that our beliefs are prone to irrational influences, including the social and cultural milieu, in writings other than *On Liberty*. See Fred Wilson, "Mill on Psychology and the Moral Sciences," in *The Cambridge Companion to Mill*, ed. John Skorupski (Cambridge University Press, 1998), pp. 203–254.

[47] See Kleinig, *Paternalism*, pp. 69 ff.

forcibly constrained in their choices. They are prevented from acting on what are, in Kleinig's second sense, their voluntary choices. This does allow paternalism in more cases than Mill wants. Mill thinks that once you've told the man on the bridge about the danger of falling, his choice to nonetheless cross it is not one you can rightly interfere with. Mill, like Feinberg, seems to think that on the whole, if a normally competent adult is familiar with the facts, he will then decide in accordance with his own ends. We see, though, that this is not the case, and this calls for what is normally called "hard" paternalism. Hard paternalism is contrasted with soft paternalism in two ways: it may mean forcing people to act (or refrain from action) rather than simply manipulating choice in less invasive ways, as libertarian paternalism does. And, it may mean imposing actions upon people that they themselves would not choose, even if properly informed; where soft paternalism only makes (or entices) people to do what they themselves would want, if they knew the facts. I argue for hard paternalism in both senses. Certainly we need to constrain people's actions, because merely incentivizing good actions, as the soft paternalist would recommend, is not sufficient. And, we will need to get them to do things they would not choose even if properly informed, because being informed is no guarantee of an instrumentally rational decision. This, then, is indeed a hard option; but it is one we need.[48]

Coercive paternalism will probably prove controversial to most people, because it argues against allowing you the freedom to do what you want to do even when you know (as we would normally construe that) all the facts. It is intended to advance your ends, but interferes with your ability to choose your means, and this is seen as offensive. There is, though, a strong prima facie argument in its favor, since it would help us to avoid destructive tendencies to which we are all prey, and would help us to end up in situations that we want; situations that in some cases are definitive of whether or not our lives count as a success. We have seen, furthermore, that properly understood, it does not entail disrespect for persons. Why, then, is it so generally opposed? Much of the answer seems to lie in its imagined effects. The fear is that a system that allows coercive paternalism in more than a very few cases will be one which, to put it most simply, results in unhappiness rather than happiness and unfairness rather than fairness. Sunstein and Thaler, for example, argue that government is

---

[48] The issue of whether it is really controversial to impose actions on people who don't entirely understand what it is that they are doing wrong will be taken up again in Chapter 6 below, in light of suggested applications of coercive paternalism.

fallible, that modern life is too complex, and that the pace of technical and global change is too rapid for "rigid mandates" for improvement (as it is, they say, for the status quo of "dogmatic laissez-faire"). They feel that libertarian paternalism, since it allows a greater range of responses than does coercive paternalism, will be in the long run the most productive system.[49] I will now turn to those dangers that many fear will result from the application of coercive mandates, and will show that, while any policy can have bad results when implemented badly, there is no more reason to expect this of coercive paternalistic practices than of any other set of governmental practices, and furthermore that the expected benefits are very great.

---

[49] Thaler and Sunstein, *Nudge*, p. 253.

CHAPTER 2

Individuality

So far my argument has been simple. Given that we allow paternalistic intervention in some cases (seat belts, prescription medicine) where we think intervention is very, very likely to make a person better off, we should allow it in other, similar cases. We believe intervention in these cases is justified because we believe the person left to choose freely may choose poorly, in the sense that his choice will not get him what he wants in the long run, and is chosen solely because of errors in instrumental reasoning. We do not consider this disrespectful, since it is a rule applied to everyone equally and which does not undervalue people's actual decision-making abilities.

It is possible, though, that even if interventions are justified when considered as individual cases, the accretion of such interventions has a cumulative effect which is itself so negative as to outweigh the individual benefits of intervention. One person who seems to have believed this is John Stuart Mill. Mill is the best known and most influential opponent of paternalism, and is furthermore a philosopher of striking intelligence and an astute critic of social policy. If he thinks there is something wrong with a policy, this gives us prima facie reason to think the same thing. Thus, we must turn now to his criticism.

Mill published *On Liberty* in 1859. It is a striking defense of individual freedom of action, thought, and speech. Mill argued that paternalism, given that it is a restriction on freedom, would result in a stunting of individuals, that it would make them unable to grow and develop in a naturally human way, and leave them, as he put it, like a Chinese lady's bound foot, unnatural, full of pain, and useless. Such a perversion would cause these individuals, in many cases, to be unhappy with themselves and with others: unable to live in the only way that would lead them to flourish, and alienated from, and exasperated with, the society that so trammeled them. As if this were not an ugly enough picture, Mill thinks that these harms, while likely to be felt most immediately by a minority (the minority typically being most at odds with prevailing mores), will result in losses to everyone in society. Originality, innovation, and genius are necessary, on Mill's view, for society to progress, and the domination of conventionality which will result from paternalistic laws will make these at best rare, at worst impossible. If Mill is right in even some of these charges, then the case against paternalism is very strong. I will argue, though, that Mill is wrong; that he was misled by a relatively unsophisticated view of human psychology and an unduly pessimistic view of government. Contemporary accounts of both can show that in fact paternalistic constraints on behavior can be liberating and provide the best means to the very thing Mill wants to defend, individuality.

THE HARM PRINCIPLE

Probably the most influential argument ever made against paternalism is the position that Mill takes in chapter 1 of *On Liberty* and which we now call the Harm Principle. Mill, as the leading proponent of utilitarianism, generally assessed the rightness of policies in terms of their consequences. Since paternalism is a practice wherein people are forced to perform actions that bring about good consequences for themselves, Mill naturally foresaw that his view could be thought to justify paternalistic policies. This, however, he believed to be quite wrong, and he wrote *On Liberty* at least in part to prove it.

The object of this Essay is to assert one very simple principle, as entitled to govern absolutely the dealings of society with the individual in the way of compulsion and control, whether the means used be physical force in the form of legal penalties, or in the moral coercion of public opinion. That principle is, that the sole end for which mankind are warranted, individually or collectively, in interfering with the liberty of action of any of their number, is self-protection. That the only purpose for which power can be rightfully exercised over any member of a civilized community, against his will, is to prevent harm to others. His own good, either physical or moral, is not a sufficient warrant. He cannot rightfully be compelled to do or forbear because it will be better for him to do so, because it will make him happier, because, in the opinions of others, to do so would be wise, or even right. These are good reasons for remonstrating with him, or reasoning with him, or persuading him, or entreating him, but not for compelling him, or visiting him with any evil in case he do otherwise. To justify that, the conduct from which it is desired to deter him must be calculated to produce evil to some one else. The only part of the conduct of any one, for which he is amenable to society, is that which concerns others. In the part which merely concerns himself, his independence is, of right, absolute. Over himself, over his own body and mind, the individual is sovereign.[1,2]

---

[1] All citations to *On Liberty* and *Utilitarianism* are taken from the Meridian edition (1971).
[2] *On Liberty*, p. 135

The harm principle seems relatively clear as to its import. The question is what justifies the conclusion Mill articulates so resoundingly. In this same chapter Mill has said that he will not rely on "abstract" ideas of right, distinct from utility. That is, he will not argue that paternalistic intervention is somehow inherently wrong. If it is to be shown to be wrong, then it must be shown to have bad consequences. Mill was aware of Kant's arguments that our treatment of one another should be based on respect for freedom, regardless of the consequences, and rejected those arguments. This is why Mill's position seems initially odd: if we truly want to promote human happiness, and use the promotion of happiness as our standard of right action, the fact that people do things that undercut their chances of happiness should suggest *instituting* some restrictions on what people can do to themselves, rather than justifying a ban on any such restriction.

Some argue that Mill, at least in *On Liberty*, believes liberty to be intrinsically valuable, not just valuable as means to the distinct end of happiness. As a consequentialist, even while rejecting Kant's deontological emphasis on rules *qua* rules, he can still argue that liberty is one of the valuable things whose production we should promote. In *Utilitarianism*, published two years later, in 1861, Mill discusses the constituents of happiness, and argued that not all pleasures are on a par – some are higher than others, and are on that account preferable.[3] John Gray has argued the exercise of choice is itself one of the "higher pleasures" that Mill extols in *Utilitarianism*.[4] C.L. Ten argues that when Mill speaks of maximizing happiness, he intends liberty to be a constitutive part of individuality, which is itself, on his account, a constituent of happiness, such that without it, happiness is not possible.[5] These arguments that liberty (or its exercise) may have intrinsic value may well be correct, both as exegesis of Mill's position and perhaps as more general statements about the nature of happiness. And these claims do give liberty more prominence than it would have if it were merely one means among others to bring about happiness, since it is at least logically possible that any given means may prove to be unnecessary in the production of a given end. Still, even regarding liberty as part of the end to be promoted doesn't constitute a good argument against paternalism. Paternalists can, after all,

---

[3] *Utilitarianism*, ch. 2.
[4] John Gray, "Mill's Conception of Happiness," *in J. S. Mill, "On Liberty": In Focus*, ed. John Gray and G. W. Smith (London and New York: Routledge, 1991), p. 193.
[5] C. L. Ten, *Mill On Liberty* (Oxford: Clarendon Press, 1980), especially ch. 5.

value liberty as an end in itself. My brand of paternalism, which promotes the satisfaction of people's long-term desires, is certainly open to this, since people do want, among other things, to be free. The paternalist position, though, is that whatever the final good consists in, it will sometimes be permissible, or indeed perhaps obligatory, to constrain what people do in order to help them reach that end. Even on this interpretation of Mill, then, where liberty is one of the constituents of happiness and thus something that should be promoted, it would make more sense to admit that at times the best way to promote it overall is to curtail it in particular cases.

This, though, is clearly not his position: he says "[t]he only freedom which deserves the name, is that of pursuing our own good in our own way, so long as we do not attempt to deprive others of theirs, or impede their efforts to obtain it."[6] While paternalistic policies do aim to promote the person's own good, they obviously do not aim to allow him to pursue it in his own way; the justification for paternalism is precisely that choosing one's own way is so often antithetical to actually achieving one's own good. So, while the paternalist concedes that all things considered, it is good to have more liberty rather than less, the paternalist would say that sometimes we need to take away someone's liberty so that in the end they can have more liberty. Mill thinks this is wrong – but why?

Mill has a number of answers to this question. One is that the immediate efficacy of paternalistic actions is often doubtful. Mill believes, as he says above, that we can interfere with your liberty if you are about to harm someone else. A major difference between that kind of intervention and paternalistic legislation is that the latter is likely to be misconceived. When we prevent a thief from stealing your television set, or punish one who has, we address an obvious need: you don't want your television stolen and are happy to testify to this. There is no doubt that anti-theft legislation typically addresses a real harm. That in itself doesn't mean the legislation is justified, of course, since in some cases a given harm will be outweighed by benefit to others, is not worth the costs of enforcement, and so forth. However, when we assess the overall consequences of theft, and the overall consequences of making theft illegal, we arrive at the decision that it is best, all things considered, to make stealing illegal when the object stolen is over a certain value.

In paternalistic legislation, however, we take someone who seems happy with his situation – because if he were not, he would change it,

---

[6] *On Liberty*, ch. 1, p. 138.

Mill seems to believe, as long as we don't prevent him – and then make him do something else which is contrary to what was making him happy. It is much harder to argue in a case like this that there is an obvious harm being addressed, and Mill thinks that when it comes to paternalistic legislation, usually no harm is being addressed. Mill thinks that paternalistic legislation is more likely to address the needs of the legislator than the needs of the object of that legislation – the person whose life is being changed. The legislator may simply be acting out of a sense of distaste for a certain kind of living – a sense, for example, that the use of drugs is degrading – regardless of any harm it does. More benevolently, and less judgmentally, he may genuinely believe this kind of living must make those who live that way unhappy, and mean to rescue them from their own poor judgment. Such a third-party judgment, though, is likely to be mistaken. He is mistaken in thinking it is his business to prevent self-degradation, even if he could be trusted to be free from mere prejudice in identifying it, and he is likely to be at least an equally poor judge of what makes someone other than himself unhappy. Generally, Mill thinks, the individual can be trusted to care most about his own happiness, and to know best what he wants.

On questions of social morality, of duty to others, the opinion of others, the opinion of the public, that is, of an overruling majority, though often wrong, is likely to be still oftener right; because on such questions they are only required to judge of their own interests; of the manner in which some mode of conduct, if allowed to be practiced, would effect themselves. But the opinion of a similar majority, imposed as a law on the minority, on questions of self-regarding conduct, is quite as likely to be wrong as right; for in these cases public opinion means, at the best, some people's opinion of what is good or bad for other people, while very often it does not even mean that; the public, with the most perfect indifference, passing over the pleasure or convenience of those whose conduct they censure, and considering only their own preference.[7]

At the same time, the individual

is the person most interested in his own well-being ... while with respect to his own feelings and circumstances, the most ordinary man or woman has means of knowledge immeasurably surpassing those that can be possessed by any one else. The interference of society to overrule his judgment and purposes in what only regards himself must be grounded on general presumptions; which may be altogether wrong, and even if right, are as likely as not to be misapplied to individual cases ...[8]

---

[7] Ibid., ch. 4, pp. 214–215.   [8] Ibid., pp. 206–207.

While this is a reasonable argument, it is too simplistic. First, it does not adequately differentiate means and ends. It is quite possible that only a given person can say what he himself enjoys.[9] It is another to say that he is the best person to choose the means to reach that end. As I have discussed in Chapter 1, we are too prone to errors to be able to assume that our knowledge of ourselves necessarily leads us to choose the means most conducive to achieving the life we want. This is true whatever our goal may be. That we do harm ourselves Mill admits; in discussing it, he says that when people harm themselves they have only themselves to blame, as if this gives us a reason not to interfere[10] – but if our motivation is benevolence, considerations of desert should not stop us from preventing harm, whoever may be at fault. The harm done is assignable, as Mill insists is required when we make laws restricting harm done to others – we can name the particular person whom the act harms[11] rather than trying to prevent hypothetical, indirect harms. And, he gives several circumstances where he thinks we can justifiably interfere with your liberty when you are about to harm yourself. First, there those who are still children, those societies in which "the race itself may be considered as in its nonage" – that is, those whose judgment, whether for reasons of age or culture, is not sufficiently developed. (He hastens to add that his readers do not fall into this category; those whom he addresses are beyond the state of incapacity that would require they be subject to a benevolent dictator.) Furthermore and secondly, even those who are competent adults in a sufficiently sophisticated society may be interfered with in a couple of specific cases: the first is that of the broken bridge (discussed briefly in Chapter 1 above), where we can interfere with someone who is justifiably believed to be ignorant of the dangers he runs with a certain course of action; and the second is that of the slavery contract, where Mill says a person should not be allowed to use his liberty to sign away his future liberty.[12] This implies that, not surprisingly, we sometimes act in a way that is at odds with our own interests, and that at least sometimes interference with such actions is not only permissible, but obligatory. Given that we can make other mistakes, and that these mistakes can also be grave, it seems reasonable that in particular circumstances it makes the most sense to interfere with people's

---

[9] Even this needs to be qualified, since sometimes therapists and even friends can tell that a person is not in fact enjoying something he is committed to thinking he enjoys.
[10] *On Liberty*, ch. 4, p. 210.   [11] Ibid., p. 212.
[12] Ibid., ch. 5, pp. 235–236. The literature on the slave contract is vast, and many different explanations of Mill's thinking are offered. Here I only draw attention to the fact that it is a case where Mill thinks liberty can indeed be infringed upon.

liberty in order to promote their good, even where their good is understood to include as much liberty as possible. If we want to promote happiness, even the "higher quality" happiness he champions, it seems that interfering with liberty is sometimes called for.

Individuality

The most reasonable position capturing Mill's general concerns, whether or not it is in fact Mill's, and one endorsed by many critics of paternalism, is that the danger is not so much any one paternalistic act but the effect of an accretion of paternalistic laws. If one paternalistic intervention is allowed, it is reasonable to think others will be allowed, at least when the cost–benefit analysis reveals the same net gain to be garnered. While a particular instance of paternalistic intrusion might be beneficial, state intrusion will be much more far-reaching. Mill believes that general formal intrusion (through regulation, prevention, or sanctions) into personal life results in the loss of individuality.

Freedom is necessary for individuality, and the development of individuality, for Mill, is essential to personal and social flourishing.

If it were felt that the free development of individuality is one of the leading essentials of well-being; that it is not only a co-ordinate element with all that is designated by the terms of civilisation, instruction, education, culture, but is itself a necessary part and condition of all those things; there would be no danger that liberty should be undervalued, and the adjustment of the boundaries between it and social control would present no extraordinary difficulty.[13]

And again,

individuality is the same thing with development, and ... it is only the cultivation of individuality which produces, or can produce, well-developed human beings.[14]

What Mill means by individuality is not entirely clear, as he says many different things, not all of which seem applicable to the same concept. Richard Arneson has differentiated three of the things Mill seems to include.[15] First, there is the simple difference from others – uniqueness rather than similarity. Some critics have decried Mill's emphasis on simply being different from others as encouraging idiosyncrasy for idiosyncrasy's sake, and thus as bringing about its own form of artificiality – the

---

[13] Ibid., ch. 3, p. 185.   [14] Ibid., p. 193.   [15] Arneson, "Mill Versus Paternalism," 470–489.

requirement to see what others do, and do differently, may be as constraining and unnatural as conforming one's behavior to others'. Still, since Mill
thought that diversity of ideas was always a good thing, even when this
included the articulation of false ideas, the support for the cultivation of
difference *qua* difference, like the admonition to "think outside the box,"
can be productive, even if the thinking inside the box is actually pretty
good. The injunction to be different amounts to an injunction to explore
untraveled paths, which may then prove to be worth pursuing at greater
length. Second, Arneson finds in Mill's praise for individuality praise
for excellence rather than mediocrity. Mill extols the development of
our uniquely human capacities, our higher abilities. This sounds surprisingly like Aristotle's argument in the *Nicomachean Ethics* that humans
(like other organisms) have a unique function which makes them what
they are and whose excellent performance is necessary to living a truly
human life: "to conform to custom, merely as custom, does not educate
or develop in him any of the qualities which are the distinctive endow-
ments of a human being."[16] Mill's praise of individuality as necessary to
living the happy life may thus bring his conception of happiness close to
Aristotle's concept of eudaimonia, in which subjective contentment is
only one element among others of human flourishing. In any case, for
Mill, the pursuit of individuality clearly entails the development of one's
human intellectual and creative capacities. Third, Mill sees individuality
as involving the development of the self, the set of traits and desires that
are truly one's own: "A person whose desires and impulses are his own –
are the expression of his own nature, as it has been modified and
developed by his own culture – is said to have a character."[17] In this third
area, according to Arneson,

perhaps two conditions for individuality are being asserted. One is self-culture,
achieved when a person freely posits a character ideal and makes efforts to
conform himself to that idea. The second requirement for individuality is
appropriateness, achieved when the character ideal posited by the individual is
chosen in light of some accurate perception as to his own basic proclivities and
talents.[18]

This sounds very much like what contemporary philosophers have
described as authenticity, the cultivation of a self which is somehow
rooted in one's true character and values.[19] Mill's suggestion may be that

---

[16] *On Liberty*, ch. 3, p. 187.   [17] Ibid., p. 189.   [18] Arneson, "Mill Versus Paternalism," 479–480.
[19] For a detailed discussion of authenticity, see Chapter 3 below.

even if the standard of human excellence is the same for all humans, this is consistent with more specific goals that may be unique to the individual – perhaps like choosing a life of politics over the life of a poet, or the life of a single person rather than one including a big family.

In any case, Mill may have intended to promote all of these – diversity, excellence in human function, and authenticity – in his praise of individuality, and clearly believed that without it, society would fail. Once state intervention is allowed, we will be prevented from developing in our own, unique, natural way, and rather forced into one socially acceptable mold, which will cause losses along all three spectra. Such a loss is clearly not worth the relatively small benefit of occasionally saving persons from hurting themselves. The benefit in question is small, first, because Mill believed the occasions upon which people need to be saved are relatively few: left to their own devices, they will typically choose for themselves that course which is best for them, given their particular desires,[20] even where this leads them to run risks another might not.[21] Secondly, we have other, less costly, ways of preventing people from harming themselves: we have control of the formation of their values and tastes from an early age to adulthood, and can more efficiently introduce rational habits there than by enforcing them through law once people have attained their majority.[22] So, intervention does great harm, and only a little good, and that little good can typically be achieved more efficiently in other ways. From a consequentialist perspective, this is a complete argument.

Mill's problem in this argument against paternalism lies not in its validity but in the truth of the premises. I will argue that Mill is mistaken in his analysis – in his evaluation of the costs of intervention and his belief that only very few benefits can arise from it. First, Mill is mistaken in his belief that, left to their own devices, people will be efficient in the development and pursuit of their own goals. As we saw in Chapter 1, people are simply not as instrumentally rational as Mill and others of his era believed, so they do not choose effective means to their ends. Second, he overestimated the degree to which humans would develop in varying, individual, and authentic ways if left without government controls. Third, he assumed that government intervention would always be a conservative influence, imposing the social conventions of the majority and repressing innovation, and this need not be the case. The first problem, our inability to reliably choose good means to our ends, has been discussed in Chapter 1. Here we want to discuss the

---

[20] *On Liberty*, ch. 3, p. 187; ch. 4, pp. 206–207.   [21] Ibid., ch. 5, p. 229.   [22] Ibid., ch. 3, p. 186.

second and third of Mill's beliefs, that we naturally pursue individuality, and that government intervention always represses individuality, to see where Mill's arguments go wrong.

Mill's claims arise from several beliefs. First, he thinks individuals don't need the help of society to develop in distinct and individual ways because that is their natural tendency. All they need from society is that it not interfere in the unique development of each human organism. He cites the work of Alex von Humboldt to this effect. Our goal, says Humboldt, is "individuality of power and development," and for these there are (apparently only) two requisites: "freedom and variety of situation." From the union of these arise "individual vigour and manifold destiny."[23] Given the appropriate requisites as a child (where paternalism is appropriate), the individual will achieve the "privilege and proper condition of a human being, arrived at the maturity of his faculties, [which is] to use and interpret experience in his own way."[24] Independence of thought and individuality of lifestyle are our natural ends.

Along with this natural tendency to develop individuality, though, there is an equally natural tendency to want to impose our standards on others. We believe our way of life is the right one, and want others to adhere to it. To this end, we will use the social sanctions at our disposal to prevent both different ways of thinking and different ways of living. One way to do this is simply through noninstitutional social pressure; by intentionally causing the suffering of those who deviate, and by ostracizing them from the society, entry into which is required for most sorts of success, society forces compliance. Instead of the cultivation of individuality that produces a well-developed human being, we get people who "need no other faculty than the ape-like one of imitation."[25] This social pressure is bad enough, but it becomes worse when society uses government to sanction these rules. Then, escape from social pressure into a deviant life becomes almost impossible.

And, Mill seems to assume that a representative government will typically allow itself to be so used; it will do nothing to hold back the effects of general social disapproval, but will rather enforce them. Mill may think that those who are in the government are likely to have the same values as the majority of their constituents. For one thing, they, too, are subject to the same despotism of custom, and will have had their distinctive beliefs pruned by common opinion. Further, in common with members of government today, they may be subject to a self-interest

---

[23] Ibid.   [24] Ibid.   [25] Ibid., p. 187.

which would make them act in accord with majority opinion even when they don't agree with it: legislators have to reflect the habits and beliefs of the majority of their constituents, since only by acting in accord with the majority will individual representatives be re-elected. Thus, the state will use its coercive powers to enforce laws that the majority wants. Even sincere attempts at beneficial intervention on the part of the government will only reflect shared prejudices of society: "No government by a democracy or a numerous aristocracy, either in its political acts or in the opinions, qualities, and tone of mind which it fosters, ever could or did rise above mediocrity." The only exception is when the masses are willing to be guided by some elite: they do better "insofar as the sovereign many have let themselves be guided (which in the best times they always have done) by the counsels and influence of a more highly gifted One or Few."[26] And this, Mill seems to think, is depressingly rare, since we generally react to new or unusual ideas with horror rather than appreciation.

Mill himself provides one counterexample to this. One occasion on which paternalistic government intervention is successful at promoting, rather than depressing, individuality is education. Mill was, more than most, aware of the value of education in the very development he promoted. While he did not approve of a state mandated and funded curriculum, again fearing the conformity it would engender, he did think the government was right to require that parents educate their children. Education is necessary for the development of the talents and abilities which both individuate us and contribute to the development of genius and, ultimately, civilization. Mill may have thought that government could be successful in forcing a practice which involves rising above inertia and thinking about new things, because the population upon which it is forced doesn't vote. As long as the parents are willing to support it, the government may act with impunity towards the unwilling youths who trudge grudgingly to school. Forcing improvements upon the adult population is quite a different thing. Since adults vote, the state can't make them do anything they don't want, or they will make the government change. Those in power want to keep it, and so to please the majority of adults, they will simply enforce the majority's values, rather than forcing upon them the means to diversity and individuality. Once the government, with its powers of enforcement and sanction, acts to eliminate different lifestyles, these are truly in danger.

[26] Ibid., p. 196.

Conformity

The problem with these claims is that they are, in large part, false. Mill believes that, first, uninhibited by social sanctions we will develop the diversity, excellence, and authenticity necessary to a flourishing society; and second, that government interference must always reinforce the social conservative bent towards preservation of the status quo, thus preventing the development of diversity, excellence, and authenticity. Neither of these is correct.

Modern studies in social psychology and behavioral economics show us different explanations of the social conformity Mill sought to explain, and they allow us to offer different recommendations as to how to harmonize the development of individuality and the pursuit of happiness. In truth, people are likely to conform to custom without any social sanctions being brought to bear. It does not take the fear of ostracism, or other harms, to make us do what those around us do – "gravitation to the norm" is the normal human tendency. Second, government can succeed in being a liberating force rather than one that simply reinforces the status quo. This is true for at least two reasons. For one thing, while it is true enough that people distrust those who have different values, Mill did not realize that people are also apt to disapprove of their own behavior, because their own behavior does not, often, reflect their values. There are occasions upon which, then, they may welcome deviation from their own practices, because they disapprove of these. As a result, they may welcome government action that interferes in people's common behaviors, because that action may bring them to live more in accord with the values they endorse. And, government action, while certainly in many cases reflecting conservative social views, sometimes proposes greater toleration of difference than society itself wants to allow.

The objection to Mill's first premise is one we might support anecdotally, even if social psychology did not support it more formally. The mere fact that a behavior is common tends to make us want to live in that way, without any social sanctions being applied. What we see as normal we see as acceptable and desirable. Psychologists identify two sorts of conformity that are of particular interest here. First, we often change an opinion if that opinion deviates from what we perceive to be the majority opinion. This "informational social influence" has been tested in a number of areas. The classic work by Muzafer Sherif took subjects who were recording their estimate of how far a light in a dark room moved. Answering alone, they provided one answer. Given the same task within a group, of whom the majority were confederates of the tester who were giving a false answer, they revised their opinions to fit those of the majority. Tested a third time, again alone, they held to the answer they had arrived at in the group. Here, no social ostracism was offered: they honestly came to believe the opinion of the majority was right.[27] This tendency has recently been attributed to "hard wiring" in the brain: seeing that your own opinion differs from that of others causes a "negative emotion,"[28] perceivable in brain scans, and it provokes neural response, which seems to cause an adjustment in the long term to an individual's own opinion.[29] The explanation seems to be the general efficacy of social learning – over the long run, we believe that the majority is probably right, and adjust accordingly, a tendency that was presumably evolutionarily useful. Unfortunately, though, the bad side of this tendency is a natural bent towards quashing original observations – we tend to doubt ourselves simply because what we believe is different from what other people believe, without sanctions of any sort being present.

Secondly, and more familiarly, we modify our behavior in response to "normative social influence." We want to do what others do because the more we are like them, the more we will fit in to the social group.[30] (Consider the embarrassment of being inappropriately dressed at a social gathering – regardless of whether anyone reacts to this.) This consciousness of social rules is evident even in very small children – it is something we pick up on early.[31] Interestingly, the same behavior is manifested in other primates – chimpanzees will follow a new method of doing obtaining food when it is introduced by a high-ranking chimp from their own group, but not when they are simply exposed to it without someone high in the hierarchy having adopted it first. It isn't worth copying until someone worthy of copying does it. This suggests, again, that it is not merely an effect of our particular culture but something deeper in the human (or, primate) psyche.[32]

---

[27] Sherif, Muzafer, *The Psychology of Social Norms* (New York: Harper, 1936).
[28] G. S. Berns et al., "Neurobiological Correlates of Social Conformity and Independence During Mental Rotation," *Biological Psychiatry* 58.3 (2005), 245–253.
[29] Vasily Klucharev, "Brain May be Wired for Social Conformity," *Neuron* (January 15, 2009).
[30] This has been studied in great depth by a number of authors, but see particularly the seminal studies by S. E. Asch: "Opinions and Social Pressure," *Scientific American* 193 (1955); and "Studies of Independence and Conformity," *Psychological Monographs* 79.9 (1956).
[31] Charles Kalish, "Reasons and Causes: Children's Understanding of Conformity to Social Rules and Physical Laws," *Child Development* 69.15 (June 1998), 706–720.
[32] Andrew Whiten, "Conformity to Cultural Norms of Tool Use in Chimpanzees," *Nature* 437 (September 29, 2005), 737–740.

So, while Mill is certainly correct that social sanctions can exacerbate this tendency towards conformity, it occurs even without these. In the absence of a significant push towards rethinking behaviors and values, we tend to conform. People like to do what is normal: to have the same style of house, of activities, even the same size family, as do their peers. Sometimes this is not problematic, but sometimes, of course, it is; both when the customs voluntarily adopted are positively bad ones, and when they simply prevent the discovery of new and advantageous ways of life.

Regulation and liberation

In *Considerations on Representative Government*, Mill expiates at length on the dangers of inertia, enervation, and mental passivity. However, he associates these almost exclusively with despotic governments, where no role is given to the individual citizen to exert himself. This is why even benign despotism is bad; it breeds, at best, a false sense of satisfaction, where "the great mass of seeming contentment is real discontent combined with indolence or self-indulgence."[33] The result is that we fail to strive for more: "[i]nactivity, unaspiringness, absence of desire are a more fatal hindrance to improvement than any misdirection of energy."[34] What Mill does not see is how likely these tendencies are to flourish, as far as we can tell, under any form of government; that they are not induced through a corruption of the self by despotism but arise naturally unless they are actively opposed. People left to their own devices, rather than developing with special vivacity and originality, relax instead into both inertia and irrationality in discovering and pursuing appropriate means to ends, even in a situation of participatory government. Instead of pursuing education, which opens them to varied ideas and opportunities for development, they may, without state requirements, do nothing but watch television. Mill may be right that such a life leaves us unhappy, but was wrong in thinking that the response to unhappiness is to try to change our situation. Rather, our response may be to avoid thinking about our situation, or to accept it as inevitable, or to assume that others' situations would be worse, or simple denial, where we tell ourselves we aren't living a life in which our primary feelings are boredom, irritation,

---

[33] *Considerations on Representative Government*, in *Collected Works of John Stuart Mill*, vol. XIX, ed. J. M. Robson (University of Toronto Press and London: Routledge & Kegan Paul, 1977), ch. 3, p. 409.
[34] Ibid., p. 410.

and anxiety. The mere fact that a person dislikes an unsatisfying way of life does not mean he will take measures to improve it; instead, he may indulge in temporary palliatives designed to make that boredom bearable (the equivalent of channel-surfing) but which are themselves unsatisfying. We remain stagnant in what he later describes as an "intellectual culture . . . of that feeble and vague description which belongs to a mind that stops at amusement or at simple contemplation."[35]

Given this, we can see a role for government intervention which is paternalistic and which imposes on people things they would not and do not do themselves, but which need not result in that government's being thrown out of power. It may take intervention to save people from themselves, and people are not incapable of recognizing this. Governments can act in ways that secure us our goals, and when we recognize this, we can react with support for that program and that government. Thus, governments need not reflect in its laws what people actually do to stay in power, because that status quo may not actually be the state the majority wants to be in. Left to our own devices, we typically do not save for old age, much less engage in a mutual system where we contribute to one another's retirement, but when the government makes us do this it does not result in a groundswell rejection of Social Security. We are glad to be forced to do what we know we should do, but don't. Would we accept government legislation geared to developing our individuality per se? I am not quite sure what all such changes would be, but certainly health and solvency seem useful means to cultivating whatever aspects of ourselves we want to. And if individuality indeed provides the highest kind of happiness, it seems that we would. Indeed, we have accepted the requirement of education, and while this is, it is true, often justified in terms of having an economically profitable workforce, we don't teach only those things needed to be good workers, but try to include a relatively well-rounded humanistic education. Legislation and enforcement can promote well-being and the development of individuality in ways in which private citizenry, left to their own devices, would not, without this resulting in the overthrow of the government, or even, more prosaically, voting out everyone who votes for requiring certain actions of us. Insofar as the paternalism involved here is about means, rather than ends, it does not provoke the outrage that Mill imagined would follow from imposing on people in ways that deviate from convention.

Mill thinks that people want their lives to remain undisturbed, but he does not reckon, perhaps, on how discontented even free people may be

---

[35] Ibid., p. 407.

with their own lives. Mill, as a believer in people's rational agency, thinks that if people are unhappy, they will change their lives, as long as there are no external obstacles to such change. He does not recognize what internal obstacles there may be, and thus, that government action may help remove these latter. Being unhappy with ourselves does not necessarily lead us to change, and we may be grateful to those who force us to behave in a way that is more consistent with our own values.

Lastly, we know that government sometimes forces us to do things that don't reflect our present values, and can be more engaged in the promotion of liberty than we, as a society, actually want. And, in such cases, even while its deviation from convention is unwelcome, the government can persist, and the changes it brings about can eventually be accepted. In the US, judicial acceptance of interracial marriage, for example, preceded widespread social acceptance of it: while there were, of course, those who supported (and tried to engage in) it at the time it was found to be constitutionally protected (1967), it was certainly not believed by the majority to be morally or socially acceptable. This was a case where the government itself made individuality, in Mill's sense – greater variety in life choices, greater ability to act on one's own values and desires – more available than if it had not acted. The 1964 Civil Rights Act was widely unpopular and yet succeeded in allowing vastly greater freedom of opportunity. Certainly the government has sometimes failed to protect such freedom – both laws against homosexual activity and the judicial decision that protected such laws (Bowers *v.* Hardwick) were arguably based on social convention very much at odds with the Constitution and judicial precedent. We cannot assume government will be in advance of society. But we need not assume it will simply reflect the bias of the majority. The case is much more complex, and the causes of legislative variance from, and conformity to, popular opinion are not easy to understand. Certainly, though, we do not have to assume that law will do nothing but impose the prejudices of the majority on the minority.

And, we need not assume that being in advance of society will cause revolution, or generally cause those who bring about unpopular changes to lose office. For some of that, of course, we may be grateful to the very conventionality that Mill deplores: there's an extent to which we accept the legality of something as an argument in favor of its being justified, and so change our beliefs to reflect laws. Some acceptance of racial equality has followed, not just caused, the implementation of the Civil Rights Act. This tendency to accept government action as justified simply because it has been performed is not always a good thing, to be sure, but it does mean that the threat of being voted out of office (or suffering a revolution) is not one that the government really needs to fear when it imposes a law at odds with accepted mores. While Mill was pessimistic about anyone outside of a creative elite giving birth to innovative ideas, even he acknowledged that when they do arise, "[t]he honor and glory of the average man is that he is capable of following that initiative; that he can respond internally to wise and noble things, and be led by them with his eyes open."[36]

ONE SIZE DOES NOT FIT ALL

Even if we accept that we often need help to achieve our goals, not just on the rare occasions Mill seems to have imagined, and if we accept that people, left to their own devices, naturally tend to conservatism rather than individuality, and that government can actually stimulate individuality, questions remain. Contemporary critics of paternalism often point out that, even if many people need the help that paternalistic constrains provide, not everyone needs this. Some individuals may be, overall, less prone to cognitive bias, and very likely not everyone is prone to each sort of bias in just the same degree on each occasion. Tests that show a majority of people being influenced by framing, for example, do not show that 100 percent of people in the study succumb to the effect of varying frames. In any given case of cognitive bias, there will be some people who can and do make a rational judgment. It is argued, then, that paternalistic legislation, however helpful it may prove to those who are thinking poorly in a given situation, will unfairly force those who are not thinking poorly to bow to the unneeded intervention of the state. Jeffrey Rachlinski gives an example of reinsurance executives, who, while falling prey to the conjunction fallacy[37] when estimating whether the US would be hit by a terrorist attack, resisted it when estimating the likelihood that the US would be hit by a damaging hurricane, "an event with which they had tremendous experience."[38] Not everyone needs paternalistic interference all the time.

---

[36] *On Liberty*, ch. 3, p. 196.

[37] The conjunction fallacy is one wherein two facts fail properly to conjoin: using Rachlinski's example, they may estimate the likelihood of California being hit by an earthquake as higher than the likelihood of the US being hit by an earthquake.

[38] Jeffrey J. Rachlinski, "Cognitive Errors, Individual Differences, and Paternalism," *University of Chicago Law Review* (winter 2006), 207–228.

Worse, paternalistic interference may be downright harmful to some individuals – it may prevent them from achieving well-thought-out ends. Obviously, different people have some different goals and needs. How *much* difference there may be in our basic needs, such as for good health or solvency, is debatable, since clearly for most people these are useful to reaching most goals. Still, granting this degree of underlying similarity, it must be acknowledged that there are people for whom any given set of regulations will be an obstacle to achieving what they want. Not all people will flourish under these regulations, even if most do: while for most of us, attempting to jump the Snake River Canyon would be downright stupid, for Evil Knievel, it was probably really worthwhile, as were the many other jumps he did (or attempted) that did not follow what we would normally regard as basic safety rules. A reasonable paternalistic legislator might well forbid canyon jumping, thinking of teenagers meeting an early death, and that would genuinely have harmed Evil; indeed Evil, as we know him, might never have come to be. His imagined food counterpart, Trans-Fat Knievel, may be entirely frustrated at having his own pursuits constrained, at least if he lives in New York, a city which has enacted perfectly reasonable dietary regulations which would prevent him from doing what he truly wants.

I don't see any way around the factual claim included in this objection. Surely, some people – the outliers Mill wanted to protect – will be prevented from doing what they truly want to do when paternalistic legislation is in place, even though most will be aided to do what they want to do. The question is whether this is a definitive reason to prevent paternalistic legislation. Legislation is by its nature general: a given rule applies to many sorts of people in many sorts of circumstances. There are times, I would posit, that action in accordance with any given rule does harm rather than good. We accept third-person rules as justified when they generally do good, even though it is, of course, possible that in some specific cases they actually produce net harm. We accept rules against theft because on the whole theft is a bad thing. However, it is true that at times theft is acceptable and even useful. It is not just that it may benefit one person more than it harms another, although that is certainly true. It may even benefit everyone involved. If my television were stolen, I would be annoyed, but I might well live a better life – less bored, more active, in the long run. The theft of the television might be a boon to me and to the thief, who wants it for his bedridden mother. Similarly, taxes are sometimes used for projects which are just bad ideas. Still, we think that making people pay taxes is a good idea. Even if we consider that laws are not so much about benefit but about justice, many people might agree that sometimes laws makes injustice possible – Walmart is allowed to move in next to the mom and pop store and drive them out of business with its low prices and underpaid workers. It seems unfair, but those who endorse free enterprise would presumably argue that in general allowing such things is fair. Given our numbers, and the variations in our ideas and our circumstances, it just won't work if we try to make rules so specific as to accommodate every situation. So, we accept that even good rules will sometimes be counterproductive. We cannot expect to make a rule that is beneficial in all real, much less imagined, circumstances, and yet we find law to be justified. Rolf Sartorius has said Mill can justify his ban on paternalism by arguing that if most members of a class action are wrong, and it is difficult to distinguish wrong ones from right ones, it is justified to ban the entire class.[39] If we change the calculus, though, and argue that most of a certain type of self-regarding action are wrong in that they are injurious to the self, and that it is difficult to know which are right and which are wrong, we might argue that it is justified to ban that class of actions.

If this is true, then it seems that laws that aim to benefit people by constraining some of their actions can be justified, even if they are not uniformly successful. We accept laws that require you to refrain from harming others even where those are not uniformly successful, and we accept at least some laws that require you to benefit others, even where those efforts are not uniformly successful. In both cases, someone can certainly claim that his own welfare has been sacrificed for the sake of others; that is, his welfare has been sacrificed for the sake of a policy that has benefited others, but not him. This is a loss to the individual. For what it is worth, though, such a loss is not typically a major one. It does not typically involve the loss of something we might say you have an inalienable right to. Requiring that people save more than they now do, that they don't amass huge debts through avaricious credit schemes, that they don't buy cigarettes, that they don't eat things with likely lethal effects, doesn't seem to interfere with the basic life choices rights are intended to protect, even in those cases where such requirements fail to benefit. It is like the policy that requires people to pay property taxes to support the school system even when they themselves have no children or when they send their children to private school. We don't seem to think you have a right to pay taxes only if you derive a personal benefit from it.

---

[39] Rolf Sartorius, *Individual Conduct and Social Norms* (Belmont, Calif.: Dickenson Publishing, 1975), ch. 8, section 3.

The fact that some people will be prevented from doing what is in fact good for them – from fulfilling some of their goals – is not in itself a reason to prohibit the legislation that prevents such actions. As with all legislation, we need to measure the costs and the benefits – how many are affected, the degree to which they are affected, the way they are affected. We want to craft the most fine-tuned legislation that is practically possible, so as to minimize the number of people who are harmed by a generally beneficent piece of legislation.

INFANTILIZATION

But if we intervene in people's lives, even on the best-case analysis, where we have entirely benevolent motives, efficient means, and certain knowledge of the good to be achieved, will we rob people of the ability to assess their own choices and make good decisions? An objection to paternalism which is frequently voiced is that it will lead to infantilization – that treating people, arguably, like children will result in them becoming childlike in bad ways. Joel Feinberg has said, "If adults are treated as children they will come in time to be like children. Deprived of the right to choose for themselves, they will soon lose the power of rational judgment and decision."[40] We can imagine a long-lived, healthy, solvent population, stimulated into rewarding activities and creative exercises, who are nonetheless unable to assess risks, weigh competing claims, or define what their interests consist in. Whether or not we think, as Mill may have, that the ability to make decisions is the quintessential human activity, without which we do not live as humans, we can agree that it is a good ability, one we must have in order to live successfully. The fear is that where people are saved from the costs of bad decision making, their skills at decision making will not improve, and very likely will deteriorate. Like the passenger in the back seat of the car, they will not learn the route, but will wait passively to be debouched in the correct location. If something happens to the driver, they are lost, and even without that, we may feel contempt for their failure ever to take charge. This is a different sense in which individuality can be lost – instead of developing into fully functioning persons, they remain unfledged and undefined. They are incapable of functioning as adults, in the sense of making reflective choices, including the all-important choices that further determine our identities.

---

[40] Joel Feinberg, "Legal Paternalism," in Rolf Sartorius, ed., *Paternalism* (Minneapolis: University of Minnesota Press, 1983), p. 3.

A related objection was discussed in Chapter 1. There, the objection was that paternalistic measures are unnecessary, because people will learn from their mistakes and will make better decisions, at least when the costs of bad decisions are sufficiently high. The answers given to that argument were: (a) in many cases we don't learn from our mistakes, because biases interfere with our acknowledgement of relevant evidence, including the results of our past actions; and (b), in some cases where we do learn, we learn too late for that knowledge to be useful. The objection here is stronger, in that it says paternalism is not just unnecessary, but positively harmful. To some extent, though, the previously given replies hold. Our ability to learn from our mistakes in our present relatively laissez-faire situation is not as great as it would be if we were the purely rational creatures we would like to be. Even if we lose some of our decision-making skills, there is a limit to how good at making decisions we can get as it is. Since our skills are not all that great to begin with, progress, while possible, is, generally, finite. And again, some lessons, which we might learn without the intervention of paternalism, are learned too late to be applied, barring reincarnation.

Still, it would be foolish to deny that using decision-making skills can improve them. The act of making a decision, of having to make up our minds, with its requirements that we consider the options, speculate as to the most likely outcomes and their desirability, and then make ourselves act as a result of this consideration, is something that we get used to and in many ways get better at. It requires the intellectual ability to do realistic speculations about the future. Then, too, there is an emotional aspect to making decisions, which also needs to be developed: a willingness to actually determine the future through making a choice, something which can be scary for those not used to it. Given this, it has to be conceded that if we haven't learned to make decisions, we will lack both the intellectual skills and the emotional strength needed to do that when we need to. Even if, somehow, the need to make a serious decision never arose, we would lack a lot of what Mill (and not only Mill) would consider one of the constituents of human excellence, the ability to make critical choices. If, on the other hand, we are allowed to make decisions but are always saved from bad consequences when we make poor decisions, then that will inevitably diminish our sensitivity to bad consequences. We are blithe about drawing to an inside straight if all we're playing for is plastic chips, and if suddenly transported to a high stakes table in Las Vegas we, while no longer blithe, are hardly able to formulate on the spot a knowledge of the odds that will allow us to negotiate a successful game. Depending on others (as the back-seat passenger does) and indifference to outcomes, since no bad ones are possible (the plastic chip poker player) could combine to make us unable to negotiate in cases where, had we been left to our own devices and unprotected from loss, we would have learned what to do in this specific occasion, and more generally would have learned how to learn what to do in new, costly choice situations. This presents a serious problem: given our lack of skills, we may not be able to figure out how to get certain things we need in specific cases, and more broadly we might not know how to proceed in the pursuit of tools that we need for the development and maintenance of individuality.

Institutional support

However, these dangers can be overstated. As concerns the possibility of losing goods we need for our development, it is interesting that Mill himself provides, inadvertently, an argument against overblown claims about the dangers of dependency. Mill opposed government-provided education, primarily, as mentioned above, because he thought it would deprive us of individuality. Another important reason he provided for opposing it, though, was that it would create a dependency on the state, which, in the event of the state failing to continue in its maintenance of education, would leave people without the wherewithal to educate their children. That is, we could be infantilized, as it might now be put, in the sense that we would no longer know how to go about educating our children once the support of the state was withdrawn. Certainly, Mill was to some extent right. Now that we do have public education, we are entirely dependent on it. If somehow states were to fail in this fabulous endeavor, the free education of all, most of us would have no idea how to provide education for our children. A very few, of course, could, as some now do, pay for private education, but this not an option for most of us, and the result would be chaos and, inevitably, uneducated children and adults. This is hardly seen by most people as an argument against the provision of public education, however. Rather, it emphasizes how important it is that such public education continue. To provide no help on the grounds that such help makes people vulnerable to its loss would undercut most social programs, and there are very few who would endorse an ideal of such hardy self-sufficiency. This is true in part because the appeal to such hardy self-sufficiency relies on mistaken ideas about what people will do if left without help. In fact, the idea that in the absence of public education we would all procure good educations for our children, and the idea that in the absence of Medicaid and Medicare we would all somehow acquire adequate funds for health care, and the idea that without social security we would take care to put more away in savings, have simply been proven false. Obviously, we were without such provisions for most of history and did not rise to the occasion by providing for all our needs. Without government provision of help, most people would simply suffer, at great cost to themselves and to society.

Furthermore, such dependency no longer seems as dangerous as it once may have – we don't fear that a new government administration will suddenly decide that public schools are a bad idea. People debate how much to spend on their local schools, and by extension, on the quality of education they are willing to pay for, but everyone agrees that there must be public schools. While new social programs are often seen as unnecessary, once they are indeed depended upon, our need is generally reflected in government policies. The program becomes entrenched, something sometimes decried, but just as often celebrated when the program is a good one – such as public education, social security, and for those lucky enough to have it, public health care. Rather than decrying our dependency on the government for some significant benefits, and promoting individual planning to substitute for government benefits, what we need to do and generally try to do is see to it that the government provides these benefits as effectively as possible. Most governments are strong supporters of stability, and doing away with programs upon which most people depend is not likely to maintain an administration's grip on power. This is not to deny that government programs are sometimes ended, especially when economic recessions mean that the government is short on funds. Such a relinquishment of aid gets a lot of public debate, though, and diminutions are generally phased in, and again, do not aim at the programs which are most necessary to most people.

So, one answer to the infantilization argument is that dependency on others to save us from ourselves is not in all cases a bad thing, since those needs met by others in most cases simply can't be met by ourselves, and we can generally rely on the most essential help continuing to be forthcoming.

Habituation and education

However, while this addresses the practical impact of the inability to figure out how to address certain problems, it doesn't address the perhaps more significant issue – that the ability to make important decisions is a kind of human excellence that we don't want to give up, even if we don't suffer any external consequences from our failure. A second response to the infantilization argument takes issue with the results of constraining options on character. The claim against paternalism is that, in making our decisions for us, it will leave us unable to make good decisions when we need to. It may well be, though, that by restricting our options in some cases, we will actually make better decisions in cases where we are not restricted. We can develop finer discernment and the more mature emotional qualities we need for decision making through guidance. In the *Nicomachean Ethics*, Aristotle argued that proper education was essential to learning to do the right thing, and for education to be effective it was not sufficient to be told correctly, and to believe, which actions were proper. Rather, one had to be habituated to right action – the process of education had to include actually doing the proper thing. In Book II, Aristotle discusses how one learns to be virtuous, but "virtue" in the Aristotelian lexicon does not denote only what we might consider moral virtue, but a wide area of practical decision making – the general area of making good choices. He emphasizes the importance of performing right actions in order to learn to act rightly:

> it is by doing just acts that the just man is produced, and by doing temperate acts the temperate man, without doing these no one would have even a prospect of becoming good. But most people do not do these, but take refuge in theory and think they are being philosophers and will become good in this way ...[41]

But while choosing the appropriate action is essential, it is not easy. For any given situation, there are many wrong choices, and only one right one. Thus, there are many ways of becoming vicious, since by practicing vicious actions, we habituate ourselves to vice: and we will end by having vicious characters – we will become used to doing wrong things, and will take pleasure in those. Once sufficiently habituated to vice, we will find virtuous actions painful. While any of us might manage a good but painful act upon occasion, we won't generally do the right thing unless we take pleasure in it, for Aristotle, so habituation determines where we will end up – we cannot be expected to do the right thing in the face of a settled disposition to do the wrong thing.

How, then, do we become habituated to doing right actions? For Aristotle, we cannot rely on a natural orientation towards the good. What we have by nature is the ability to learn to be virtuous, but equally an

---

[41] *Nicomachean Ethics*, Book II, section 4, 1105b9–18 (W. D. Ross translation [Oxford University Press, 2009], p. 28).

ability to learn to be vicious. In order to do virtuous things before one has actually become virtuous, then, you need help from others – you need good teachers, teachers who will train you to do the right sorts of thing by having you do the right sorts of thing: "it makes no small difference to be habituated this way or that way starting from childhood, but an enormous difference, or rather all the difference."[42] That is, we develop a virtue through habituation, which involves doing the right thing even though we are not yet virtuous; and given that we are not virtuous, we must, in the early stages, be taught by someone else, who makes sure we do the right thing. Such teaching appears to continue into adulthood, since Aristotle says that the legislators must also concern themselves with habituation in the construction of a constitution: "for legislators must make the citizens good by forming habits in them, and this is the wish of every legislator."[43] Necessary to proper habituation, says Aristotle, are good laws.

But it is difficult to get from youth up a right training for excellence if one has not been brought up under right laws; for to live temperately and hardily is not pleasant to most people, especially when they are young. For this reason their nurture and occupations should be fixed by law; for they will not be painful when they have become customary. But it is surely not enough that when they are young they should get the right nurture and attention; since they must, even when they are grown up, practice and be habituated to them, we shall need laws for this as well, and generally speaking to cover the whole of life; for most people obey necessity rather than argument, and punishments rather than what is noble.[44]

Aquinas, one of the first and leading philosophers of law, develops a similar claim in the *Summa Theologica*, where he discusses the role of law as an aid in habituation: whereas for Aquinas, some may be persuaded "by words," others need laws, so that "they would both leave others in peace and be themselves at length brought by habituation to do voluntarily what they hitherto did out of fear, and so become virtuous."[45]

Doing good things is necessary for developing good habits, which in turn will result in your doing more good things, and in order to get started along this trajectory in any given area, you need help from others. The pertinence of this to the present question is clear: rather than weakening people's ability to make good decisions, paternalistic legislation can help habituate them to making good decisions, so that in those

---

[42] Ibid., Book II, section 1, 1103b23–25.   [43] Ibid., Book II, 1103b2.
[44] Ibid., Book X, section 9, 1179b32–1180a5 (Ross translation).
[45] *Summa Theologica* I–II, Question 95, 1st Article.

areas where there is no legislation, they will continue to make good decisions. Constraint does not weaken, but strengthens, the likelihood of good outcomes when people are making their own choices. Training both attunes us to the relevant features of a situation and develops in us a taste for doing what is right. Of course, the fact that Aristotle has said it does not make it so. Still, one reason Aristotle's consideration of habituation has received so much attention is that many people find it plausible. I am inclined to think that if the local police went on a strike, most of us would still not steal things from our neighbors, even though adolescents are notoriously free-handed. After a while the training takes hold. This is one reason that towns don't need more police than they have – for most of us, it isn't the fear of getting caught that slows us down. Some of us can remember when it was not illegal to litter, and when, sure enough, there was trash all along the highways. The illegality of littering transformed people's habits, and this has become a change in values – littering is now not only illegal but looked down upon. We perceive the harm of littering, and don't want to litter. Laws make this happen at lot more effectively than public service messages exhorting us to be good, because they effectively constrain our behavior. Good habits help us make good decisions, in part because we not so tempted by bad decisions as we might otherwise be – we don't find them attractive – and in part because we have developed a feel for what a good decision consists in – we aren't completely at sea when it comes to determining what is a safe driving speed, or a reasonable approach to trash disposal, even in a new situation. Even as Aristotle thought, legislation helps us inculcate good habits, and thus to make good decisions, rather than leaving us in an infantile state of waywardness.

Legislative limits

Lastly, and most obviously, we should remember what it is that the paternalist is trying to accomplish. No reasonable paternalist (and this includes me) thinks that legislation should control every aspect of life. Legislation shouldn't control even most aspects of life. Legislation should intervene when people are likely to make decisions that seriously and irrevocably interfere with their ability to reach their goals, and where legislation can reliably prevent them from making those bad decisions, and where legislation is the least costly thing that can reliably prevent them from making these bad decisions. The majority of decisions we make do not meet these conditions.

Opponents of paternalism insist that the worst-case scenario is the one that should guide us in considering whether or not paternalistic measures should be adopted. They forget that while worst-case scenarios are good to bear in mind, we need to consider their probability, not just their disutility. There is no reason to think things will turn out for the worst, or that most paternalistic decisions will be destructive ones. I am reminded of one of Mill's defenses of utilitarianism, that "[t]here is no difficulty in proving any ethical standard whatever to work ill, if we suppose universal idiocy to be conjoined with it."[46] Paternalism is not totalitarianism, and there is no reason to think paternalist legislation would interfere in so many corners of life that people would lose their ability to make decisions. What would be the point of such a cumbersome, costly, and in the long run ineffective system? The point of (at least, intelligent) paternalistic policies is not the avoidance of all pain, but the avoidance of serious and irreparable harm to persons, where, as above, harm is defined as something which stands in the way of their preventing their long-term goals, where those would be much more likely to be reached without the harm being present – such as long-term health problems or financial insolvency. This does not call for intervention in most aspects of life, and thus certainly does not call for the elimination of decision making, with all its concomitant skills and emotional maturity.

CONCLUSION

We see, then, that many objections to paternalistic policies are mistaken. Paternalism in some areas will not cause our abilities to atrophy. It will not lead to social conformity. It can in fact work against the inertia and conservatism to which we are naturally prone, and in so doing leave us better able than we would otherwise be to develop our own characters according to our own choices.

---

[46] *Utilitarianism*, ch. 2, p. 275.

CHAPTER 3

Alienation, authenticity, and affect

PSYCHOLOGICAL COHERENCE

We may still wonder, though, if enough has been said about the subjective effects of paternalistic policies. No matter how appropriate the legislation the paternalist envisages, the fact remains that these policies are in place to make people do things they would not otherwise do. One question that gets scrutiny, especially in the popular consciousness, is what the effect of legislation is on how we feel and how we think. We looked in Chapter 2 at the possible effects that removing decisions from people would have on, as it were, their outward vision: how much it would constrain their assessment of various lifestyles, and whether it would inhibit their ability to weigh consequences in considering options. However positive one might be about these, there remains the possibility that people will be handicapped in some aspects of what we might call their relationship to themselves. The fear is twofold: the easiest to understand is that people will simply feel bad; that being subjected to paternalistic laws, being told what to do, will result in depression or anger, no matter how good the quality of the laws. The second is that they will lose a kind of introspective skill necessary to being an authentic person, and to choosing in light of that. The question is what the psychological effect is of being constrained by laws, and perhaps by the more general sense that other people have precedence over ourselves when it comes to decisions that affect our personal well-being. Even if they make all their decisions correctly, choosing programs geared to promote individuality, critical thinking, and all-around wholesome, healthy psyches, there is the thought that this kind of control will inevitably backfire. The mere fact of external control will be destructive.

Philosophers (with some exceptions, of course, notably Mill) have not given as much attention to these possible effects of paternalism as to the issues of rights and respect, but it clearly is a sufficient issue for many people to make cautionary treatments of paternalistic states popular in both fiction and film. Many of these scenarios deal not so much specifically with paternalism as with any state in which there is a proliferation of legislation, but people often imagine that paternalism makes the proliferation of regulations especially likely: while third-person legislation might be limited to areas in which there are actual complaints about others' behavior, paternalistic regulation, since it doesn't require actual complaints about behavior to be justified, may seem to have no natural boundaries. It is imagined, then, that paternalism will give rise to lives largely managed by outside regulations, and that this, in turn, will have deleterious effects both on people's feelings and on their ability, generally, to engage in the critical introspection required to know who they are and what they want. If people cannot act on their own decisions, what is the point of self-knowledge? The general fear is that there will be a loss of psychological coherence, and without this even the most enlightened legislation can't be successful.

When we look at fictional portrayals of paternalistic states – and there are many of them – such portrayals seem to fall into either of two camps: depictions of either alienation or of inauthenticity. In the first scenario, at least portions of the citizenry are depressed and/or resentful, frustrated by the intrusions into what might normally be called their private life. They are alienated from their own lives, in finding them unfulfilling or downright hateful, as well as from the society that has so orchestrated their lives. In, for example, Ray Bradbury's *Fahrenheit 451*, the protagonist, the confused Montag, becomes initially alienated from his own life as a burner of books and husband of an essentially soporific wife, and eventually joins an underground of rebellious citizens who fight against the totalitarian government. One scenario, then, is that government interference, even when benevolently intended, produces either depression, or anger, or both.

In the second scenario, perhaps seen as worse, members of paternalistic societies are shown as unrealistically contented: Stepford citizens, whose happy smiles and wholehearted endorsement of their own chains suggests they have lost touch with their real feelings, goals, and values.[1] In Lois Lowry's 1993 Newbery Award winning *The Giver*, for example, a society has evolved in which pain and conflict have been eliminated. People live

---

[1] Ira Levin's satirical novel, *The Stepford Wives* (1972) actually described a society in which the wives had been replaced by robots remarkable for their servile yet contented behavior. It has come to serve as a term for anyone remarkable for excessive conformity to oppressive norms and unnatural docility in that performance.

entirely in harmony, engaging in informal family therapy each morning, working at jobs to which they have been (apparently correctly) assigned according to their skills and affinities, married to spouses who have been selected by those in charge on the basis of genuine compatibility. While Lowry goes further than most in actually showing some attractive elements to this society, in the end we discover that the sacrifices they have made for happiness are too much – they cannot see color, they cannot hear music, and they cannot, in short, experience anything beyond the most moderate stimulation or emotion. They are contented, but without any real sense of who they are or what they might be.

If we combine these prospects, the suggestion is that the effect of paternalistic laws will be either of two things. They may produce alienation, where people feel disenchanted both with their government and with their own lives, encompassed and confined as they are by nagging reminders of what they are supposed to be doing, and threats as to what will occur if they don't. Or, people may accept the legitimacy of such intervention, and wholeheartedly accept that what the government wants them to do is what they themselves want to do, in which case they seem overwhelmingly inauthentic. Many of these science fiction descriptions of paternalistic societies combine both effects – an angry and/or depressed protagonist, struggling in the midst of an unhealthily contented population. The examples I've given are fictional, and thus are not evidence of what people have experienced in paternalistic societies. They have to be speculative – while there have been totalitarian societies, there have not actually been truly paternalistic (in the sense of genuinely benevolent) totalitarian societies, so we can only guess at what they would be like. The popularity of such depictions, though, demonstrates the fear that many people have that societies intending to control personal choice would inevitably be destructive, no matter how benevolent their motives. Neither alienation nor inauthenticity is an acceptable outcome, even to the paternalist.

It is true of all laws, of course, that they interfere in our lives and keep us from doing what at least some of us want to do. Criminal laws keep a few people from doing what they may want to do very much (kill in anger, for example) and keep most of us from doing what we might want to do to some extent (paying the government less in taxes than it demands). For the most part, critics do not object that the obedience to law per se results in either alienation or inauthenticity, at least in a democratic society. (As I say, for the most part: there are certainly enemies of "big government" who think all laws pose the danger of our becoming a passive and psychologically enslaved citizenry, and who react to regulations with anger, alienation, and even threats of militancy. Most of us, though, don't find the existence of laws designed to protect third parties, including indirect aid through environmental legislation, to be psychologically destructive.) The difference seems to be that paternalistic laws are especially intrusive. Some of this may be for the reasons addressed in Chapter 1, especially the belief that such laws may be taken to be disrespectful. I have argued there that as long as paternalistic concerns are not allowed to justify a class system, where some people believed to be of superior judgment create regulations for those they believe to be inferior, and as long as it accurately addresses, rather than exaggerating, people's needs, it is not disrespectful. Even if we assume this, though, and imagine paternalistic laws crafted, as it were, by the people and for the people, without prejudice, they may appear to be more intrusive simply because of their scope: while it may be intrusive to tell me how to treat other people, it is more intrusive to tell me how to treat myself, because the law intervenes in a more intimate connection. It comes between me and my plans for myself. It is one thing for law to drive a wedge between what I want to do to or for other people and what I can actually do to them; for law to drive a wedge between what I want to do for myself and what I can actually do is intrusion in an area which means much more to me, my relationship with myself. We always have to accept some sort of arbitration in cases of conflict of wills, and we are used to doing that, even before it gets institutionalized in laws: practically from birth, we have to come to terms that we can't always get what we want from other people, that we have to agree to terms on how to treat each other, and that sometimes third parties will arbitrate between us, whether it's Mom deciding whose turn it is on the swing or the Supreme Court deciding whether our land can be taken by eminent domain. We are certainly not used to such conflict, or such arbitration, within the self. Of course, we experience conflicts of desires within the self, but typically we feel both sides of such a conflict – two desires which can't both be fulfilled, for example – as emanating from ourselves, and we at least think we can decide in terms of what we most want, which yields internal satisfaction. And, we get to do the deciding ourselves. The idea that external agency will enter into our decisions about actions that affect no one but ourselves may, then, be experienced as a novelty, and not a happy one. Such, at least, seems to be the thinking behind those who depict paternalistic laws as creating a society of, as seen above, people who experience deep feelings of alienation, or who avoid alienation at the cost of inauthenticity and the atrophying of skills of introspection and evaluation.

This is a criticism the paternalist needs to address. In these states psychological coherence has been lost, and paternalists don't want either a situation in which people are, to put it most simply, unhappy, or one in which they feel happy only because they have given up on crafting genuine lives. Regulations which intend to help people bring about their own ends are not successful if people living under them cease to have ends of their own. So, the question is whether paternalistic systems are indeed likely to have these destructive effects. We will look, then, at the specific arguments involved in each claim, and will reflect on the paternalist's response.

ALIENATION

Bernard Williams began what has been something of a cottage industry on the nature of integrity. In Williams' well-known examples, two conscientious, thoughtful agents are presented with dilemmas. Both Jim and George must do something they find personally repellent, for the sake of the greater good. Jim feels he must kill an innocent person because he believes it is morally right to do so – right, because the evil Pedro will kill nineteen innocent people if Jim does not. George, a fervent opponent of biological and chemical warfare, discovers that due to an unfortunate confluence of circumstances, the most effective way to retard such warfare (and meanwhile take care of his family) is actually to take a job in the biological/chemical weapons industry. These are not, of course, examples connected to the implementation of paternalistic policies. Rather, Williams is making a point about the demandingness of morality and whether such demandingness is somehow destructive. His conclusion is that under a sufficient conflict a person may lose his "integrity." Insofar as moral demands, even demands whose truth he recognizes, cause him to live in a way that is at odds with his central plans and values (in Williams' terms, his "ground projects"), he will lose a sense of himself and of the things which give his life meaning.[2]

Even if Williams' claims are overblown, as a number of people have argued, we can see why someone might feel that life in a paternalistic society might, for some, result in a similar reaction. The conflict is not in this case internal in origin, as it is for Jim and George – the irony for them is that they believe in the moral demands which are made on them, even while feeling that conceding to those demands is destructive of their lives.

[2] Bernard Williams, "A Critique of Utilitarianism," in Bernard Williams and J. J. C. Smart, *Utilitarianism: For and Against* (Cambridge University Press, 1973).

To some extent, a conflict arising from the external imposition of law may appear to be less destructive, since it is not a set of inconsistent internal motivations that are tearing the person apart. For Williams, though, a good part of the danger seems to be simply that one is forced to give up one's central ground project, and this danger certainly persists when the conflict is between one's own commitment and external agency. The fear is that in a paternalistic society we might be sufficiently interfered with by outside agency as to feel a divide between ourselves and the ends we want to pursue, and in so doing lose a sense of ourselves as we lose the sense of coherence that pursuing a central project provides.

This loss could be experienced as either disenchantment with our own projects, or with society, or both. In the first case, constant frustration in doing what one wants can lead to losing the desire to do that thing; not so much in the salutary (perhaps) sense that one simply gives up on it and goes on (the way you might give up your desire to act when you discover you have no talent, and move on to working backstage instead), but in the sense that you look upon your own projects with something like resentment. Think of Freud and repression of the sex drive – its frustration can yield neurosis generally, and an inability to enjoy the forbidden object even when it is eventually made available (as in disinclination towards sex once it is finally allowed between the socially acceptable married couple). Or, we might turn our frustration outwards, and feel hatred towards the system that oppresses us. Living in constant resentment of others, particularly those who have control over our actions, is not itself conducive to psychological harmony. Generally, the frustration of desire is associated with anger, depression, aggression, and stress. This is the vocabulary of psychology rather than philosophy, but it surely connects to the loss of a sense of wholeness, the loss of integrity, which Williams sees as a result of the intrusive demands of morality.

And, even if the regulations proposed do not interfere with specific "ground projects," in the immediate way that Williams imagined, we must acknowledge the possibility that simply being under someone else's control can itself be a source of frustration and disheartenment. When what one is told to do is not, in any given case, particularly contrary to one's overall wishes, being told what to do can nevertheless be an irritant. No one wants to be nagged, even if on any particular occasion one is only nagged to do something that isn't itself particularly bothersome. Joel Feinberg has said that the conditions of self-governance, of the sort that slaves lack, provide a sense of "responsibility, self-esteem, and personal dignity," and presumably this is true even if the slave were not forced to do anything he didn't want to do.[3] The accretion of controls itself can create a sense of confinement. States that enact paternalistic laws are sometimes called "nanny states," and while this is presumably supposed to suggest that they belittle their citizens by giving them a childlike status, as discussed in Chapter 1, it can also suggest the irritation that arises when we are nagged – picking a sock up off the ground is not so bad, but being told to do it, and then to brush your teeth, and then to take your vitamin pills, and then to eat your vegetables, collectively constitute an intrusion. Rational paternalistic states would not, presumably, suggest quite such fine-tuned intervention, since the costs are prohibitively great, but by the nature of paternalism it will, of course, be intrusive, and again the accretion of such interventions can take away a sense of control which, some will argue, is central to happiness.

INAUTHENTICITY AND "PERSONAL" AUTONOMY

The second imagined area of danger concerns the complicated relationship between authenticity and what its proponents typically call "personal autonomy." Those who value authenticity, and this certainly includes Mill, are worried about the possibility that people will cease to be truly themselves, and will simply, chameleon-like, take on the desires, values, and even affect of the society around them. We may feel contented enough, in this Stepford world, but only because we have not sufficient motivation, knowledge, or skills to know what we really want, much less to assess if what we are doing is congruent with those genuine desires. There are two related issues here. First, there is the danger that with greater legislation there will be more, and more clearly enunciated, and more clearly celebrated, public values. As society tells us what to do, not just in our treatment of others but in our own lives, we may be more likely to adopt those standards just because they are publicly supported. We will not adopt them because of a well-considered estimation of their value, but simply because society pushes us in that direction.

Many people have felt that in order to truly be a person, in the sense of a responsible moral agent, a person has to have some character traits and values that are in some ways not a function of random social influence. The criteria for the requisite sort of stability and independence vary with particular writers, but they have in common the intuition that there is a difference between some people, who have genuine feelings and opinions, and others,

---

[3] Feinberg, *Harm to Self,* p. 31.

whose pronouncements are neither really lies nor yet expressions of their own beliefs, but simply what they hear and therefore take on as their own. Someone whose ideas change with every fashion seems to us to be lacking in some fundamental stability needed to make them an agent rather than just a continuous body with a continual flow of ideas and desires. This having a "real" self, while construed in different ways, is referred to as authenticity. The danger is that the greater the social pressure included in a paternalistic world, the greater the incentive to abandon the pursuit of our own values; and this will yield faint-souled inauthentic shadows of persons.

In addition to this sort of institutionalized peer pressure, paternalistic regulations place an overall restriction on what we can do. Another fear is that where some actions are impossible (or at least difficult, in being illegal), we may lose the incentive to do the sort of introspection we need to do either to know what we are, or to know what we would want to be. This sort of introspection and critical evaluation is referred to by many of its proponents as personal autonomy, and its loss, for them, is tantamount to a loss of agency, for some even to the loss of personhood.

Proponents of personal autonomy have focused not so much on the possibility of external action that might follow a choice as on the articulation of appropriate internal conditions for choice, and the aspects of choice they celebrate – reflection and self-knowledge – certainly appear to be desirable. They seek to describe the psychology of the chooser, and to understand what the qualifications are for having a healthy psychology in which choices are not the random operation of forces through a person but in some way are actually a person's own. The criteria for satisfactory internal conditions have varied: Kant, of course, embraced the proper use of the metaphysical free will. Mill, while unlike Kant in many ways, sometimes sounds like him, in thinking that for a choice to be really one's own it must be unaffected by others: he speaks of "home-grown" characteristics, and deplores the person who "lets the world, or his own portion of it, choose his plan of life for him, [with] no need of any other faculty than the ape-like one of imitation." On the other hand, the person who

chooses his plan for himself, employs all his faculties. He must use his observation to see, reasoning and judgment to foresee, activity to gather materials for decision, discrimination to decide, and when he has decided, firmness and self-control to hold to his own deliberate decision. And these qualities he requires and exercises exactly in proportion as the part of his conduct which he determines according to his own judgment and feelings is a large one . . .[4]

---

[4] *On Liberty*, ch. 3, p. 187.

To be unaffected by others is apparently the best path, perhaps the only path, to being capable of making decisions.

More recently, those who write on personal autonomy have eschewed the idea of the Kantian metaphysical free will, and along with it the possibility that a person can make decisions unaffected by socialization. Instead, Gerald Dworkin, for example, has promoted an idea of personal autonomy that is not so much based on freedom from influence as on reflection on those influences.

Autonomy is conceived of as a second order capacity of persons to reflect critically upon their first order preferences, desires, wishes, and so forth and the capacity to accept or attempt to change these in light of higher-order preferences and values. By exercising such a capacity, persons define their nature, give meaning and coherence to their lives, and take responsibility for the kind of person they are.[5]

Personal autonomy, thus construed as an evaluative enterprise, is connected to the existence of the authentic self discussed earlier: the relationship between the two is dynamic. Dworkin says that autonomy is "not merely an evaluative or reflective notion, but includes some ability both to alter one's preferences and to make them effective in one's actions."[6] For Diana Meyers, another who, like Dworkin, construes autonomy as more of a set of introspective and evaluative skills than a function of free will, authenticity requires having a genuine self, but the genuine self is not so much a set of traits one is born with as it is something one creates, through the use of one's skills as an autonomous being: it is "a self-chosen identity rooted in the individual's most abiding feelings and foremost convictions, yet subject to . . . critical perspective."[7] Natural character may place parameters on what we are able to make of ourselves, but an important component of our self-identity is a function of the decisions we have made. This requires the use of judgment, where a person does not adopt an idea or a value until he or she has scrutinized and deemed it worthy of adoption. Thus, authenticity and autonomy come together: to be autonomous, a decision must been made in light of the actual traits, values, and so forth of the person, that is, of the authentic self: "the core of the concept of personal autonomy is the concept of an individual living in harmony with his or her authentic self";[8] and again, "[t]o live in harmony

[5] Gerald Dworkin, *The Theory and Practice of Autonomy* (Cambridge University Press, 1988), p. 20.
[6] Ibid., p. 17.
[7] Diana Meyers, *Self, Society, and Personal Choice* (New York: Columbia University Press, 1989), p. 61.
[8] Ibid., pp. 49–50.

with one's authentic self, one's current life plan must be consonant with one's contemporaneous authentic self, and one's evolving self must not persistently violate the personal ideal included in the current life plan."[9] At the same time, the authentic self is in turn created, at least in part, by autonomous choice: "The autonomous individual is engaged in a dynamic process of meshing a self-portrait with a life plan that provides for an integrated personality."[10] We build ourselves, as we reflect on what we want to be. For Meyers, the authentic self consists of traits one has endorsed, and this endorsement is not a mere liking but a reflective approval. Judgment, then, is necessary for having an authentic self. Another proponent of autonomy, Marina Oshana, has yet a different view of the relationship between authenticity and autonomy: she does not believe that autonomy requires authenticity in the sense of a set of endorsed traits, and neither is such authenticity sufficient for autonomy. However, she accepts that autonomy may require authenticity in the distinct sense of an acknowledgement of what one's traits actually are.[11] That is, autonomy requires self-knowledge. Such knowledge will enlighten the choices that one makes, since choosing paths inconsistent with who one is or what one is capable of is fruitless.

These views suggest that there may be a problem for the paternalist. I have argued against the importance of autonomy in the sense of freedom of action. The concomitants of authenticity and the skills described as personal autonomy, however, are ones desirable in any healthy society. Self-knowledge is generally good; having an authentic self, which one creates through reflective choices as to what traits and projects one can endorse, is good; exercising the ability to make reflective choices in general certainly is good. The problem for the paternalist is that many proponents of these desirable traits see them as having their natural expression in external action. For Oshana, autonomy, in addition to internal elements of decision making, also requires freedom of action – a person is not autonomous unless such appropriately arrived at decisions can be turned into action: "if a person is to be autonomous, the circumstances to which he authentically assents must grant him the latitude to choose to live in a self-directed fashion."[12] And again, "[b]eing autonomous is not simply a matter of having values and preferences that mirror

---

[9] Ibid., pp. 61–62.   [10] Ibid., p 84.

[11] Marina Oshana, "Autonomy and the Question of Authenticity," *Social Theory and Practice* 33.3 (July 2007), 411–429.

[12] Marina Oshana, "Autonomy and Self-Identity," in *Autonomy and the Challenges to Liberalism,* ed. John Christman and Joel Anderson (Cambridge University Press, 2005), pp. 77–97, at p. 91.

those that a person holds under conditions in which control is absent. Rather, being autonomous is a matter of directing one's life according to such values and preferences."[13] Oshana says this differentiates her from what she calls "internalists" about autonomy, but even Meyers, while concentrating on the internal criteria for autonomous choice, assumes such choices are ultimately to be expressed in action: the function of autonomy competency is "self-governance – controlling one's life by ascertaining what one really wants to do and acting accordingly," and while she feels this description of self-governance is by itself unedifying – we need to add the more definite aim of securing an integrated personality to see how to go about this – she does not reject the emphasis on its ultimate expression in action. The problem is this: once we have curtailed external freedom of action, there may seem to be no need for either authenticity or personal autonomy.

Logically, the possibility of external action, on the one hand, and the possibility of authenticity and personal autonomy, on the other, are distinct. Nonetheless, from the point of view of the agent, curtailing external freedom of action may undercut the motivation to develop either authenticity or the skills of personal autonomy. One might wonder what the point is to (internally) autonomous procedures of decision making, if such decisions can't actually be acted on. If one's autonomy of action is constrained, the critic may say, there is no real point to reflective consideration of what to do. There is no point to self-knowledge, when there is no opportunity to choose how to live in light of that, and no point to thinking what sort of person one wants to be, if there is no possibility of putting that decision into action. One may as well make no decisions at all, or, "decide" only in accordance with the bounded path one is legally allowed to pursue. If such choices aren't made, then there is a collapse of the structure of authenticity – there is no way to reflect and build the authentic self, in Meyers' and Dworkin's sense, and no need to acknowledge what one's true self really is, in Oshana's sense, since such self-knowledge may be felt as moot in the absence of choice. This is what underlies the depiction of totalitarian societies as places where people simply concede their decision-making capacities to those in authority – the idea that if our decisions can't be put into action, we will cease to make them.

We need to avoid inauthenticity, with its superficiality of affect, and to promote personal autonomy, insofar as that signifies engagement in

---

[13] Marina Oshana, "How Much Should We Value Autonomy?," *Social Philosophy and Policy* (2003), 99–126, at 101.

critical reflection on one's values and goals. The paternalist needs to show that substituting restrictions by law for freedom of action doesn't have these destructive psychological effects.

As if this weren't enough of a problem, both alienation and inauthenticity (with its concomitant loss of critical reflection) may be accompanied by something that worried Mill a great deal – what we might call a loss of affect. While much of Mill's discussion of individuality pertains to the diversity of human desires, and to their origins, and to their role in the development of human character (as discussed in Chapter 2 and in the section above) there is, as a subcontext to all these discussions, a concern for the *strength* of desires. Mill felt that one of the most unfortunate results of conventionality was that people would cease to have strong feelings – both strong desires and strong emotional reactions.

[T]he danger which threatens human nature is not the excess, but the deficiency, of personal impulses and preferences. Things are vastly changed since the passions of those who were strong by station or by personal endowment were in a state of habitual rebellion against laws and ordinances, and required to be rigorously chained up to enable the persons within their reach to enjoy any particle of security. In our times, from the highest class of society down to the lowest, every one lives as under the eye of a hostile and dreaded censorship ... I do not mean they choose what is customary in preference to what suits their own inclination. It does not occur to them to have any inclination, except for what is customary ... [B]y dint of not following their own nature, they have no nature to follow: their human capacities become withered and starved: they become incapable of any strong wishes or native pleasures.[14]

It may not be the case that all philosophy is autobiography, but certainly in this instance we think of Mill's own youthful breakdown. As he writes in his *Autobiography*, he had been brought up by extremely strong-minded adults (primarily his father, but with the aid and advice of Jeremy Bentham) who took his education entirely in charge, isolated him from other children, and, with the goal of making him the perfect utilitarian, inculcated him with utilitarian values. At age 19, Mill realized he had, in fact, ceased to care about anything: "I was thus, as I said to myself, left stranded at the commencement of my voyage, with a well-equipped ship

[14] *On Liberty*, ch. 3, p. 190.

and a rudder, but no sail; no delight in virtue, or the general good, but also just as little in anything else ... all feeling was dead."[15] For Mill to rediscover the possibility of joy, he had to turn from the values in which he had been steeped (not disavowing them, but ceasing to make them the center of his life) and cultivate his very personal responses to music and the poetry of Wordsworth.

For this, and perhaps for additional reasons, Mill was extremely sensitive to the fact that under certain social conditions, feelings could be so constrained as to atrophy entirely. For Mill, such social control, "if acquiesced in, dulls and blunts the whole nature."[16] The modern standard "express or tacit, is to desire nothing strongly" and the result is "weak feelings and weak energies."[17] Lest it not be immediately obvious to us that such a loss is grievous (and Mill thought it might not be obvious, given what he believed to be society's tendency to abhor strong feeling), Mill goes on to argue that strong feeling is necessary to any achievement; it is the very stuff of which character is made. Without it, progress is not possible, and society becomes nothing but an enervated mass incapable of any activity other than imitation. Less hyperbolically, Wendy Donner points out that for Mill, much of our motivation to help others, and more generally to promote the greatest happiness, arises out of sympathy, feeling other's pleasures as one's own;[18] thus, if we cannot feel pleasure for ourselves, we are not likely to feel other's pleasures, either, and that motivation to help others will be wanting – as is consistent with Mill's report of his own breakdown, where he saw that even the complete achievement of his altruistic dreams would yield him no joy. It is not that one would necessarily cease altogether to work for the betterment of others (judging from Mill's autobiographical account), but that such work would naturally become less rewarding, and to that extent, more likely to falter. Failure of affect, then, has far-reaching repercussions, as well as constituting an immediate loss. While the chances of any of us being subjected to the kind of narrow and intense education Mill received are almost nil, it is still worthwhile to consider whether excessive regulation, even in the best of causes, can result in this sort of diminution of feeling.

---

[15] John Stuart Mill, *Autobiography*, Riverside Editions (Boston, Mass.: Houghton Mifflin, 1969), ch. 5, p. 85.
[16] *On Liberty*, ch. 3, p. 192.   [17] Ibid., pp. 199–200.
[18] Wendy Donner, *The Liberal Self: John Stuart Mill's Moral and Political Philosophy* (Ithaca, N.Y.: Cornell University Press, 1991), p. 120.

SELF-ESTEEM

Similarly, it is feared by some that the sense that we have lost control of (some of) our personal choices can result in a loss of self-esteem. This might be caused either because of the specific areas of loss – you can't choose your own degree of debt, and this makes you feel less worthy – or because of the understanding of the more general rationale for such losses of control. If the imagined paternalistic state is transparent in its machinations, as I recommend it should be (see Chapter 5, below), citizens will be aware that the rationale for paternalistic intervention is that they are simply not very good choosers. We would be reminded every day, then, through the existence of paternalistic laws, that we're not competent to make choices, at least in certain ways, and also that, insofar as we're not occurrently conscious of our cognitive biases, our self-knowledge is flawed. We don't know what we are doing – we are bad at choosing how to get to our ends, and we can't recognize the flaws that make us choose badly. For people who pride themselves on being responsible and intelligent (which includes all of us), this constitutes a loss of status. While I have argued that paternalistic regulations do not manifest disrespect towards those subject to them, it is still quite possible that people will lose esteem for themselves when they are confronted by regulations that systematically sow doubt about their abilities. There is a degree to which self-doubt is healthy, but in excess it can paralyze action and undercut our sense of purpose. Self-esteem is something we want and need.

These concerns about alienation and authenticity, and their effect on our capacity for emotion and for self-esteem, are legitimate, and they clearly have captured the popular imagination. I think, though, that they rest on confusions. First, paternalism is not totalitarianism; most decisions are not placed outside one's power in a paternalistic system. Second, making decisions is not always subjectively rewarding – to the extent that some decisions are removed from one's control, one may find that this actually allows more latitude for engagement, reflection, and emotional attachment. More choice is not necessarily better. As it is, we already live in a world of restrictions and do not find that it has made us inauthentic or reduced us to an affect-less state of apathy. Lastly, self-esteem does not rise and fall with an objective estimate of our abilities. Our capacity for self-esteem is more elastic than that, perhaps precisely because we are not entirely rational beings. Paternalistic legislation, by allowing us to focus on what is important in our lives, and allowing us to better achieve our goals, will, if anything, help us to hone introspective skills and achieve psychological coherence.

ALIENATION: RESPONSE

The fear here, we recall, was that paternalistic legislation could create an overarching sense of alienation. Paternalistic regulations might conflict with our fundamental commitments, Williams' ground projects. Or, while compatible with any given ground project, paternalistic regulation, merely by being in place, might constitute a nagging presence that would give us both the sense that we have lost control, and a resentment towards those who do control us. Neither of these is conducive to the health of the individual or of society.

These things are possible. The fictional depictions of government intrusion that are shown to have these results are depictions of totalitarian governments, though, and there is a reason for that: it is under totalitarian governments that such effects are likely. Totalitarian governments, as the term "totalitarian" suggests, are ones that try to control every aspect of life. If we imagine a totalitarian paternalistic government, then, one thing we probably imagine is that it will impose ends on the citizens. That is, rather than helping them achieve the goals they themselves have, it will intervene to try to make them pursue what it imagines as better goals. This is, to say the least, a bad idea. It is this sort of thinking which led the Taliban to ban chess, and music, and to destroy the ancient images of Buddha – a belief that a certain way of life was the only good one to be lived, and that citizens should be forced to live that life. Such an intervention might, conceivably, be entirely benevolent, but there is simply no reason to think that imposing certain ends upon people actually makes them better off. (This will be discussed at greater length in the next chapter.) Even if it makes conceptual sense to speak of one particular kind of life as being objectively better than another, where that means something other than that being a life in which the person attains his ends, it is clearly controversial what that objectively better life consists in. The paternalistic restrictions argued for here, as discussed in Chapter 1, are those that assume agents' ends as given, and try to substitute external regulations for what is likely to be poor instrumental reasoning.

Given this, it is much less likely that "ground projects," or other personal commitments, will be prevented by the imposition of paternalistic regulations. It is, first, simply less likely that there will be as many restrictions in a paternalistic society as in, for example, a religious totalitarian society, as has been argued before. Second, the goal of this paternalistic legislation is to allow us to be more like ourselves, not less. It is to let us be closer to our ideal selves, not in the sense of idealized selves who may have every socially recognized virtue but who are completely unlike our actual selves, but rather the selves we want to be. As we saw in the last chapter, it is, of course, conceivable that a particular person will have a personal commitment that is at odds with regulations which generally promote the achievement of ends. This will not be a general phenomenon, though, since the laws envisaged here are those that typically give people more and better options for doing what they want to do. There is a clear difference between a paternalism about ends and a paternalism about means, and that difference means that much of the fear that individual lives will be subsumed under some foreign system of values is, in this case, not applicable.

Furthermore, we are, under our present laisser-faire system, all too likely to become unable to pursue our ground projects. The truth is that we too often pull the rug out from under our own feet by making bad choices. If George has massive debt from his unrealistic mortgage, he will have no choice but to take the highest paid job, no matter how repellent it is. Perhaps the idea that our ground projects could be undercut by so prosaic a thing as debt seems unlikely to someone like Williams, whose concerns are with the abstract grip of an objective moral system, certainly a more grandiose, and more theoretically complex, scenario for conflict. In real life, though, a massive debt can be at least as restricting as George's internal conflict between moral beliefs and personal commitments. Illness, too, can be a real stumbling block on the way to achieving one's life's goal. Since many of the regulations proposed here concern such prosaic prerequisites for goal fulfillment as good health and financial solvency, they should, on the whole, support the commitments that give life meaning.

It is still true, though, that the second concern expressed here about paternalism, that the general accumulation of rules that tell you what to do, even when none of those is in itself particularly oppressive, may create a sense of alienation: the nag effect is real. Of course, one easy answer is to say that a wise paternalist will not create so many rules as to have these be so burdensome. As we saw in the discussion of infantilization in Chapter 2, when the costs of legislation outweigh the benefits, then that legislation has become excessive. While noting the dangers of excess is not the same thing as avoiding it, this is an exercise at which we have some practice: just as we know that outlawing every third-person offense is counterproductive (fining people who are rude, for example), we know that trying to prevent everything that people may do to harm themselves is not worth the intervention. While part of the costs that make such intervention impractical is simply the administrative cost of promoting obedience, another is certainly the resentment of those who would, for example, be fined for rudeness, and the same holds true here: insofar as nit-picking, nagging rules irritate, that is a reason to minimize them.

This much is clear. What is perhaps not as obvious is that regulation can itself free us from some of the same sorts of nagging concerns. I hate having to review all my health insurance options, pension options, mortgage options, and credit card options, to see which of these are actually helpful and which are liable to leave me in penury. This, presumably, is part of the reason people don't do this. I don't even like reading articles about food to see what it is bad for me to eat, and then having to read labels to see if they contain those things. I am fortunate enough not to be addicted to cigarettes, but if I were, I can imagine vividly that I would hate either giving in to that addiction, knowing its costs both in terms of dollars and of health, or, trying to quit, a process that obviously consumes attention and effort. I hate the time that self-regulation takes from things that I actually am interested in. It is true that I am not forced to self-regulate, in the sense that under a paternalistic system I may be forced to give up cigarettes. I can eat without worrying about it, smoke, and allow the friendly mortgage salesman to decide how much debt I can handle. These, though, have obvious costs. I would far prefer it if someone with my interests in mind reviewed the options and made the decision for me, so that I could use such time to pursue decisions that concern things I enjoy thinking about.

While some people write as if every time a freedom were taken from us we kick and scream and feel deprived, others, more realistic, recognize that the responsibility for making such choices is a burden, and one that we are often quite willing to give up. Most of these people will argue, though, that it is a burden we ought to carry – the burden of responsibility for our personal lives is part of what makes us human, makes us adults, makes us moral agents, and so forth. To some extent this is true – deprivation of all choice would leave us, as conceded in the last chapter, as something less than human. Not all choices are equally worth our time, though, and whether or not they are worth it is not just a function of how important to us the outcome of the choice will prove. It is very important to my continued existence that my car be safe, but I do not want to have to come up with a reasonable set of auto safety standards. It's just not how I want to spend my time. I am entirely uninterested in cars. I don't even want to be in charge of inspecting my car to see if it meets the standards that someone else has created, even though I could presumably do that at least somewhat more quickly. Not only do I not want to do these things, I don't think my agency, humanity, or anything else of value would be enhanced by being in charge of these or other, similar, decisions. If the government were to do the research and ascertain that trans-fats are bad for my heath and then remove trans-fats from my diet options, I'd be grateful. With all of these things, not having to think about them seems liberating rather than demeaning. I don't think we would be glad to be rid of these decisions (and I expect most of us would) just because we think we are geniuses who should be released from quotidian concerns so we can do fabulous work elsewhere. That might have been a reason to release Mozart from some sorts of chores, but not most of us. It may be that there are some decisions that we are better at; some that we enjoy more; some that use skill sets we care about; and some that mean more to us. There are some decisions, too, that are clearly subjective, in that no one else really can make them for us. Even as I don't want to consider what is an acceptable amount of rust in a car, I do want to consider what color to paint my dining room, although I would be the first to concede that the structural integrity of my car is more important than finding a shade that coordinates with the colors of both the kitchen and the living room and still shows my cherry table to advantage. There are, probably, an infinite number of ways in which we can use our powers of discrimination, and for most us, some are simply not that fulfilling. When such unfulfilling decisions are also difficult, requiring expertise, and important, such that a failure in their regard can substantially alter our quality of life, it can be liberating to have them taken out of our hands.[19]

INAUTHENTICITY AND PERSONAL AUTONOMY: RESPONSE

The dangers here were that paternalism would (a) make us more prone to influence through socialization, and thus less stable and less genuine in our characters; and that it would (b) discourage the development and use of the powers of critical reflection. There are two things the paternalist can say to the charges that those in a paternalist society will be more subject to the pressure of others' opinions, and thus likely to adopt the values of others. First, socialization is inevitable. There is no such thing as a self that is unsocialized, uninfluenced by current opinions and current methods of

[19] Some of this discussion was prompted by a conversation with André Grahle, who said he would find it a great relief if he were (at least sometimes) forced to do what he thinks is morally right, instead of relying on himself and (at least sometimes) failing.

thinking. Kant, Mill, and other thinkers before Marx, before Freud, and before feminists' reconfiguring of the possibility of objectivity and resistance to culture, may have thought that such independent, well-formed characters arise from nature. For nineteenth-century thinkers, and twentieth-century thinkers who held to nineteenth-century ideals, socialization merely serves to pervert and destroy the real nature of the person. Once we accept that socialization is inevitable, though, our picture of what it is to be an authentic individual changes. Whatever it may be, it cannot be someone who rises above cultural influence to evaluate his own abilities or suitable life plans.

Diana Meyers has recognized this, and points out that the crucial question is not whether, but how, we are socialized. Meyers does not address paternalistic regulation in particular, but her discussion of socialization is pertinent here. Whether socialization is a bad thing depends on the values it instills in us. Social mores can teach us, as she discusses, that women should behave in a certain circumscribed way, or it can teach us that they have all those abilities that men have.[20] It can teach values that liberate or that cripple. Our very plasticity can help us to be open to the possibility for improvement, as well as for the adoption of social standards that are harmful. The likelihood of increased peer pressure in paternalism may not, then, be a bad thing. It could be a bad thing if our society has gone awry or if measures intended to be beneficent are instead harmful and yet their implicit values widely accepted. The conclusion to be accepted here is not that a paternalistic society might not do harm, but that its influence, while likely to be more pervasive than that of a society which tries to avoid institutionalizing values, is not necessarily bad. Social pressure can encourage us to find ourselves, or, as Meyers would have it, to create ourselves, in better ways.

Again, when it comes to the need for the particular skills applauded by champions of personal autonomy, self-knowledge, and critical evaluation, Meyers points out that we cannot in fact come to know ourselves, or come to be able to assess our lives and then construct them according to our values, without the skills and knowledge provided by socialization. It is for this reason, for example, that we support education, even while we recognize its capacity to influence – part of the socializing it does is to encourage our capacities for critical thinking. To the extent, then, that paternalistic legislation will influence people's beliefs and values, it is not intrinsically different from other forms of influence, and not necessarily something that saps

---

[20] Meyers, *Self, Society*, Part 3, sections 1–3.

people's capacity to reflect. Some sorts of socialization make the person more reflective, more able to decide what she wants to do, and allow more options. Other sorts close off possibilities, including the possibility of self-knowledge and of self-cultivation. Paternalistic legislation is intended to open options. To the extent that it influences us in our beliefs about ourselves – in particular, that we need help in some decision making circumstances – this again is designed to help people know what they are capable of and what they are not capable of. Reality checks don't close off options, although they sometimes may reveal that we don't have options we mistakenly thought we had. This, of course, helps us recognize our true options.

It is true that paternalistic legislation will be felt, generally, as an immediate restriction, whatever its long-term effects. And it is also true that knowing certain things can't be done may well keep us from considering, in our reflections, whether we would want to do them, whether they would suit our ambitions, and so forth. To that extent, an occasion for the introspection and critical reflection championed as personal autonomy is lost. However, we should realize that if constraints on our actions discourage us from reflection and deliberation, then reflection and deliberation are already lost causes.

Meyers, for example, thinks that considerations of moral autonomy precede those of personal autonomy, as she puts it.[21] That is, if certain projects are immoral, the personally autonomous person really can't choose them. She uses the example of someone whose particular love of daring and danger orients her towards being either a paid assassin or a mountaineer, and for whom, given the immorality of being a paid assassin, only being a mountaineer is really an option. Marina Oshana thinks that autonomy restricts other sorts of choices one can make about one's life – that one cannot, for example, embrace a life that is not itself autonomous, and thus can't choose to be a slave, or to submit one's choices to domination by a cult leader; "Being autonomous is not simply a matter of having values that are authentic, but of directing one's life according to such values."[22] These particular imagined restrictions arise according to particular conceptions of autonomy and what it entails, but

---

[21] Ibid., pp. 14–15.

[22] Marina Oshana, "Personal Autonomy and Society," *Journal of Social Philosophy* 29.1 (spring 1998), 82. This is a controversy among those who promote appropriate internal conditions for personal autonomy: Gerald Dworkin thinks it is compatible with personal autonomy to choose a life without choice, to choose "to be the kind of person who acts at the commands of others – [whose] autonomy consists of being a slave" ("Paternalism: Some Second Thoughts," in *Paternalism*, ed. Sartorius, pp. 105–123).

they suggest more generally that even proponents of the skills of personal autonomy think their development is consistent with certain restrictions on action. In point of fact, experience tells us that whatever one's view of autonomy, if it is to be possible at all then it must be consistent with our inability to choose all sorts of things.

After all, we are constantly constrained in what we can do by circumstances beyond our control. I think novel writing has more value than does the writing of philosophy, and I would love to be a novelist. Sadly, however, I just don't have any talent. Given this recognition of an internal constraint, my options are accordingly reduced, and I don't spend a lot of time using my introspective or evaluative skills considering the life of novel writing: I don't consider whether it would really make me happy, whether I want to do it because I truly value it or because I think other people would admire me more if I were engaged in it, how consistent it would be with my other values, and so forth. My lack of talent dissuades me from giving careful consideration to one particular course of action in my life, but this doesn't seem, in itself, to reduce my powers of reflection and deliberation, even while it removes one possible area of deliberation. A constraint has been placed on my choices, and this makes it useless (even harmful) to engage in the considerations relevant to authenticity or to use the skills of personal autonomy, but such engagement isn't destroyed just because its use in a particular course of action is made moot. This sort of roadblock occurs in our lives all the time, and yet we continue to think authenticity and the critical reflection designated as "personal autonomy" are possible.

It is true that constraints arising from moral considerations and those that are a function of personal ability may both be seen as internal in origin, and thus very different in their effects from constraints that are placed by a foreign entity, even if that is a democratically elected government. Even if moral requirements are objective, it takes the agent's own belief in a requirement for it to serve as a stumbling block for his action, as is the case with Meyer's assassin/mountaineer. For my failed career as a writer, even if my lack of talent is a real fact, it is something about my own nature that is preventing me from achieving the creative life of the novelist. Paternalistic restrictions are external, in the obvious sense that they are imposed from outside. In some cases we may be glad they are there, as they save us from temptation, but in other cases they may simply seem like roadblocks in our way to, for example, purchasing our dream home, the only one that (we think) can give us a sense of fulfillment, and so forth. Are external restrictions on action peculiarly destructive of the reflection, deliberation, evaluation, and so forth, that these writers think of as personal autonomy?

Again, if they are, then there is no hope for us. For one thing, we are already restrained by laws, and don't find that in itself debilitating. More, though, we are constantly revising our plans as to what we can do, and dismissing some altogether from consideration, in consideration of unwelcome external restraints. The cost of a college education can and does seriously affect how many children we choose to have. The sad need for money for food and shelter constrains us to work, when perhaps a life of leisure would really express our nature and allow us to embody our goals more fully. We don't, typically, consider seriously how to spend an unlimited amount of leisure time because it isn't a possibility. Indeed, as Meyers believes, the ability to adjust to and move on from definitive roadblocks may seem itself an exercise of the choice and creativity that goes into constructing our authentic selves.

Of course, when science fiction writers present dystopian visions of an alienated and/or inauthentic citizenry, this is not a pure flight of fancy. Knowing that we can't do what we want may well dishearten us. There are people who wanted all their lives to be doctors, only to find that the field was too competitive for someone with their particular MCATs to have a chance of getting into medical school, and surely some of those people feel alienated and angry, just as others may plaster Stepford-like smiles on their faces and pretend to themselves that being a medical technician was all they really wanted, anyway. Dystopian visions extrapolate from these responses to external constraints to imagine one where more general constraints produce more general alienation and inauthenticity. This is a reasonable thing to think about. More commonly, though, people who find that there are things they can't do move on and focus on something else. The pre-med may well take satisfaction in some other medical career, not through pretending to like it, but by actually coming to enjoy its benefits. Or, inner reflection may reveal that he really doesn't want to be a med tech, because what he wanted from medicine was power and prestige, and so he may choose another career that can provide those, no matter how far removed from medicine. Restrictions on action require the very skills of introspection that are praised here, because people need to re-evaluate their goals, values, and abilities in the face of opposition. Life is structured around the negotiation of obstacles, of which paternalistic laws are typically the slightest.

AFFECT: RESPONSE

If these arguments – that alienation and inauthenticity needn't arise from ceding some control over our personal lives to others – are effective, then the question of lost affect raised above might appear moot. I think, though, that it deserves some consideration. Certainly Mill may have been on to something. The mid-nineteenth century certainly indulged in a high degree of social disapprobation for those who did not obey the rules (including, to some degree, Mill himself and his romantic partner Harriet Taylor). This may indeed have brought about a degeneration of normal human feeling.

> The general average of mankind are not only moderate in intellect, but also moderate in inclinations: they have no tastes or wish strong enough to incline them to do anything unusual, and they consequently do not understand those who have, and class all such with the wild and intemperate whom they are accustomed to look down upon.[23]

This may be overstated: Victorian England, for all its conventionality, produced political reformers, including Mill himself, and innovative authors such as the Brontes and George Eliot, who, while they all suffered because of Victorian conventions, showed no lack of energy and originality. And if emotions were repressed, much of that, as Mill recognized, was not a function of law so much as custom. It was not law that Mill and Harriet Taylor should be disapproved of because their friendship went beyond the norms of nineteenth-century male–female friendship, even while it remained (apparently) Platonic during the life of Harriet's husband. It was not law that dictated that George Eliot could no longer be received in society after she had decided to cohabitate with George Henry Lewes, himself married to another woman, even while Lewes himself was generally welcomed. These were social conventions arising from a long history of norms concerning sexual behavior and gender. Still, it is likely that a paternalist should concede that the nineteenth century, if one can generalize over centuries, suffered in some ways from a surfeit of prudence and social control, and that this had some dampening psychological affect, and that it is prudence and social control that paternalistic laws promote. It may be, then, that we see a diminution in the intensity and impulsivity of emotion encouraged by paternalistic laws.

Is this necessarily a bad thing, though? Imagine a teenager who wants to drop out of college to be with his girlfriend, thinking they can marry, work as waiters, and survive on love, laughter, and song. He may know

---

[23] *On Liberty*, p. 199.

that this will be a poor path to worldly success, but believe that world well lost for love. The parent, on the other hand, opposes this, in the belief that love may fail but a college degree, like a diamond, lasts forever. Say that the child concedes to the parent's persuasion, and eventually decides that it was the right thing to do – the girlfriend dumps him eventually, and he's glad he's got the college degree that allows him to pursue any number of options. If he internalizes such prudence in future, it may well be that he never is quite so carried away again. He may look at future relationships more rationally, judging whether the two of them are really compatible, whether he's ready to make a commitment, whether it would make more sense to wait until he's settled somewhere and find someone in the same place so he won't have to have a commuting relationship. Prudence may be inimical to passion, just as Mill feared. Passion, on the other hand, is no guarantee of happiness. Just as we often choose when we are older to experience less intense emotions for the sake of more rewarding ones, so we may choose a world in which some heat is lost. I don't see that the specific sort of prudential constraints I am proposing would stand in the way of passionate love, actually, so this a hypothetical, but I concede that under some imagined circumstance it might, and certainly it is an endorsement of prudence overall which might have more general effects on our wild and crazy ways. This hardly entails, though, that we have no tastes strong enough to incline us to do something unusual. I think that, given the satisfactions and dissatisfactions in life overall, in the long run we will think it is worth it for its enhancement of our overall happiness.

SELF-ESTEEM: RESPONSE

Will thinking of ourselves as the kind of creatures who need to be controlled diminish our self-esteem? The existence of paternalistic laws will surely remind us of our failures to do, and/or abide by, appropriate instrumental thinking. I expect that we will continue to think well of our judgment even as we recognize that our decisions are often flawed. Fortunately, we are the kind of creatures who don't have any trouble believing in two contradictory things at the same time. The fact that we know our decisions to be flawed in many cases will not lead us to stop making them, or trusting in ourselves as generally good judges. Graham Priest has argued that "many, in fact most, of us believe contradictions. The person who has consistent beliefs is rare ... the moment one realizes one's beliefs are inconsistent, one does not ipso facto cease to believe the inconsistent things."[24] Because we are not purely rational creatures, the realization that we are not purely rational creatures is not likely to have the impact that it otherwise might. We typically celebrate both our freedom and, antithetically, our inability to control many things about ourselves. Philosophers and political theorists tend to pass over our enjoyment of the latter, but it is certainly in evidence: we take refuge in the idea that what we do is outside of our control, even as we feel that we are in control: we attribute our behavior to syndromes, to disorders, to inheritance, and even to the stars. We deny responsibility for some aspects of our character, even as we exhort ourselves to change. A recognition that we are all prone to error in certain ways is perfectly compatible – perhaps not logically, but emotionally – with the feeling of responsibility for, and of pride in, our choices.

Self-esteem, too, is not really determined by an objective consideration of our merits. That's why people full of accomplishments, merit, and virtue can feel worthless, while people who've never accomplished anything they've set out to do can feel confident about their worth. Psychologists have studied the sources of self-esteem since William James (at least), and have attributed its presence or absence to various factors: "Early affective experience" (how your care-givers treated you) is one source.[25] Another appears to be simple predisposition – some of us have "negative affectivity" – we are more likely to be gloomy than others, and negative in our judgments of ourselves as well as of other things.[26] Some of it derives from what importance we attach to what we perceive as our areas of success or failure.[27] One thing to which they have *not* attributed the development of self-esteem is how good, or smart, or accomplished people actually are. One more fact about ourselves, even a big fact that changes our romantic self-conception (and which, indeed, was never consistent with our empirical observation of error) is not going to be destructive of our self-esteem. Lastly, we may note that since the goal of paternalistic legislation is to allow people more easily to reach their own goals, and thus to be successful in those areas that they themselves do think important, it will aid, to the extent that recognition of success in one's personal goals can do, in building self-esteem.

---

[24] Graham Priest, "Contradiction, Belief, and Rationality," *Proceedings of the Aristotelian Society* 86 (1985/86), 102.

[25] C. Alan Sroufe, "Attachment and the Roots of Competence," *Human Nature* 31 (1978).

[26] David Watson and Lee A. Clark, "Negative Affectivity: The Disposition to Experience Aversive Emotional States," *Psychological Bulletin* 96.3 (1984), 465–490.

[27] Brett W. Pelham and William B. Swann, Jr., "From Self-Conception to Self-Worth: On the Sources and Structures of Global Self-Esteem," *Journal of Personality and Social Psychology* 57.4 (1989), 672–680.

CONCLUSION

All in all, the dangers of paternalistic regulation per se for psychological health are not great. While it does constitute a loss of control in some areas, those losses are not likely to be experienced as significant, and are furthermore compensated for by improvements that may allow more meaningful choices. The recognition that we need help in certain areas is not in itself destructive, especially when the help we need is provided. Insofar as the fear of an overwhelming paternalistic presence that destroys self-esteem, initiative, attachment, and integrity has rational roots, its roots lie in the envisaged misuse of paternalism: the fear that a state with paternalistic powers will not restrict itself to those measures where the benefits of legislation truly outweigh the admitted costs. It is to that fear, the fear of misuse and abuse, that we now turn.

CHAPTER 4

Misuse and abuse:
perfectionism and preferences

Most people grant that paternalism is a good idea in at least some situations where people pick poor means to their ends. However, even if we accept that paternalistic policies can, in principle, be extended to other cases where faulty reasoning results in great costs to the individual, there is, for most people, a significant stumbling block: the fear of misuse. Even if we believe paternalism to be morally justified in specific contexts, recognizing those contexts and taking only those measures appropriate to them is, in practice, difficult. Recognizing the legitimacy of paternalism in one area may serve as the thin edge of the wedge: before we know it, it is feared, governments will have taken the rationale offered for legitimate interventions in personal life and will use it for "paternalistic interventions" in areas that are not at all legitimate. Once we have established that personal decisions don't always have to be respected, it may be hard to say when they should be respected. We imagine a government agent standing behind us, making us eat our vegetables, switching the channel from *The Biggest Loser* to public television, and dragging us to exercise class. Even if these are things we wish we ourselves did, we typically don't want someone else making us do them. Worse, we may imagine a government imposing entirely foreign values, forcing us to live in ways that have nothing to do with what we want. Even a government quite sincerely attempting to do what is good for us may be wrong-headed about what our welfare consists in, and can impose actions that lead us entirely in the wrong direction. Torquemada may have been entirely benevolent – after all, surely anything is better than an eternity in hell – but this is little comfort to those who face the rack. This is a repellent picture, and to that extent it is a reasonable objection to paternalism: we do not want to introduce a policy that will inevitably be misused. We don't even want to introduce one that has a high probability of misuse.

The question is whether such misuse is inevitable or probable, as many seem to think, or whether it can be averted, so that we can enjoy the palpable benefits of appropriate paternalism without the costs of misuse. There are two main points to consider here: (1) whether government can be prevented from foisting upon us values and goals that are at variance with our own; and (2), whether using our own goals as the guideline in paternalistic practice is practically possible, given the effect of bias. I will argue that, while any policy (taxation, public education, democratic elections) can be grievously mishandled, this is no more likely when it comes to paternalism than it is in any other potentially beneficial but complicated process. The point is not to avoid paternalistic legislation, but to legislate properly.

ERRORS OF SCOPE

There are those who try to prevent abuses of paternalistic policy by arguing that certain areas of decision making should simply be placed off-limits to paternalistic interference; that certain types of personal decision, should, on principle, be left up to the agent, even if such decisions are likely to be significant in terms of happiness or unhappiness, and even if there is a good chance of failure for individuals who try to make the correct determination. The idea is roughly that the value of autonomy, of self-determination, is very great. It can sometimes be overridden for the sake of other valuable things (like continued life) if the decisions being made are not deeply significant, not central to one's self-conception; for example, the decision as to whether or not to use a seat belt is one we tend to make simply on the basis of convenience, rather than as part of a personally significant set of values, so interfering here is permissible. However, the value of autonomy is so significant in other areas that there it will almost always outweigh mere prudential concerns. Peter de Marneffe, for example, in defending paternalism from the charge that it creates a government too likely to believe itself *in loco parentis*, suggests that those who implement paternalistic policies might accept that

paternalistic interference with the basic liberties of freedom of thought and expression, freedom of worship, freedom of movement and political liberty is impermissible, and paternalistic intervention with any other liberty is impermissible unless it protects goods that are essential to our well-being or continued autonomy.[1]

I am averse to declaring certain areas of freedom off-limits in principle to paternalistic intervention, though. If the justification for paternalism is

---

[1] Peter de Marneffe, "Avoiding Paternalism," *Philosophy and Public Affairs* 34.1 (2006), 68–94, at 84.

that we often make decisions that are inefficient in, or downright contrary to, the promotion of our goals, not through some sort of corrigible bad character but because we are susceptible to certain errors of instrumental thinking, then it seems that interference might possibly be justified where such errors may be made. Whether or not it is *worth* it to interfere – whether the benefits outweigh the costs – would, on my account, be an empirical question, not a matter of principle, and it is this question of efficacy that would determine the appropriate policy. Of course, in considering costs we must include the feelings of the person who is constrained by paternalistic legislation, and in particular his feelings that, at least in certain areas, he doesn't want to be bossed around. While these emotional reactions are relevant, though, they should not be taken to be definitive of policy. The overall determination of whether a paternalistic procedure is appropriate will require many things, including the consideration of such feelings, of precedent effect, of the likelihood of its actually achieving its goal, the costs of implementation, the possibility of the policy being abused, and so forth. If interference has more costs than benefits, then, obviously, it is not a good idea. In many areas this will prove to be the case. However, even with the proviso that a paternalistic course of action which is ineffective is not one that a paternalist would endorse, it is clear that the paternalistic program envisaged here is wider than those that are more commonly accepted, even among those who defend paternalism. The fear arises, then, that a policy which doesn't even allow for prima facie exclusions, that will allow the paternalist to weight anything and everything to see if paternalistic interference is justified, will easily lend itself to excess. This could happen not only in insignificant areas but in decisions that are central to our lives. With no limitations to rein them in, even well-meaning practitioners might extend these policies beyond what we would consider acceptable, and ill-meaning practitioners could make our lives a totalitarian hell. We need to consider the criticism that open-ended paternalism is just too dangerous.

Perfectionism versus subjective welfare

While I think there are no limits, in principle, to the areas of decision making to which paternalism can be applied, there is a limit to the sorts of goals it can be used to advance. The goal of the paternalism recommended here is the advancement of individual welfare, and that is individual welfare construed as the maximization of the fulfillment of subjective ends. The standard of welfare is, then, what is typically termed a subjective one – based on the desires of the subject. Paternalism is not perfectionism, and it is perfectionism that is far more likely to permit of abuses.

Perfectionist views are those that recommend the pursuit of lives of objective value rather than simply the satisfaction of desire. The problem with perfectionism is not with individuals who have beliefs about object-ive value and wish to live according to those beliefs; this is not only not a bad thing, it is hard to imagine living in any other way. Rather, perfec-tionism, as a political view, recommends that governments should try to make people live lives of what the government (or more broadly, the culture) considers to be objective value, as opposed to helping them live the lives they want to. This is a problem. It is this practice, I think, that has given paternalism some of its bad name, because we imagine pater-nalists forcing us to do things in which we have no interest whatsoever. I think, though, that reasonable paternalists will avoid any kind of perfectionism, not simply because it is unpopular, but because it is unjustified.

Moral perfectionism

There are two sorts of (supposed) objective value that may come into play here: moral perfectionism and welfare perfectionism. The first advocates making people *morally* better. The idea is that it is morally bad to act in certain ways – to be a drunkard, for example, or to engage in morally wrongful sexual inclinations – and that the role of the government is to make us morally better people. This is the sort of theory that might lead governments to try to stamp out sin, eliminating, say, pornography, not because of its possible effects on others, but because it's just bad to enjoy it. Many religions have endorsed a kind of moral perfectionism, where the end of life is to be morally good, no matter how much suffering this entails. Beating someone to rid him of his tendency to think wicked thoughts would qualify as a morally perfectionist practice, although of course there are others more benign.

The second strand of perfectionism is not moralistic but nonetheless may be a justification for very intrusive policies: the belief in objective standards of welfare.[2] Those who believe in welfare perfectionism think

---

[2] As with so much philosophical terminology, "perfectionism" may be described in more than one way. L. W. Sumner, "The Subjectivity of Welfare" (*Ethics* 105.4 [1995], 764–790) uses "perfectionism" to describe only the view that there are objective accounts of what constitutes welfare, and differentiates the pursuit of objective moral goodness from perfectionism. Others, however, use perfectionism to describe both objective accounts of welfare and objective accounts of moral goodness: see F. H. Buckley, *Fair*

that there are certain necessary constituents of human welfare, such that you simply cannot be well-off if your life fails to include these goods. You may feel entirely satisfied – you've achieved everything you want – but this is not sufficient if your life does not include certain states or activities. A standard example is the person who does nothing but lie stoned in the basement watching bad sitcoms – even if he is entirely satisfied with such a life, and derives more pleasure from it than most of us do from our more active lives, many share an intuition that this life is not a good one. Gerald Dworkin, for example, says, "In my own view, someone who leads a boring, conventional life without close friendships or challenges or achievements, marking time to his grave, has not had a good life, even if he thinks he has and even if he has thoroughly enjoyed the life he has had."[3] Many will view such a life as unsatisfactory even if the person is able somehow to do good to others, and thus satisfy moral duties: imagine the stoner has set up a charity from his trust fund, which automatically dispenses money to whatever organization his computer program, "Passive-give," determines to be the best. He's happy, he's charitable, and yet, to many, the life is seriously wanting.

This distinction within perfectionism, between the pursuit of objectively good moral ends and objective standards of welfare, is to some degree artificial – certainly there are those who have tried to argue that the two are at least co-extensive, if not identical; that the better off you are morally the better off you are in terms of welfare. Socrates argued to a skeptical Athenian public in the *Apology*, for example, that he could not be harmed by his enemies, since these could not make him a morally worse person: while they could cause his death, or drive him into exile, or deprive him of civil rights, "no evil can happen to a good man, either in life or after death."[4] While Aristotle criticized Plato for suggesting that moral virtue is sufficient for a good life, he, too, in propounding his view of man's happiness as the excellent (virtuous) performance of human function, and his inclusion of justice, courage, and temperance among these, suggested that the attainment of moral virtue is at least necessary for achieving full welfare. Given our contemporary understanding both of what morality

---

Governance (Oxford University Press, 2009) and the *Stanford Encyclopedia of Philosophy* (http//plato. stanford.edu/entries/perfectionism-moral/). I have decided to follow the second, more inclusive, usage. More recently, Gerald Dworkin has differentiated "morality" from "ethics," where morality consists of to duties one has to others, and where ethics is the domain of the good life. Dworkin argues that to be good, a life must meet certain objective standards. ("What is a Good Life?," *New York Review of Books* [February 10, 2011], 41–43.)

[3] Dworkin, "What is a Good Life?," 42.   [4] Plato, *Apology*, 41c–d (Benjamin Jowett translation).

requires, and of what welfare consists in, though, we will typically differentiate between the two. While we generally think moral goodness plays some instrumental or even constitutive role in our welfare – it is hard to think of the serial killer psychopath being well-off – we are apt to think of moral concerns and concerns of welfare as two distinct things, which may interact causally but which are measured on different scales of value. The person who throws himself on a hand grenade to save his companions is morally good precisely *because* he sacrifices his welfare for that of others.

The distinction is evident in the relative popularity of the two kinds of perfectionism. At present, the idea that a government should enforce moralistic perfectionism is not popular, and there are good reasons for that. While we typically endorse moral views that enjoin constraints on behavior towards others (that it is wrong to murder, for example), it is harder to insist that behavior that affects no one other than yourself, and which you approve of and engage in voluntarily, is nonetheless morally wrong. It is even harder to argue that you should be prevented from doing that. In the case of murder, there is an identifiable loss of something the victim did not want to lose, whereas "immoral" behavior that is desired by the only party involved is tied to no identifiable harm. We tend to associate such an assessment with fanaticism, often religious, of the sort that has condemned homosexuality, masturbation, and even "impure" thoughts, no matter how welcome these are to the participants. We are wary of such judgments, which have led to standards of behavior that seem pointlessly oppressive and often simply mistaken, lacking in any justification but an unfounded belief in one's own direct access to God's opinion, or just as unlikely, one's own infallible intuition as to what objective morality consists in. Judgments which hold human behavior to a standard that is external to it – judgments not based on what we are like, or on what we want – seem increasingly controversial, and inhumane, and have become less and less popular.

Welfare perfectionism

Judgments about objective welfare, however, do not suffer from the same stigma. Many philosophers advance arguments that some lives are objectively better than others without feeling that they are open to charges of prejudice, much less fanaticism, because their positions on what constitutes the good life are founded on arguments about the nature of humanity itself.[5] They thus seem, to many, to allow a more rational assessment.

---

[5] The position that some lives are better than others is not taken to entail that some people are worth more than are others.

Whereas we may not have a sure handle on the metaphysical realm of the good, we do have humans ready to hand whom we can examine. The argument here is that (a) we have a better sense of what objective welfare consists in, and (b) when we fail to live that way, there is a sense in which we are harmed, even if we feel satisfied, because being human is essential to us, and such failure makes us less good humans. We can make sense of saying a plant has been harmed by having lost its leaves and branches to parasites, even though the plant is not suffering any dissatisfaction. It is perhaps for this reason that those who avoid arguing that we should strive for the attainment of objective moral values may nonetheless feel comfortable insisting on objective notions of welfare. Philippa Foot has worked to revive an Aristotelian notion of functioning, where we take what is definitive of a human's being human and then use that as a standard by which to measure the quality of human lives.[6] Richard Kraut, more recently, has introduced a broader picture of what could constitute an objective standard for well-being.[7] Martha Nussbaum's capabilities approach reflects the belief that some of our capacities are more important than others, and that the development of these more central capacities is essential to a good human life. She includes bodily health, practical reason, and the ability to live with concern for other species, among others.[8] None of these authors, I hasten to add, supports any form of coercion, governmental or otherwise, in implementing these values. Most of them are concerned with delineating the appropriate private pursuit of what they consider objectively good states of well-being, and Nussbaum, who is in favor of government action in the support of the achievement of the good life, argues only for a system where the government makes such features easier to achieve, not one where the government forces certain sorts of lives upon the public. Paternalists, however, are obviously willing to intervene in people's lives, and if a coercive paternalist were convinced that there existed an objective state of welfare, we can imagine such a paternalist trying to impose it.

This is one of the things that the opponents of paternalism fear. If we are willing to designate certain sorts of life as objectively better than others, what would stop the paternalist from insisting that people be coerced into living in these supposedly superior ways? Why rest with

---

[6] Philippa Foot, *Natural Goodness* (Oxford University Press, 2001).
[7] Richard Kraut, *What is Good and Why: The Ethics of Well-Being* (Cambridge, Mass.: Harvard University Press, 2007).
[8] Martha Nussbaum, *Women and Human Development: The Capabilities Approach* (Cambridge University Press, 2000).

furthering the satisfaction of desires, if the satisfaction of desires will result in a lower quality of life than might be otherwise achievable? If good health, practical reason, social interaction, and artistic expression are truly constitutive of a better life than the life that lacks them, why wouldn't the paternalist get everyone out for early volleyball, art lessons, philosophy class, and mandatory conversational exchanges – no matter how much they hate it?

It's a good question. There are those who oppose the imposition of even correct values on an unwilling public because they think that doing so infringes on autonomy, but this is not an argument that is open to the coercive paternalist, who is perfectly willing to infringe upon autonomy when the benefits are sufficient. The paternalist wants to make people better off, and if we have an idea of what constitutes objective well-being, it seems reasonable to think the paternalist would impose this on people, even though we really don't want this.

The rejection of perfectionism

It's not clear that the objective notion of well-being that is necessary for conceptualizing welfare perfectionism makes much sense. Aristotle's belief about objective welfare is that what defines someone as human is his ability to reason, and that the best life for a human is naturally the life in which he is fulfilling his distinctive function well – that is, the best life for a human is the life of theoretical reasoning. This view hasn't had many takers, and this is presumably because it, like so many candidates for the uniquely best life for humans, seems unattractive to many people. Even if, for the purposes of argument, we accept that humans as a class have a distinctive function that defines them, and accept that this involves reasoning, many resist the idea that maximal participation in the life of theoretical reasoning is necessary for a successful life. Some people argue that they would not enjoy the life of theoretical reasoning, and the idea that they would nonetheless be better off seems deeply unconvincing. Others are willing to sacrifice some enjoyment, but in pursuit of their own goals, goals that they feel define them as individuals, rather than as members of a species. Whatever the reason, few people accept Aristotle's conclusions, even when exposed to the specifics of his argument.

One natural response from the welfare perfectionist is that this is a problem for Aristotle rather than for objective welfare theories – Aristotle may just have hit upon a particularly unappealing account of what our flourishing consists in (appealing, perhaps, to a philosopher, but not so much to the general public). Someone else might stress our capacity for choice as what makes us distinctively human, or our capacity for love, or our ability to produce art, and such an account of our distinctive function might accommodate more of our intuitions about what constitutes the good life. The problem, though, is ultimately the same. Whatever the account, there are those who do not see it as being important to their fulfillment. There are those who can imagine a perfectly good life in which the capacity for choice is surrendered – we often enjoy relying on others to make our decisions, or we might make a principled commitment to surrender our will to some greater authority. We sometimes criticize people who abnegate the power to decide, but more because we disapprove of the particular authority they have chosen – the wrong God; the wrong loyalties – than because we disapprove of such a surrender itself. Others may see love as something that is good for other people, but not for themselves – St. Jerome's solitary life of asceticism and study, so beloved of medieval artists, may appeal to them as the apex of human achievement. The value of art serves as the basis for the construction of a life for some, but of course, not for others. Presumably one difference between being solitary in the way that St. Jerome was, and being solitary in the way of someone who is frantically trying out all the on-line dating sites, is whether they have chosen solitude, either as a goal or as a necessary concomitant of a chosen goal. It is the subjective commitment that makes the difference.

Of course, one might have accounts of objective welfare that do not, as Aristotle's does, depend on a unique human function. These could either (a) suggest that there is more than one distinctive human function, or could (b) give up the function argument altogether. These attempts to square our beliefs about value with objective welfare accounts still fail the test for intuitive plausibility, however. Again, our identification of ourselves as human, with, on this account, a set of distinctive activities, rather than just one, may not seem a sufficient base for the orientation of our lives – what if being human just doesn't matter that much? Even if there is a relatively varied set of essentially human activities, I may not value, or excel, at any of them. It seems I might reasonably choose to be deformed *qua* human in the interests of some other goal.

And then there is the problem that some distinctively human activities seem particularly unworthy of pursuit. Kraut's developmental account says that there are some capacities that humans shouldn't develop. For example, we are the only species capable of deliberate cruelty, but Kraut argues that this should not be included as a necessary constituent of human flourishing. This is a problem: first, accounts that base their account of objective welfare on "the potentialities, capacities, and faculties that (under favorable conditions) they naturally have at an early stage of their existence"[9] appear inconsistent if it turns out that "some natural powers are bad for the person who has them."[10] If not all aspects of our nature actually count, then it's hard to say what role our nature actually plays in the justification of the argument that we should develop certain capacities.[11]

The truth is that good of the individual need not be tied to the good of its species-being. Since Babe the pig excelled at herding sheep, that made him a poor pig, whose function is to do distinctly piglike things, not distinctly Border Collie-type things; but herding sheep was clearly conducive to Babe's welfare, because it allowed him to reach his goals – community, self-respect, and avoiding being served for dinner.[12] His identification *qua* pig is less important to his welfare than his identification *qua* Babe, with his own distinctive set of characteristics and goals.

Some who argue for objective accounts of welfare do abandon the argument that your welfare is tied to being an exemplar of your type – in our case, to being a proper human. James Griffin, for example, without relying on Aristotelian function, has suggested that the good life may be a combination of intrinsically good states: lives realizing different combinations of these fundamental values may all be good.[13] This bypasses the problem of justifying a particular activity or set of activities as the distinctive human function, but still suffers some of the same problems as such views. What if none of the proffered standards of a good life appeal to us, even after we have been sufficiently exposed to them to understand what they consist in? Griffin's account, for example, gives no value to sensual pleasure, and it has been persuasively argued that to many people this a primary, perhaps even the most significant, component of the good life.[14] What, then, founds the argument that a certain kind of life is objectively good? Saying that the good life is the one that includes the

---

[9] Kraut, *What is Good*, p. 131.   [10] Ibid., p. 147.

[11] In the end, Kraut's account seems to be something of a hybrid – while he uses the language of Aristotelians and neo-Aristotelians, where the good consists in the flourishing according to one's nature, capacities (at least for humans) also have to pass additional tests as to their value.

[12] See *Babe: The Gallant Pig* by Dick King-Smith (New York: Crown Publishers, 1985; first published in Great Britain as *The Sheep Pig*, 1983.) Also an exciting motion picture, *Babe*, directed by Chris Noonan, 1995.

[13] James Griffin, *Well-Being: Its Meaning, Measurement, and Moral Importance* (Oxford University Press, 1986), part I, pp. 7–72.

[14] David Braybrooke, "Review Essay: Thoughtful Happiness," *Ethics* 99.3 (1989), 625–636.

optimal combination of objectively valuable things – activities, feelings, states of affairs – sounds good until we look at any given proffered list of objectively valuable activities and then see that the activity we care for is not on it, and that ones we don't care for are. Such claims seem to bring us back to moral perfectionism – the argument that there are simply good states of being, and that you ought to pursue them, whether they mean anything to you or not. The problem with objective standards of welfare seems to be that, as L. W. Sumner puts it, it would be strange if "my life can be going well despite my failure to have any positive attitude toward it."[15] It reminds us of those who argued that slaves were better off enslaved than living according to their own (presumably inappropriate) wishes. No matter what the account of the objectively good life, it seems to have something missing – our own adherence to it as reflecting the way we want to live.

Lastly, such objective accounts are unlikely to succeed as blueprints for government policy. It can feasibly be argued that for a government policy to be justified it has to work, at least most of the time. One problem with objective accounts of welfare is that even if there is a correct one, there just isn't enough agreement on what such an account would be, as we have seen, and there is no obvious way of resolving our differences of opinion. It looks as though no account of the good life that focuses on one definitive good-making feature, or one limited set of features, will be accepted by even the majority of people.

Some of this is because our accounts are likely to be wrong. We know it is too easy to endow a personal goal (I will feel like a horrible failure if I don't learn to do a side snap kick properly, instead of constantly confusing it with a side thrust kick) with what we take to be objective value – something that everyone should pursue. I do recognize that pursuit of the perfect side snap kick is not something I can wish on everyone, but what about reading *Middlemarch*? There, I often find myself willing to believe that what is (in a more rational moment, I can concede) a personal value is really objectively valuable – everyone should put down every other book and pick up George Eliot instead. Of course, there are sound arguments that George Eliot is a good writer, since we can judge her vis-à-vis the standards of a genre, but no good ones that say we are justified in establishing a mandatory George Eliot reading hour across the nation.[16]

---

[15] Sumner, "Subjectivity of Welfare," 764–790.
[16] I actually think this is a great idea, but I assume this just goes to show that one person's sense of a clearly objectively valuable aspect of life is another's anathema.

The fact that the George Eliot Appreciation Hour reflects only my personal preference, not the good, is one reason that it can't be effectively forced on people. Another is that even if we had a correct account of what objective welfare would consist in, it's not clear that objective goods can be forced upon people. We discussed above the fact that moral perfectionism is an unpopular view. One reason was that it was hard to make sense of, but another is that it would be hard to use moral perfectionism as a guide in transforming people's lives. The argument here is that moral perfectionism has to be rejected because forcing people to achieve moral purity is simply not possible. H. L. A. Hart wrote that while one might legislate "moral" behavior, that is, action that mimics what morally good people would do, this does not in itself yield morally good behavior, since that depends on having the appropriate motives, and fear of government sanctions is not one that produces truly moral behavior:

> It is difficult to understand the assertion that conformity, even if motivated merely by fear of the law's punishment, is a value worth pursuing, notwithstanding the misery and sacrifice of freedom it involves. The attribution of value to mere conforming behavior, in abstraction from both motive and consequences, belongs not to morality but to taboo.[17]

Morally appropriate behavior without the accompanying motivation is no longer morally appropriate behavior. Being forced to attend a church in which you do not and don't want to believe, as Locke pointed out in his *Letter on Toleration*, does not make a person into a believer. Even if we knew what constituted moral perfection, we can't force moral virtue, but at best can only force mimicry of what morally virtuous people would do.

It might at first seem rather different when it comes to objective accounts of welfare. If it is objectively good to live up to some particular standard of human health, for example, we could presumably be forced into better health, no matter how much we hate it. However, many conditions that are suggested as being objectively valuable may indeed depend on the person having the proper motive, in the same way that moral virtue does, and that motive may not be achievable by force. For example, it is hard to imagine the appreciation of art achieved through legislation that mandates it. Taking busloads of people to the art museum, even making them listen to informative and insightful lectures on the relationship between Titian and Tintoretto, is not enough to make them actually care for art. (I've heard a number of lectures on the relationship

---

[17] H. L. A. Hart, *Law, Liberty, and Morality* (Oxford University Press, 1963), p. 57.

between Titian and Tintoretto, and my only reaction is that, granted a certain skill in depicting fur, the paintings of both leave me cold.) One might think that if it is objectively better to read poetry than to play pushpin then we can ban pushpin and have mandatory poetry readings in the square, but again, this seems unlikely to achieve what is really wanted. It's not enough that our ears take in the sound of poetry; we need to actually enjoy and gain insight from it. Those predisposed to like poetry might well enjoy it if poetry readings were mandatory, and there is an argument for giving people a chance to go to such activities, so that those who do turn out to like it can enjoy it. Others, though, would go from indifference to poetry to downright hatred. Forcing everyone to engage in the activity just doesn't achieve the desired end. So, practically speaking, trying to impose values doesn't have the desired results: it might lead to certain behaviors, but insofar as what we want is internal states of engagement, forced activity just doesn't make that happen.

In an individual life, not being sure what sort of life has value is not necessarily so bad. If we decide that what we're doing isn't valuable, we often can change, or at least modify, our life in light of that conviction – the way someone changes when they stop (or start) believing that a certain sort of life is dictated by God. While sometimes our irresolution about what has value is depressing, it can also be rewarding to reflect what kind of life we believe to be objectively valuable. Being locked into the pursuit of an "objectively" valuable life in which we don't believe by a government policy, though, allows neither the ability to change nor the sense of reward of an individual's pursuit. This is the situation we are likely to find ourselves in if we allow welfare perfectionism.

Welfare perfectionism, as a program of government intervention, has the same flaws as moral perfectionism. One is that, given reasonable disagreement about what welfare consists in, we may well err in what we impose. The second is that, given the same lack of agreement, we are unlikely to accept and internalize, in any meaningful way, any imposition of values that do not reflect our own desires. The result is that such a policy will result in disaffection, disorder, and disunion. This, in addition to its other failures to convince, makes it an impractical policy for improvement.

ERRORS OF CALCULATION

This emphasis on subjective welfare may seem to get us out of the frying pan only to land us in the fire. The subjective view, where we operate from people's preferences, may seem too slippery – can we know what preferences are? Are there preferences at all? To promote welfare so conceived, we will need to figure out what needs and goals people actually have, and to craft policies in accordance with those. Some have questioned whether we are astute enough to do this. Others have even questioned whether such "preferences" exist. In what follows, I will argue that designing paternalistic programs around people's own needs, goals, and values is, in fact, as practicable as creating any other sort of regulation.

Cognitive error

The government is made up of (more or less) normal human beings. I have argued (in Chapter 1) that the need for paternalistic intervention does not justify a class society, since the sorts of flaws that lead us astray are common to all people, and those who are in the position of legislator have no reason to think they are immune to the same problems that beset us all. This, though, obviously entails that people in government are just as likely as private individuals are to make errors. To some, this suggests that the very existence of cognitive bias, which may be seen to justify paternalistic intervention, also provides an argument against it. Sunstein and Thaler have argued that one reason why their libertarian paternalism is typically superior to coercive measures is that it allows citizens a safeguard: they can always elect to opt out of policies that may reflect the confusion on the part of boundedly rational planners.[18] The idea is that legislators suffering from cognitive bias will create poor legislation – laws whose efficacy is thwarted by the very bias it is designed to circumvent – and so we naturally need to be able to protect ourselves from their errors.

The mechanisms that could allow for such failures are familiar. One argument is that our inability to make good distinctions will lead us down a slippery slope, from (possibly) reasonable paternalistic interventions to unreasonable ones.[19] Our bias against extremes will generally lead us to choose whatever seems to be the middle course of action. We have a certain policy that is the status quo. In the interests of improvement, we are willing to change this most familiar course of action, but not too far.

[18] Cass Sunstein and Richard Thaler, "Libertarian Paternalism is not an Oxymoron," *University of Chicago Law Review* 70 (2003), 1200–1201.
[19] Douglas Glenn Whitman and Mario J. Rizzo, "Paternalist Slopes," *New York University Journal of Law and Liberty* 2.3 (2007), 411–443.

What constitutes "too far," though, is not a function of intrinsic merit but of the options we are given. If the speed limit on the edge of town is 45, and there is an argument that it needs to be changed, and the two suggested options are 35 and 25, we are more likely to take 35 as being a reasonable speed, not because it is actually preferable, but because it is the middle course of action. At the same time, as this becomes the status quo we are familiar with, we are more likely to move, incrementally, to options which might previously have seemed beyond the pale, but which now are merely the middle course between the familiar and newer extremes – so, once we become familiar with the speed limit of 35, moving it to 25 no longer seems so unreasonable, while changing it to 15 seems clearly excessive. We know that, for example, the idea of banning smoking outside would once have seemed ridiculous; however, as we become familiar with banning smoking indoors, banning it from exterior door- ways that lead indoors seems reasonable; once we've banned it outdoors near entrances, banning it from whole campuses and entire parks seems reasonable (at least reasonable enough that such bans are becoming more and more popular). While some might think that this is because we're more familiar with the dangers of second-hand smoke, the argument here is that it is more likely to be because we are irrationally willing to accept incremental changes that fall between two extremes, regardless of their intrinsic (sometimes lack of) merit.[20] The same cognitive biases which prevent us from individually arriving at fully reasoned assessments of courses of action will prevent us from recognizing which extensions of policy are well grounded and which arise from our bias towards the "middle" course. Mild, and possibly justified, paternalistic practices will, on this account, almost inevitably morph into ever more extreme measures.

"Slippery slope" arguments – arguments that if you take position A and cannot define a precise cut-off point where cases are substantially differ- entiated, you are inevitably led, through incremental steps, to accept its extreme extension, Z – are generally thought of as fallacious. The fact that there is no clear cut-off between A and B, between B and C, and so on, does *not* entail that there is no distinction between A and Z. The critic of paternalism, however, claims that in the case of paternalistic policies, the slope really is one we are likely to slip down, because while progress from A to Z doesn't follow logically, we are, just as the paternalist maintains, far from entirely logical. Especially where concepts are imprecise, the hapless lawmaker is much more likely to go from a possibly justified

---

[20] Whitman and Rizzo's example (see ibid.).

policy to one that is not. And when it comes to paternalism, the argument continues, the concepts are imprecise in just this way: paternalist policies are there to advance welfare, but there is no consensus on what precisely welfare consists in. "Different decision makers will naturally approach the problem with widely varying notions of welfare and well-being."[21] Given the reasoning problems to which we are prone, and the difficulty inherent in planning social policy around an inchoate notion such as "welfare," there is no reason to think that legislators will do any better than will private individuals in recognizing which are good means to ends.

The trouble with this argument as it stands, though, is that it is not so much an argument against paternalism as an argument against legislation in general. Laws that protect third parties must also use vague concepts: such laws are intended to prevent us from harming others, but "harm" is no more specific a concept than "welfare," upon which it arguably depends. And the concept of "desert," surely, is even harder to get a handle on, yet we use it continually in order to assess punishments and include it in a complex calculus of considerations including actual harm done, degree of ill intent (as in murder vs. attempted murder), and the cost of enforcement. (Philosophers of law point out that even traffic law, seemingly straightforward, yields its share of conceptual puzzles – does an intoxicated person in an electric wheelchair qualify as a drunk driver? Does a path closed to vehicular traffic admit of horseback riding?) Just as with paternalistic laws, what may at first seem extreme, relative to the norm, can come to be seen as the status quo, which enables a step to what was considered extreme now appear moderate, and thus acceptable, regardless of merit. Yet, we are convinced that laws are generally good to have, especially insofar as they act to protect us from the actions of others. My argument here is certainly not that our experience of criminal and other third-person laws shows that we need not fear the existence of cognitive bias in their construction or their application; rather, the argument is that we think it is worth it to have these laws, whatever their failings. At least sometimes, we can discover that the thinking that led to their creation was mistaken and we fix them. And sometimes, sadly, we don't. When this happens, it is bad: unjust, costly, counterproductive. We don't, though, give up on laws, because on the whole our imperfect system of law is better than no system: more just, less costly, and more productive than the alternative. So, the fact that paternalistic laws are liable to these same failings is not much of an argument against their production.

---

[21] Ibid., 421.

A more vexing argument for the paternalist is that paternalistic laws are not merely *as* likely to include errors as are other laws, but *more* likely. Edward Glaeser argues that legislators are prone to more bias than are individuals seeking to promote their own welfare, so their decisions will be correspondingly worse.[22] This suggests a disanalogy with third-party laws – while laws protecting us from harm committed by others have their problems, it is hard to argue that we could do better if we left it up to private individuals to make their own decisions in such matters. Since we have to assume that lots more people would decide to rob and kill if there were no law enforcement to prevent them, even flawed laws keep us safer than no law. If, on the other hand, lawmakers using paternalistic laws do a worse job at promoting welfare than do private citizens, they shouldn't be in the business of promoting welfare through paternalistic laws.

The question is whether it is true that individuals make better prudential choices than do legislators on their behalf. Glaeser's argument is that (a) individuals have a greater incentive to do what is in accordance with their own welfare than lawmakers do to create laws in accordance with the general welfare; that (b) individuals have a greater incentive to make specific decisions that promote their own welfare – buying wisely, for example – than they do to vote for legislators who will do a good job doing that; and that (c) it is easier for lobbyists and the like to affect the decisions of legislators than to sway the public, simply because there are fewer legislators, each wielding more power, than there are private citizens. Given these three things, he concludes, lawmakers will be more prone to error than will individual citizens.

There is some truth to these claims. The first two depend on the argument that my incentive to make prudent purchases is quite strong, stronger than other relevant motivations that I may feel, and stronger than any concern the legislator feels on my behalf. This seems likely: it is more painful to me if my purchase of a big new house drives me into debt than it is to my legislator, who may view my poverty with relative indifference, just as I am more rewarded for my saving for my old age than is she by my prudence. So yes, I care more, even if my legislator is reasonably altruistic. The problem, though, is that I am also much more tempted by imprudence. I am much more tempted to buy this fancy but realistically unaffordable house than she is tempted to make laws that let me buy it, since I'm the one who's going to enjoy it, who is daydreaming

---

[22] Edward L. Glaeser, "Paternalism and Psychology," *University of Chicago Law Review* 73 (winter 2006), 133–156.

about the Hollywood-style parties I will throw there, who is thrilled at the impression I'm going to make on my friends. I'm also the one who has unbounded optimism about my future prospects, optimism an unbiased third party is very unlikely to endorse. While I have more incentive to avoid the pain of foreclosure or whatever economic pressure that may occur when I buy things I can't afford, I am also the one who is irrationally inclined to buy those things, and my felt motivation is influenced by things that will not influence the legislator.

There is no doubt that, in many cases, it is the temptation of the current moment that allows us to fall sway to cognitive biases. That is why when we are not in the grip of temptation, we are much more able to do a reasonable analysis of the costs and benefits of a course of action. When we make that shopping list at home we do not write, "whatever smells really good, no matter how fattening, cholesterol-laden and sugar-filled." We plan to buy only the fruits and vegetables that we like just fine and that will be good for us. But then – that counter covered with hazelnut and dark chocolate cupcakes, with the smell of baking in the air – we're goners. We make lists of desirable properties in a romantic partner (at least some people seem to), but then go for the cute guy with the unbounded charm and tendency to lie. We plan to buy a reasonable house, but when the real estate agent shows us the much nicer one and tells us they know a company who will finance it, we give in to the fantasy. If the fact that we are the ones who will suffer a loss in a situation made us better at calculating, and caring about, the risks of that situation than other people would be, then there would be no problem here. There is more to decision making than this, though, for better or worse.

Incentives are not felt as static: while the facts remain the same, our appreciations of those facts, and our motivations to act, vary with the situation, including, importantly, whether we ourselves are liable to benefit from a certain good. Glaeser perceives this, but thinks it means that those who stand to suffer from a loss will be extra cautious. He apparently does not recognize that as we stand to benefit from a gain, we also become extra incautious. As our motivation varies – as we want something more – we are more prone to miscalculate about its harms and its benefits, and the probability of both of these. Of course, this is not rational. That's the whole problem. When I'm being more rational – when I'm away from temptation, which can mean at home, and not in the bakery, or when I am considering the desirability of a purchase I myself am not making, I am pretty good at looking simply at the figures and seeing if it is a good idea. Glaeser has granted that we are prone to cognitive bias, and is right to think that incentives can affect our judgment. The incentive to avoid costly mistakes, though, is only one among many. Glaeser seems subject to a lingering hope that we will calculate risks rationally, which the facts don't uphold. As a consequence, he has missed the highly pertinent fact that legislators – like anyone who considers a decision from the perspective of a third party, not subject to its seductive qualities – are in a better position to see what is, and what is not, a good bet. Similarly for voting: while our incentive to vote prudently is not as strong as it might be, and we vote often in less than informed ways, we are at least not subject to the temptations of self-delusion to the degree we are when we make (at least some) decisions that affect our whole future. We don't have as much investment in voting badly as we do in buying badly.

Lastly, as concerns Glaeser's final reason for worry, lobbyists: lobbying is always a problem. It is possible, of course, that legislators may be more prone than people in general are to suasion by lobbyists when it comes to paternalistic legislation. A legislator may have no personal interest in whether there are milk subsidies, and thus may be open to being pushed either way by lobbyists. Because paternalistic legislation, on the other hand, is intrusive into personal lives, the legislator may be more willing to consider its true merits, since he, too, will be affected by them. We can't assume this, though. Legislators may be so corrupt that they intend to have access to their own private store of cigarettes, cheap trans-fats-filled pastries, and offshore financing, and be entirely indifferent to the personal effects of paternalistic legislation, and thereby they will not bother to consider the relative benefits and costs. Or, they may take bribes so great as to offset any costs to themselves. Or, effective lobbying may be able to hide the negative effects of the legislation they contemplate, and so they make incorrect even if well-meaning decisions. So yes, the possible deleterious results of lobbying are as real here as in all other legislation. It seems to me, though, that rather than failing to attempt legislation because lobbyists might affect it, we might rather try to limit the effects of lobbying. If legislation is otherwise good, but only dangerous because lobbyists interfere with democratic processes, the cure doesn't seem to consist in avoiding legislation. The claim that it does merits the response given to the first argument above: that if lobbying here argues against legislation then it does so in all cases, yet, we believe in legislation.

These three arguments against paternalistic legislation fail, then. Of course, not all cognitive biases are affected by incentives. I dwell on these because this is what Glaeser sees as the reason the government will be more likely to make mistakes than will individuals left to their own devices, despite our sorry record, as individuals, in making choices. While these arguments are correct insofar as they argue that people who are making laws will be subject to cognitive bias, they haven't shown that they will be more prone to cognitive bias in making paternalistic laws than in making laws in general, nor more prone to cognitive bias than individuals deciding for themselves. On the contrary, an understanding of cognitive error shows that people will be less prone to certain sorts of error – since there will be fewer incentives to self-delusion.

Mistakes about welfare

It has to be admitted, though, that just as we are likely to make mistakes in assessing what "objective" value consists in, so we will make some mistakes concerning subjective welfare and the best means to promoting that. I have argued that legislators will typically make better choices than individuals in these sorts of issues, and that, insofar as they are good paternalists, they will try to do what is good for people according to the way people themselves conceive of their good. That said, legislators make errors. Worse, once legislative mistakes are made, it can be extremely hard to undo them. Inertia is a powerful force: for many, it is hard to reconceive a law that has been in place for a while, and even those who reconceive it may be timid about proposing a change, since to many people that will seem like apostasy, no matter how foolish the law.

It has been suggested to me in several venues that at least some drug laws fit this description, and thus are evidence against the advisability of paternalist legislation. In particular, a good number of people argue that marijuana is not in fact very bad for you; no worse than the use of alcohol, which is legal, and arguably better than the use of alcohol, which has its own health consequences. Some of those who support keeping marijuana illegal seem to concede that it is not itself all that dangerous, but offer the rationale that marijuana is a "gateway" drug; that is, that its use leads to the use of more serious drugs that are arguably worse for individuals to use, and are often addictive. The argument here seems to be that those who use more dangerous drugs started by using marijuana. Obviously, the relevant point for showing a causal link between the use of marijuana and something like heroin is not just whether those who use heroin first used marijuana, but how many users of marijuana go on to use heroin – the causal argument is incomplete when we don't look at those who use the first drug and don't go on to use more. It is reasonably arguable that those inclined to use serious drugs will start with whatever is most available, whatever that may be. If it is marijuana, they still start with that; if it is something else, they would start there. There will always be some drug which is the easiest to obtain, and as long as people are interested in taking drugs, it seems likely that whatever is easiest to obtain will indeed be quite easy. The "gateway" argument is weak.

Yet, the federal government spends billions of dollars per year on the "war on drugs," and a good part of that is the attempt to prevent the importation or smoking of marijuana. Add to that what is spent on prosecuting and imprisoning people found guilty of selling and using marijuana, and you have a truly impressive amount. And, in addition to the financial costs on the part of the government, there are enormous costs to the individuals who are prosecuted and imprisoned. Despite all this, marijuana is easily obtainable in just about any American high school. Whether or not people use it does not seem to be a function of its availability, since it is generally available, but of personal choice. Furthermore, the fact that marijuana is illegal means that it is imported by criminals, and this black-market trade has resulted, in areas such as northern Mexico, in massive violence in the struggles between drug cartels for control of the market.

Thus, we have a policy where the costs are extremely high and the benefits are very few, which we nonetheless persist in pursuing. It is true that in many cases the pursuit of individuals using marijuana has been relaxed; marijuana has been decriminalized in many areas. Still, the massive spending goes on. For this reason, drug laws, as currently enacted in the United States, are often offered as an example of mistakes paternalists are likely to make: they can undertake ineffective policies, and, once the infrastructure is in place for pursuing those wrong-headed policies, continue to pursue them despite the manifest failure, even on paternalistic grounds, to achieve anything beneficial.

It is best to concede at once that a paternalistic policy might be undertaken on the basis of poor information, and that it is hard to undo laws once in place. I would argue, though, that in a case were there is a huge amount of information available about the costs of a policy, and about its failure to be very effective, something other than paternalistic considerations are apt to be at play, and this is certainly true in marijuana legislation. Its justification has relied on a combination of third-party concerns (protection of the innocent from marijuana users) and perfectionist policies, neither of which has sufficient justification.

Historically, anti-marijuana legislation was introduced primarily in the belief that marijuana use led to violent crime; not in the sense that drug dealers might engage in the kind of combat we see among *narcotraficantes* themselves, but rather in the belief that the individual using marijuana was prone to fits of violence. The claim was that marijuana could induce a sort of temporary insanity in which users would murder, rape, and generally go on bloody binges. In particular, it was seen as inducing violence among what were seen as dangerous members of society – Mexican-Americans in the west, and black city dwellers in the east.[23] A contemporary source cited by courts of the time argued, among other spurious claims, that "[o]ccasionally an entire group of men under the influence of this drug will rush out to engage in violent or bloody deeds," and that the word "assassin" is derived from the word for hashish.[24] This misinformation was believed, in part, because most Americans were unfamiliar with marijuana at that time, and in part because racism made the (supposed) activities of minority groups seem particularly dangerous. This is certainly an example of poor legislation, but it is an example of poor legislation designed to protect third parties, rather than poor paternalistic law.

Modern drug policy is different, since we know more about marijuana and do not associate it with crazed violence. The rationale for illegality now is certainly confused, but I think a good part of the impetus is perfectionist, rather than based either on immediate third-party concerns or on a concern for the welfare of the people doing drugs. Many people associate drug use with decadence of character, with a disregard for hard work and achievement and a preference for lolling about on sofas. They may be disinclined to think people will stop at mild drug use, and refrain from full-flown heroin addiction, because they think anyone so wanting in character as to use one drug will naturally want to use more. I'm inclined to think this is incorrect, at least for many marijuana users, who appear to be no more decadent than wine, beer, and martini drinkers. The important issue, though, is not whether marijuana users are wastrels, but whether their wastrel-hood should be a concern for us. There are two legitimate areas of concern: harm to third parties (we no longer believe in marijuana-crazed murderers, but some people worry that marijuana users contribute insufficiently to the economy, for example), and genuine paternalistic concerns (whether marijuana use

---

[23] See the comprehensive history of marijuana legislation and its rationales in Richard Bonnie and Charles Whitehead II, "The Forbidden Fruit and the Tree of Knowledge: An Inquiry into the Legal History of American Marijuana Prohibition," *Virginia Law Review* 56.6 (October 1970), 974–1253.

[24] Ibid., 1023–1024.

prevents people from reaching their own goals). I'm not in a position to address either of these questions with any authority, but these questions need to be asked when it comes to drug use – we make them illegal without getting evidence of harm to others and without considering whether their use is consistent with the overall life goals of those who use them. For many people, it just seems wrong that people should use drugs, and it seems perhaps even more wrong that a country should allow that people use drugs. I think it is plausible that it is this perfectionist perception, rather than an incorrect paternalist calculation, that lies behind much of the intransigence of American drug policy.

It is not always easy to avoid imposing values. Dan Wikler points out that even with regards to health, we may be moralistic rather than genuinely concerned with welfare: if we talk about health legislation to discourage "gluttony" and "sloth," we are using concepts that are morally loaded.[25] Our judgment about what should be done may reflect very personal values – as I might say that of course people should give up chips and junk food, but at the same time argue that wine appreciation is truly constitutive of welfare, whatever its costs may be to the body. So, we must be wary of cultural prejudice even when we are making what we claim to be means–end judgments, not judgments about what has value as an end in itself: "If the effect on health is not sufficient to justify the social engineering which may be required for efficacy, the health educator's paternalist rationale is open to question. Surely he is not a better judge of a culture as a whole than are those whose behavior he wishes to change." It is not always easy to avoid the imposition of foreign values, but it is only to the extent that we can do this, and help people in the pursuit of their own desires, that intervention will be effective. One suggestion is that the harm the legislation is intended to mitigate should be regarded, by those who will experience its loss, as indeed something they'd prefer, in the long run, to be without. "The harm to be avoided should be accepted as a harm, even as a primary harm, by most of those affected by the intervention."[26] And, more generally, an understanding of the difference between paternalism and perfectionism, and familiarity with the criteria a paternalistic policy needs to meet in order to be justified, will help us avoid such costly mistakes.[27]

[25] Dan Wikler, "Coercive Measures in Health Promotion: Can they be Justified?," *Health Education Monographs* 6 (July 1978), 232.
[26] Jack Lively, "Paternalism," in *Of Liberty*, Royal Institute of Philosophy Lectures Series 15, ed. A. Phillips Griffiths (Cambridge University Press, 1983), 147–165.
[27] See Chapter 6 below for a detailed discussion of the criteria for successful paternalistic interventions.

Indeterminacy

Some argue, though, that even if we were somehow free of cognitive bias when it comes to legislating ways to help people act on their true preferences, there is another sort of cognitive deficit: we can't know people's true preferences because often there is no such thing as a true preference, in the sense of one which predates, and then is distorted by, adverse choice strategies, and which could be rehabilitated through different choice strategies. In "Libertarian Paternalism is Not an Oxymoron," Sunstein and Thaler demonstrated at length that in some contexts it is the context itself that determines our preference. Whether we want fruit rather than pastry may depend on where they placed in the cafeteria line; whether we prefer government policy A to policy B may depend simply on the wording used to describe the policies, rather than their actual content; whether we choose pension plan X or pension Y depends on which of them is the default option, rather than on their respective advantages.[28] Given this, it has been argued that there is no way we can paternalistically implement preferences by altering the choice architecture: the choice architecture *creates* the preference. The architect can certainly affect what decision is made, but not according to the pre-existing preference of the chooser. Robert Sugden critizes Sunstein and Thaler for saying we should aim for the decision the person would make if they had complete information, unlimited cognitive abilities, and no lack of will power; how, says Sugden, can we know what such a decision would be? We need to apply these criteria to stable preferences, but "the whole problem is that the real human being lacks stable preferences."[29] Paul Slovic asks in what sense preferences even exist, if they are formed according to the elicitation procedure, and points out that it is hard to say they are distorted by the process if that process is what makes them what they are.[30] If I prefer A to B under one description and prefer B to A under another, how can we say that I actually have a preference at all? Critics conclude that insofar as paternalism, libertarian or other, intends to satisfy the subjective desires we would have if we weren't irrationally affected by external factors, it gropes for a phantasm.

---

[28] Sunstein and Thaler, "Libertarian Paternalism is not an Oxymoron," 1159–1262.

[29] Robert Sugden, "Why Incoherent Preferences do not Justify Paternalism," *Constitutional Political Economy* 19 (2008), 232.

[30] Paul Slovic, "The Construction of Preference," *American Psychologist* 50.5 (May 1995), 369–370.

I think there is some truth in this, but perhaps not enough for it to be a problem. In philosophy, more than economics, we differentiate between preferences for ends and preferences for means. In this context, an end is the situation we want to arrive at, where a means is the method we choose to get there. It is a distinction that goes back at least as far as Aristotle, who argues on the first page of the *Nicomachean Ethics* that there must be a final end at which we aim in order for our actions to make sense. In some kinds of preference, it may well be true that there is no pre-existing desire, no desire un-"distorted" by the peculiarities of presentation. But this is not the case when it comes to many of our preferences, and in particular, our ends appear more stable than our preferences about means. I would argue that we (most of us) have a stable desire to be healthy and prosperous, and furthermore have a relatively clear idea of what constitutes a satisfactory degree of health and prosperity, even though in choosing means to that end we succumb to poor thinking. We yield to anchoring, and so forth, when we consider whether smoking is or is not compatible with a long and healthy life; we fall for the enticing but deadly adjustable rate mortgage, despite the fact that we want to maintain financial and domestic stability by owning a house over time; but we never think that cancer is OK, or homelessness a satisfactory condition. It is precisely *because* we have ends that some of our actions may be said to be mistaken.

It is not that our ends never change; surely they do. We may value a life of freedom and adventure at one point, and a life of stable roots and strong family relationships at another. These preferences, though, do not change according to the peculiarities of a choice procedure. This is not because our ends are somehow more rational. Ends may not be chosen through reason; they may not be chosen at all. In some cases we may just be born with certain ends, or they may be formed through the vicissitudes of our psychological history, mere accidents. The point is that they seem to be more stable preferences than the particular means we choose to achieve them. Maybe as evolution has led us to rely on mental shortcuts which, however serviceable in some situations, turn out to be disadvantageous in others, it has left us with preferences about ends that endure: those who didn't care about long-term well being didn't survive long enough to reproduce. Whatever the reason, much of the indeterminacy we see seems to relate to means rather than ends. We know where we want to go, but aren't very clear on what means are best, and thus are susceptible to the influence of nonrational factors. Our choices as to what is a good gamble vary widely with the particular descriptions of benefits and percentages, but when we gamble, we all want to end up with more, not less. It is surely true that the standards we use in determining the specifics of our ends will be socially constructed – what counts as a prosperous life depends on what is available in our society, so that what might have induced satisfaction in 1611 will certain not do so in 2011. This sort of cultural influence, though, is not the same thing as indeterminacy – it just means that our standards of success are relative to the culture we are in, but that standard itself is stable.

Slovic has described the situations in which choices are most likely to be affected (or determined) by the elicitation procedure as those that involve "complex, unfamiliar task[s]." The formation of ends doesn't fit this description. For most of us, a sufficient number of our desires are fixed prior to the decision process for a third party to be able to determine what actions are consistent with our desires. Where there are no determinate desires, it is true, paternalism is impractical, but to suggest that there never ends we fail to reach because of wrong choices is contrary to life as we experience it.

CONCLUSION

Paternalism can be misunderstood. It's like democracy; if someone understands it only as majority rule, then they can justify slavery of the minority as long as most people vote for it. A better understanding of the values that justify democracy shows that slavery can't be democratic, because the principles that justify voting also make slavery impermissible. Paternalism, as a theory that justifies making people do what is good for them, may similarly be misunderstood. It is not about forcing people to live up to a certain standard of behavior that is entirely foreign to them. To this extent, the term "paternal" may have unfortunate connotations, since parents often do, in fact, try to make us live up to standards in which we have no interest. The stress should be on the other aspect of parental relationships, which is a benevolent interest in our development that at times requires interfering in our actions for the sake of our ability to (eventually) fulfill our goals.

CHAPTER 5

Misuse and abuse:
punishment and privacy

However, even if we cleave to good paternalistic theory, intending to promote those goods that people want to promote and avoiding the imposition of foreign and questionable values, the actual practice of paternalism naturally involves potential difficulties. If practical difficulties make it impossible to use a good theory effectively, there may not be much point to pursuing its merits. On the other hand, any principle of justification will require at least some difficult choices when it comes to implementation, so the fact that bad outcomes are possible is not, in itself, a reason to reject the theory. The question is whether we can easily avoid mistakes that would have excessive costs. There are a number questions to raise about how paternalism would actually work, but here I will focus on two of the most significant issues that can reasonably give us concern: whether excessive sanctions might attach to paternalistic regulations, and the unwanted exposure of information about our private selves that might result from government oversight into our ways of living.

PUNISHMENT

Observation and revelation

If we create paternalistic laws, it seems likely that we will have to enforce them, and this naturally gives rise to worries. One of the concerns we feel about paternalistic legislation is that typically the way laws are enforced is through punishment, and we really do not like the idea of being punished for imprudence – especially if we have accepted that cognitive bias is not a function of will. For one thing, this will simply result in more punishment than we have previously encountered. I feel pretty safe from punishment when it comes to grand larceny, but the temptation to be imprudent is constant. Do I save enough? Do I eat five servings of fruit and vegetables a day? Do I consider carefully the insurance and retirement options I am

126

given or simply accept the default option, no matter how inferior? I fail in all these respects, as I do with regard to my other pernicious habits – buying almond croissants without regard for whether they contain trans-fats, drinking more than the heart-healthy number of drinks per week, and a host of others. These failings make me less healthy and less financially secure than I want to be, and than I would be if I had perfect reasoning and self-control. So, I'm guilty, and if punishment is in the offing, it looks as if I'm ripe for it in more ways than one. This is disturbing.

The second troubling thing about punishment for violating paternalistic regulations is that it appears undeserved, in some sense of undeserved: cognitive bias is not typically brought about through the cultivation of vice, or even the failure to cultivate virtue. While we sometimes punish those we know had no ill intent, simply in order to teach (we speak harshly to the un-housebroken puppy in order to train him, even though his mistake is not his fault), this is not a policy we generally endorse. It just seems unfair. One of Rawls' earliest and most influential articles argued that punishment based not on desert but on the future-regarding desire for improvement is not really punishment at all. He called such actions "telishment," the giving of pain in order to achieve an end, and said that once accepted as a practice telishment, could be used to justify institutions both cruel and arbitrary.[1] We would like to think that it is at least necessary for punishment that the person who is punished had some sort of ill intent, so that he can fairly be said to deserve to suffer sanctions. Failures of rationality, on the other hand, more often serve as paradigms of the kinds of errors that don't deserve blame. It's like punishing a short person for not being very handy at getting books down off a high shelf. Those who harm themselves don't intend to do that, and while sometimes mistakes are culpable, we generally don't think they deserve the kind of treatment that intentional harms may receive.

Answers to some of these concerns, however, are implicit in the objections themselves. The brunt of the first criticism is that paternalistic punishment will do more harm than good, and the obvious answer is that it's a very poor paternalistic policy that does more harm than good. If punishment harms more than it helps, then we should not use it, even if it might change behavior in the way we want. Of course, the critic's point is likely that while paternalists will accept this obvious principle, they may not recognize precisely when the costs of punishment outweigh its

---

[1] John Rawls, "Two Concepts of Rules," *Philosophical Review* 64.1 (1955), 3–32.

benefits. In fact, though, it's a rule we have lots of practice at using. We are accustomed, in crafting laws to protect *others* from an individual's actions, to weigh whether a law is worth it. Some harms to others aren't worth making illegal, either because they'd be too costly to detect, or because any imaginable punishment seems generally greater than the harm of the initial infringement. (Imagine prosecutions for super-petty larceny – a paper clip.) Sometimes experience leads us to change our mind about what should be punished: generally, harsh words and insults in the private sphere have remained extralegal, no matter how much we deplore them, because trying to prevent them seems hopeless. On the other hand, more recently, Internet bullying has been considered for legal action, presumably because it seems more harmful than most sorts of meanness and also because it is easier to prove. So, we are accustomed to weighing costs and benefits, and adjusting our policies according to our needs.

This is the same sort of thing that would go on with paternalistic policies. Again, this is not perfectionism – it doesn't advance paternalistic policies if we create desired behavior at the cost of excessive suffering. While some perfectionists may think the achievement of the goal is worth whatever the costs, paternalism here is based on considerations of subjective welfare: it is simply not worthwhile to have dental police who ascertain whether you flossed. For one thing, it would be really expensive. For another, it would be really annoying. Psychological costs are as relevant as any other in assessing paternalistic policies. The point is to make people better off, not drive them mad with irritation. While failing to floss your teeth can, as any dentist will tell you, lead to serious gum disease, it also may not, and in any case such a condition is not likely to ruin your life. And indeed, close supervision might not even lead to compliance. Thomas Aquinas believed that laws should help make people good, but at the same time warned against laws that try to make people *totally* good: as new wine put into old wineskins splits them, says Aquinas, trying to stuff imperfect citizens too full of virtue may simply lead to rebellion against the law.[2] This is a case where soft paternalistic policies, which lack some of the psychological costs of harsher, coercive ones, might prove useful. We can continue to educate people about dental health, for example, or give insurance breaks to those who have perfect dental visits. (Or, in a better world, give free dental care to everyone!) We know that these are not entirely effective, but they might be effective

---

[2] Thomas Aquinas, *Summa Theologica* I–II, Question 96, Third Article (printed in *On Law, Morality, and Prudence* [Indianapolis, Ind.: Hackett, 2003], p. 62).

enough to justify their costs, depending on what these are. What is certain is that coercive measures intended to prevent or substantially reduce all imprudent practices are simply not worth it. The government official standing behind you snatching your fattening ice cream cone from your hand is a figment of the paranoid antipaternalistic imagination. While paternalistic laws will make things illegal that previously were not, it will be by no means as pervasive as many people seem to think.

The second concern was that punishment for these prudential errors seems unjust. It seems likely, however, that a paternalist would seldom recommend punishment of individuals in such cases, because it's not clear that punishment is the best way to create compliance. Dan Wikler, in "Persuasion and Coercion for Health," argues that punitive measures against obesity, such as a fat tax, are unlikely to work, because such behavior is involuntary.[3] If it's involuntary, introducing more motivation not to do it isn't likely to help, because motivation isn't the issue. Instead, punishing individuals for behaviors that they have a lot of difficulty controlling is likely to result in more pain, without substantial improvement. Punishment is much more relevant in cases of third-party harm, where it can introduce a motivation to obey the law that is otherwise absent – the thief may care nothing for his victim, and it is the threat of punishment that makes the difference. The person who harms himself, though, already has a motivation to stop that; he's just not very good at going about it. Adding punishment as a motivation, on top of his existing motivation to live a healthy and long life, may simply not make much of a difference – except that it makes his failure even more painful. And, the existence of punishments for self-destructive behaviors may contribute to more social disparagement, insofar as it may be easier to condemn people for an activity that is illegal as well as unfashionable. For the same reason, the fear occasionally expressed that paternalists would engage in particularly humiliating punishments, like public shaming, is misplaced. We are familiar with scores of such shaming for perfectionist reasons – Hester Prynne's scarlet letter, or Jane Eyre's being forced to stand on a stool before her classmates as a result of her supposed vices – but they make little sense in situations where the fault lies in reasoning more than in a taste for wrongdoing. Since we already have motivations not to do what is self-destructive, adding more reason, in the form of the threat of public

[3] Dan Wikler, "Persuasion and Coercion for Health: Ethical Issues in Government Efforts to Change Lifestyles," in *Paternalism*, ed. Rolf Sartorius (Minneapolis: University of Minnesota Press, 1983), pp. 35–59.

shame, will make no difference.[4] It would seem, then, that paternalistic policies would generally avoid punishment of the imprudent, since point-less punishment is, well, pointless.

There are, however, alternatives in such cases. Gerald Dworkin has divided paternalism into two kinds, pure and impure, saying that

In the case of "impure" paternalism, in trying to protect the welfare of a class of persons we find that the only way to do so will involve restricting the freedom of other persons besides those who are benefited. It might be thought that there are no cases of "impure" paternalism, since any such case could always be justified on nonpaternalistic grounds, i.e. in terms of preventing harm to others. Thus we might ban cigarette manufacturers from continuing to manufacture their product on the grounds that we are preventing them from causing illness to others in the same way that we prevent other manufacturers from releasing pollutants into the atmosphere, thereby causing danger to members of the community. The difference is, however, that in the former but not the latter case the harm is of such a nature that it could be avoided by those individuals affected, if they so chose. The incurring of the harm requires the active cooperation of the victim. It would be a mistake in theory and hypocritical in practice to assert that our interference in such cases is just like our interference in standard cases of protecting others from harm.[5]

In many cases, such institutional change is a more efficient way to bring about improvement than is pursuing each individual person, and doesn't have the costs (personal embarrassment, shame, ostracism, resentment) that pursuing individuals may have. Instead of pursuing suspected cigarette smokers with nicotine detectors, we should make the production and importation of cigarettes illegal.[6] Instead of public weigh-ins, we can get restaurants, includ-ing especially junk food restaurants, to downsize their portions. We could outlaw soft drinks, if, as well as being nutritionally void and bad for your teeth, they turn out, as some suspect, to contribute to unhealthy obesity.[7]

[4] A considerable number of politicians have blown their careers by engaging in what are publicly perceived as shameful acts, seemingly oblivious at the time of their performance to the fact that they could get caught and have their careers ruined. In the case of sexual exploits by male politicians, some have linked this to testosterone, which, it is argued, drives some to political ambition but equally to sexual conquest, and further reduces appreciation of risk. Stephanie Rosenbloom, "Scholars Discuss Weiner's Behavior," *New York Times*, June 17, 2011.
[5] Gerald Dworkin, "Paternalism," in *Paternalism*, ed. Rolf Sartorius (Minneapolis: University of Minnesota Press, 1983), p. 22.
[6] Opponents of paternalistic law often point to the failure of Prohibition to show that laws controlling popular behaviors can't work. Such objections will be discussed further in Chapter 6. Here I will say that the acceptance of alcohol is greater, and its place in our culture much more firm, than that of cigarettes, even while the harm it does is much less. Some behaviors are easier to change than others.
[7] Gary Taubes, "Is Sugar Toxic?," *New York Times*, April 13, 2011. I argue in Chapter 6 that outlawing the production of soda does not seem to be a policy that a paternalist would endorse, but that could change if we discover more evidence for the dangers of soda.

As we now control how much interest creditors are allowed to charge, we could control how much debt people are allowed to run up. Such institutional changes will be more efficient, since they (a) require less oversight than monitoring individual citizens; (b) do not call upon citizens to exercise self-control that, as Wikler points out above, may simply not be available; and (c) do not result in the excoriation of individuals for imprudence, which strikes us as unjust.

Such changes are not without costs, both administrative and personal. We will miss those supersized portions, at least initially. We will similarly want to buy things we can't afford, and will miss the credit that would allow us to borrow huge amounts. Some of these desires are malleable – if gallon-sized soft drinks stop being available at convenience stores, then we may stop thinking that a Big Gulp is what we want to quench our thirst. The idea of drinking a bucket of soda may eventually strike us as silly. Others desires may not go away – I still want to buy an island, even though I know I can't afford one, so it's a good thing that even at present no one will give me the loan they know would allow me to ruin myself. If we lowered borrowing limits, people will miss even more things they can't get. At the same time, such paternalistic policies would prevent people from making mistakes that in the long run will disappoint them when they can't get the things they want even more. Mill said of those who act imprudently,

if he spoils his life by mismanagement, we shall not for that reason, desire to spoil it still further: instead of wishing to punish him, we shall rather endeavour to alleviate his punishment, but show him how he may avoid or cure the evils his conduct tends to bring upon him.[8]

I have argued that showing him how to avoid the evils is not sufficient, given our failures of reason, but the principle that we should not generally cap failure with punishment and ignominy remains the same.

That said, a bullet remains to be bitten. There is no doubt that punishment of individuals in some cases changes behavior for the better, and is worth the costs. Drunk driving has gone from being regarded as an amusing folly to being condemned as a moral crime, precisely as it has become a legal crime. The motivation for drunk driving laws is not primarily paternalistic, but I use it as an example where, in modern times, a salutary change of behavior has taken place through the imposition of sanctions on individuals' behavior. Because of our poor ability to estimate

---

[8] *On Liberty*, ch. 4, p. 210 (Meridian edition).

our abilities to drive while under the influence, we too often think we can drive safely when we can't. The short-term, considerably lesser harm of being stopped by a policeman has, for some people, a much greater motivational effect than the mere consideration that I may kill myself driving home like this. This isn't rational, but it is real. Making drunk driving punishable has succeeded in getting lots of drunk people off the roads. Seat belt laws have clearly increased the number of people using seat belts, and these do typically involve at last some kind of sanction.[9] These acceptable cases of paternalistic punishment seem to be cases where the harm in question is severe and immediate – death in a traffic accident, for example – and the sanction is actually effective without being too severe (losing one's license for a while, not incarceration).

So, while I have argued that on the whole punishment of individuals is not the best route to take for paternalistic improvements in behavior, I certainly can't say there are no cases where it might be the best route. I can only argue that it would not be the approach of first resort, that it would have to be effective, given the overall consideration of costs and benefits, and that few behaviors are best controlled in this way.

PRIVACY

One image that is persistently associated with paternalism is that of Big Brother, George Orwell's totalitarian leader. Big Brother is not, in fact, a portrayal of a paternalist, since he was not benevolent in the slightest.[10] Still, the image persists, in part because Big Brother's state was one in which the government controlled individuals' personal activities, and one in which privacy was impossible. Even in the home, cameras reported one's every move back to a central clearing house. One thing that appears to bother people about paternalism is a vision of it, too, as an

---

[9] Compliance to seat belt laws also increases as it becomes a primary, rather than simply a secondary, infraction – that is, when you can stop people just to check their seat belts, rather than stopping them for something else and then seeing that their seat belts are not on.

[10] Hackneyed as it may be, the image crops up persistently in the writings of those who attack the Obama health plan, with its paternalistic requirement that everyone acquire health insurance: it is said that this "puts American families and small-business owners under the control of Big Brother regarding health insurance coverage decisions" (Brian Schwartz, "Obama's Health Care Proposal: Death Spiral, Huge Implicit Tax Rates, Mandatory Insurance," www.patientpowernow.org/2010/02/); that its "big brother mentality that 'government knows best' and that is their mission to provide cradle to grave 'care' of its citizens all doom America as we know it" (Bradley Blakeman, "Be Afraid, Be Very Afraid of Obama's Latest Big Brother Plan," www.foxnews.com/opinion/2009/12/10/); and that it will create "a Big Brother bureaucracy" (Scott Atlas, "Beware of ObamaCare," www. washingtontimes.com/news/2008/oct/26/).

overwhelming, intrusive, pervasive, system of regulations that will call for constant monitoring of our behavior so as to protect us from ourselves. I have argued that interventions by government will be limited by cost–benefit considerations, where resentment is clearly a relevant cost, and thus that the nightmare vision of a totalitarian nanny-state has, like so many nightmares, little bearing on reality. However, even if we accept that paternalistic interventions will be relatively limited, some are bothered by the fact that even the most well-intended and generally beneficent interventions can result in a loss of privacy.

Privacy has many meanings: Daniel Solove has distinguished six different concepts of privacy, and at least some of these may be further divided.[11] It is clearly true that paternalism will justify some interference with "privacy" under one of its meanings – freedom of action – and I have argued that this is justified given our poor ability to do what is best for ourselves. The further issue here is that even justified interference with freedom of action can lead to a different nightmare scenario: the prospect of excessive publicity, of having things known about us that we don't want known. This concerns what Solove calls "informational privacy," our ability to keep information about ourselves from others. Jeremy Bentham imagined a perfect prison, which he called the Panopticon: a system of mirrors would allow guards views of all the prisoners at all times, wherever they might be, whatever they might be doing.[12] His idea was not so much that this would allow the authorities to punish those who transgressed, as that it would prevent transgression: prisoners would know that anything they did might be seen and would behave themselves accordingly. Paternalism might seem even worse, since its interventions aren't limited to the incarcerated. For some, it conjures up visions of repressive childhoods, where well-meaning parents have, and use, the ability check up on us to see if we've done our homework, washed our hands, eaten our vegetables, cleaned our room, and so forth. Even though we love our parents, it was a supervision we were happy to leave behind. The idea of a paternalistic government *in loco parentis*, with the right to oversee our activities and keep records of our actions, is not inviting. Yet, if we intend to interfere with people's lives, which paternalistic laws clearly do, then it stands to reason that application of such laws will require at least in some cases that we observe what people are actually doing. The initial paternalistic regulation will be followed by intrusions

---

[11] Daniel Solove, "Conceptualizing Privacy," *California Law Review* 90.4 (2002), 1087–1155.
[12] Jeremy Bentham, *The Panopticon Writings*, ed. Miran Bozovic (London: Verso, 2011).

into personal life for the purpose of gathering information. Such visitations need not be punitive to be irritating – if all our parents say is "those hands aren't clean," the mere fact of being inspected constitutes an intrusion, with all that that entails. Publicity itself gives us, correctly, a sense that others have the power to view us, or aspects of our life, while we have no power to stop that; it leads to the mere sense of being watched that, for whatever reason, keeps us from being able to relax.

And it may be worse than irritating; it may be dangerous. The growing contemporary concern about loss of privacy arises largely from the harm that may be done to us by those who gather information about us: they may reveal secrets that embarrass us; they may change our relationships with commercial institutions for the worse, in more ways than one; they may affect our ability to get or hold jobs. Many such intrusions are already occurring; some through businesses which track us via our computer use without our permission; some through postings that others make about us; and some through our own voluntary activities, which often have a reach we in no way foresee. These already-existing ways in which others can find out about us have been the subject of much recent worry: if the government increases its own intrusions into our lives, that, to some, only adds to the fear of 1984 – even if, as was not the case in *1984*, the supervision is benevolent.

This not an exclusively contemporary problem. In 1890 Samuel Warren and Louis Brandeis largely inaugurated the debate about privacy in confronting the conflict between the public, who want to know about other people, either for profit or for pure titillation, and those who want knowledge of their domestic lives kept the provenance of those actually involved in them. They argued that "[p]olitical, social, and economic changes entail the recognition of new rights, and the common law, in its eternal youth, grows to meet the demands of society." The particular change that aroused their concern was a technological one, and this continues to be the source of our greatest problems: for Warren and Brandeis, "[i]nstantaneous photographs and the newspaper enterprise have invaded the sacred precincts of private and domestic life; and numerous mechanical devices threaten to make good the prediction that 'what is whispered in the closet shall be proclaimed from the housetops.'"[13] For us today, of course, this problem is computers and the Internet, but Warren and Brandeis' general recognition of the danger of "the too enterprising press, the photographer, or the possessor of any

---

[13] Samuel Warren and Louis Brandeis, "The Right to Privacy," *Harvard Law Review* 4.5 (1890), 195.

other modern device for recording or reproducing scenes or sounds"[14] seems prescient. Two factors are at play at present that they did not, presumably, foresee, and which increase the pressures on the private realm: Warren and Brandeis' particular focus was on commercial enterprises driven by a desire for profit, profit that came from revealing personal facts to those with an appetite to know about other people's domestic arrangements, especially those of the rich, famous, or peculiar. One of the most pervasive dangers to privacy today, the acquisition and subsequent trade of private information between businesses who want to know more about your buying habits than your sex life, is not one they could well be aware of. Second, they may not have imagined the absolute passion private citizens would have for putting forth information about themselves, or about others, without remuneration. Granted, the websites that post such information generally do that with the intent of making a profit, whether from advertising or selling their information, but they have the help of thousands of unpaid researchers who will work hard, for example, to find out and post the name, address, and employer of the wheelie-bin cat-chucker,[15] the "kissing couple,"[16] or the married American guy living in Scotland who (quite convincingly) pretended to be a gay, female, Syrian blogger living in Damascus – so effectively that after "her" arrest, concerned citizens used the Internet to track down the author of the blog, to their subsequent astonishment.[17] So, the search for information about others is more pervasive than anyone in a previous century could have foreseen. It has been remarked that while at one point it was feared that the Internet would provide too much anonymity, allowing posters to disseminate misinformation without accountability, just the opposite has happened – it is difficult to remain anonymous when faces in crowd photos are identified, locations tracked down, and actors thus revealed, whatever efforts they may have taken to escape detection.[18]

The result is an ocean of information about each of us, access to which we cannot control. Individuals thus stand in danger, and some would argue that in addition to individual harms, society more generally suffers:

[14] Ibid., 206.

[15] "Woman who Dumped Lola the Cat in Wheelie Bin Defends her Actions," *Guardian*, August 25, 2010. The owners of the CCTV camera, who were also the owners of the cat, put their film of the woman on the web, where she was subsequently identified and her name made public.

[16] "Back Story: Vancouver Kissing Couple Identified," June 17, 2011, http://hypervocal.com/news/2011/

[17] "Gay Girl in Damascus is American Man," June 13, 2011, www.npr.org/2011/6/13/137146192/

[18] Brian Stelter, "Upending Anonymity, These Days the Web Unmasks Everyone," *New York Times*, June 20, 2011.

first, from our wholesale pursuit of what Warren and Brandeis described as "triviality [that] destroys at once robustness of thought and delicacy of feeling,"[19] but also from a general sense that there is no longer a distinction between public and private. This disturbs us, because one thing that has not changed since Warren and Brandeis' time is our desire to keep certain things to ourselves, and we are made uncomfortable by the fact that this is increasingly difficult to do. We are willing to share many things – sometimes more than others want to know – but not everything. Many will argue, too, that even when we are willing to share, we err: those who are profligate with personal information often have no idea quite where the information they voluntarily disclose will end up. For the sake of self-protection, and perhaps, more significantly, for the sake of human dignity, critics argue, privacy needs to be maintained.

Paternalistic record keeping

Paternalistic laws look as if they may exacerbate the problem. Two of the already generally accepted forms of paternalism certainly involve publicity: seat belt laws and laws for prescription medicine. Seat belt laws, particularly where they exist as primary laws, allow for a kind of surveillance – police are allowed to look at you to see if you've got your seat belt on. Prescription laws require that a record be kept of the medications you take, thus allowing information about you to be posted out into the world.[20] In the first case, this information (if it involves legal action) may be intentionally accessible to the general public; in the second, those who have access to it are restricted, but there may be a fair number of them (especially if your medication is paid for by an insurance company) and there is always the possibility of your health records being leaked.

The harms of the first sort – public record keeping of legal actions – are obvious: if you are ticketed for not having a seat belt on when you are driving back from the beach, the very day you told your boss you were out sick, this may cause problems. The second sort of information gathering, intended to be private, at least in the sense of allowing only limited and authorized access, is also problematic. For one thing, others will have information about you that you would prefer they not have. For some,

[19] Warren and Brandeis, "Right to Privacy," 196.
[20] The distinction between surveillance and record keeping as intrusions into privacy, to which I will return below, is owed to Daniel Solove's "Privacy and Power: Computer Databases and Metaphors for Information Privacy," *Stanford Law Review* 53.6 (2001), 1393–1462.

being forced to give up information about yourself is degrading. There is a sense in which this kind of information is still "private," since access to it is limited, and we do often refer to information to which access is, by policy, limited to those who have a right to know it as "private" – this includes, for example, the financial information you give the IRS when you pay your taxes, or the health records to which insurance companies have access. In a different sense of "private," though, it is not, since it is known to other people, and furthermore known, in some cases, against your will. If paternalism requires that you buy health insurance (which, assuming measures are in place to make that practical, I think it would), then that in itself causes the (relative) exposure of certain facts: your mental health, sexual activity, weight, plastic surgery, and liposuction would be a matter of record. They would not, of course, be a matter of public record, any more than health histories now are matters of public record. They would, however, become known to some others, and you would not be able to control precisely to which others – even if you can choose your doctor, there is no way for you to pick who will process your claim form. Jonathan Wolff has argued that luck egalitarianism, where people are compensated for their unlucky lack of desirable qualities, will cause too much shame to those who have to expose those lacks to the government.[21] Someone sympathetic to this view may think it is even worse if we have to expose our failings and other personal facts without even the balm of compensation. This sort of thing already goes on (many of us would rather not let the government know how much we earn), but paternalistic policies could open up a whole new realm of information gathering. Making us refrain from self-destructive behavior will probably result in more things about us being known.

Second, there is what Solove refers to as the "database" problem.[22] Even if government agencies have every intent of keeping what they know about you completely confidential, there seem to be many ways in which others can get to this information. As more and more about you is known, more and more about you becomes accessible, despite the best efforts to limit access to it. Those who can make money from it will do their best to get access to that information, profit from it, sell it, and generally use it in ways you cannot control. While you might give up your information voluntarily in the first case – you want insurance, and thus are willing for

---

[21] Jonathan Wolff, "Fairness, Respect, and the Egalitarian Ethos," *Philosophy and Public Affairs* 27.2 (spring 1998), 97–102.
[22] Solove, "Privacy and Power."

them to have records of your health – you don't want to be besieged by offers for expensive cures for giving up smoking by those who've either bought or stolen that information, or blacklisted from employment because it's foreseen you will drive up health care costs. I think, in the end, that the last of these is the most serious threat, and it is a danger. However, as we will see, if paternalistic actions lay us open to this danger, then paternalistic reasoning also can be used to protect us from it, in ways that arguably promote our welfare more than the government's collection of information endangers it.

Government oversight
First: does the mere fact of the government's laying claim to personal information about us constitute a harm? Some argue that control over the information about oneself is essential to dignity. Charles Fried has said, "[A] threat to privacy seems to threaten our very integrity as persons,"[23] and "[t]o be deprived of this control not only over what we do but over who we are is the ultimate assault on liberty, personality, and self-respect."[24] Edward Bloustein argues that "Western culture defines individuality as including the right to be free from certain types of intrusions. This measure of personal isolation and personal control over the conditions of its abandonment is of the very essence of personal freedom and dignity."[25] These claims cannot be precisely true, however. Or, if they are, none of us has the freedom and dignity, the integrity as persons, so touted. We all have to give up information we don't want to; I give up correct information about my income on pain of punishment, and if I do try to deceive the IRS, they have their own ways of knowing the truth. There are many cases, both institutional and personal, where people know things about me I would prefer they didn't know. This isn't just a function of the modern bureaucratic age, but of living around other people. As anyone who lives in one will tell you, there are no secrets in a village – small, nontechnical societies generally allow a detailed flow of information among their members (also known as gossip). Unless we live our lives as particularly isolated hermits, this is inevitable. It is possible that insofar as we're a social species, we all lack dignity; but it is more

---

[23] Charles Fried, "Privacy," *Yale Law Journal* 77 (1968), 475–493, and reprinted in Frederick Schoeman, ed., *Philosophical Dimensions of Privacy* (Cambridge University Press, 1984), pp. 203–222, at p. 205.

[24] Fried, "Privacy," in *Philosophical Dimensions*, p. 212.

[25] Edward J. Bloustein, "Privacy as an Aspect of Human Dignity," *New York University Law Review* 39 (1964), 962–1007 (which is also reprinted in Schoeman's *Philosophical Dimensions*, at p. 165).

likely that our dignity is left unsullied by the fact that being members of a community requires some exposure to others of facts about our lives, whether we consent to that or not. For one thing, the idea that a person is somehow more dignified – more worthy – if other people can't know anything about him that he doesn't choose to let them know seems silly. It reminds us of the anachronistic belief in the superiority of the stiff upper lip – that it is somehow intrinsically better not to show pain or sorrow than to reveal one's feelings. Similarly, the idea that it is simply better that other people not know things about you seems to reflect an odd notion of worth – that you are more worthy, for example, if no one knows you have weaknesses, or likes and dislikes. Surely, though, our worth does not depend on this sort of informational impregnability.

What the claims about dignity and integrity must mean, then, to be plausible, is that it is an insult to my dignity if I can't control whether people who, for some reason, ought not to know things about me do know those things. If I can't stop people knowing stuff that it is none of their business to know, I do feel out of control, oppressed, and insulted, and not only do I feel this way, I have also lost a certain stature vis-á-vis others, those who so fail to respect my legitimate boundaries. Some facts about me are the business of some, but not of others. If I bounce a check, it is the legitimate business of the bank to know that, and (if the bank doesn't cover it) it's the legitimate business of the person to whom I wrote the check. It is not, on the other hand, the business of my neighbors, and if the bank leaked that information and embarrassed me in front of the public, I would certainly be affronted. The question, then, is not about the presence or absence of complete control over information about myself, but about the limits of *permissible* publicity. *Who* has a right to know *what*?

The thrust of the argument throughout this book has been, of course, that sometimes I need help in reaching my own goals, and that providing me with this help does not diminish my value. It recognizes an inability, but does not impose one. If accurately providing me with help requires that others know certain things about me – those that are essential to the provision of help – I don't see that this constitutes a further, distinct, infringement on my autonomy. The principle, again, is that invoked in seat belt or prescription laws; that left to our own devices, we are likely to misread what needs to be done in order to reach our goals (a long life, without brain damage; medications that are effective) and in some cases the only way we can achieve those things is by giving certain information to others. We do this without thinking in aid of others – paying our taxes, proving our identities before we fly – and it is no less justified when we do it in aid of ourselves.

Insofar as this is necessary, it ceases to be an infringement. One thing that is clear is that much of our belief about what is properly private is a matter of convention. If someone posts a picture of me in which my bare ankles can be seen, I am neither shocked nor demeaned. I don't consider my ankles "private" in the sense that someone else, even a stranger, looking at them would constitute an intrusion, whereas if someone posts a picture of me entirely naked it certainly would. It is not just, as some will claim, that I am content to let my ankles be seen only because I am secure in the knowledge that if I so chose I could wear exclusively skirts that would hide them. That is, it is not the fact of my control over others' seeing them that keeps my dignity intact. Ankles just don't strike us as private any more, the way they once would have. I don't get dressed in the morning having thought "it's my choice whether or not to expose my ankles, thank God, and inasmuch as I have tacitly permitted it, others may photograph them without injustice." I might feel that way about something that we do think of as private – that it is up to me, and that I'm glad it's up to me, to control its exposure. Thus, I might let someone see me naked, and I might not, and this does seem like something that should be up to me: because it is customarily private, I want control over the information that a naked picture would convey. But ankles just don't matter. Similarly, then, for other information about ourselves. There's some we want to be able to control, and some that we are used to thinking of as being in the public realm. And, this changes with different fashions, different technologies, different institutions, different practices. Warren and Brandeis were particularly concerned about protecting the inviolability of the home, for example, but here again conventions have changed as to what we consider inviolable: it is now considered a public matter if a man beats his wife, or parents their children, or if parents send their children to school, or fail to provide them with proper nourishment, whereas these would once have been considered private, domestic issues. Outside interference within the family would have once seemed outrageous, while now it is taken as a matter of course that the state may legitimately (a) ascertain if family members are being harmed and (b) interfere if that is what the law directs; indeed, this is not only permissible but obligatory. The boundaries of the private are fluid; that this is true seems to be upheld by the whole history of cultural change.

So, if it should come about that paternalistic laws require that more about you be known to some particular agency, and if we see that as a legitimate use of state power, that will cease to seem an intrusion into privacy, but will instead constitute a change in our idea of what is private and what is public. This has happened again and again, and will continue to do so. In some cases, what is public may once again become private – if, for example, we stopped prosecuting people for marijuana use, it would once again be a private issue whether you choose to use it. Thus, there is nothing demeaning about the state knowing something about you, per se. The state should not overstep its legitimate functioning, and what constitutes legitimate functioning will depend both on the justification for the intrusion and the procedures through which it is approved at any given time, but the mere fact of the state learning more about you than it had previously had access to does not constitute disrespect.

Second, in most cases this will not be felt as a harm. How much we care about what others know about us depends not only on what is known, but on who knows it: our selectivity extends to the knower as much as to what is known. And while it is true that there are some things we want to share only with our intimates, there are other things we would much rather share only with strangers. We are all familiar with having embarrassing experiences, and how much better we feel if we can tell ourselves that the people who witnessed it don't know us, that we'll never see them again, that, while they know something about us, they are not in a position to associate that with more general knowledge of our lives. It can be nude swimming on what we wrongly thought was a deserted beach (an incident related in a recent travel article), a pratfall on a foreign sidewalk, anything we would hate to have our friends or acquaintances witness but which we don't mind half so much being seen by people with whom we will have no continuing acquaintance. This kind of anonymous publicity is not a source of shame or embarrassment. It is not literally anonymous – there may be a name or in some cases a face attached to the embarrassing moment – but these are not people who form part of our social circle, whose regard matters to us, whose opinions support our place in society. I wouldn't generally want others to see a nude photo of me without permission, since the appearance of my body is private, as said above; but if it had to happen, how much would I rather it were circulated among the members of a remote Mongolian village that in my own town! This, presumably, is why some people seal their letters or memoirs, not just until after their deaths, but until a certain number of years after their deaths, when no one who actually knew them will have access to the information. We want privacy as a kind of protection, but there are those who pose no threat even if they have the relevant information.

Government record keeping is of this sort. It is not so much that only anonymous bureaucrats will have access to our health records, but that we are anonymous to them, in the ways that matter. It's like my tax records in the nonpaternalistic world – someone out there knows a lot about me, including that I haven't figured what Original Issue Discount is and have misreported it more than once. But this isn't like having my friends and colleagues think that I am an idiot. Having facts, even personal facts, about us known to someone somewhere just isn't a burden.

The database problem

The fact that the government has access to information about you does not mean it will make such information publicly available, since the state can demarcate which of their records are made public and which remain "private," that is, accessible only to those who need to know it in some official capacity. There are reasons why some information is kept privileged and some is easily accessible to members of the public who seek it out. If public access to information is harmful, we can change its legal status.[26] This is something we can decide for ourselves.

However, it must be admitted that there are, nonetheless, dangers that arise from having too much information about us under the control of others. Daniel Solove has argued persuasively that one of the greatest dangers that besets us now stems not so much from the threat of surveillance, government or otherwise (the Big Brother problem, as he puts it), but from the "thoughtless process of bureaucratic indifference to arbitrary errors, and dehumanization, a world where people feel powerless and vulnerable without any meaningful participation in the collection and use of their information."[27] Those who suffer the most significant loss of privacy are those who find themselves in the modern world,

without knowing who has what information, what purposes or motives those entities have, or what will be done with the information in the future. Privacy involves the power to refuse to be treated with bureaucratic indifference when one complains about errors or when one wants certain data expunged. It is not merely the collection of data that is the problem – it is our complete lack of control over the ways it is used or may be used in the future.[28]

---

[26] See Paul M. Schwartz, "Property, Privacy, and Personal Data," *Harvard Law Review* 17.7 (May 2004), 2056–2128, for the suggestion that in general governments should cut back on the public accessibility of certain sorts of records, since these can be used for identity theft. Similar considerations could dictate that personal records kept for paternalistic reasons could be kept out of the public realm.
[27] Solove, "Privacy and Power," 1393.   [28] Ibid., 1426.

Solove emphasizes that once information is out there, its use is, at least at present, impossible to control. Much of his concern is, as this quotation suggests, about mistaken or incomplete information – the person who is wrongly, and apparently permanently, identified to the public as a criminal, or the person who is correctly identified as having an arrest record but without the exculpatory explanation that his arrest arose as a result of a protest against inequality in the civil rights era. Similar concerns might arise, though, even when information is complete and correct. The person identified as having placed the friendly cat in the trash bin really did do that, and in so doing really did act wrongly. Still, we may think that identifying her to all people and for all time may be inappropriate – not only has it resulted in the possibility of material harm (she's had death threats), but generally the shame and embarrassment of having one's wrongdoing exposed to the entire world simply seems excessive in some cases. Because there is no one person or organization in charge of such information, though, there is nothing the person can do to have it – or at least certain portions of it, like her home address – expunged from the record.

Solove is clearly right that the existence of this amorphous web of information and disinformation is a problem, and a growing problem. Much of the source of the problem, though, as he describes it, is commercial. That is, it is those seeking to make a profit from information, rather than government agencies seeking to control the population, who engage in the buying and selling of personal data. We (too often) sign up for services or (free!) on-line prizes, or Facebook pages, that give others access to not only our information but also to that of those we have had either personal or business dealings with. The dangers to privacy from commercial transactions on the Internet have been well documented, and have, furthermore, been the subject of Congressional hearings.[29] Says Solove, "the process of information collection in America is clandestine, duplicitous, and unfair,"[30] but this is surely less true when it comes to the initial collection of data on my income or criminal record by the state – I'm pretty well aware that I am handing this over. It is when I am dealing with businesses that I often don't realize what I've signed up for, especially when it comes to the secondary market for my information.

This is not to say that the collection of information necessitated by paternalistic measures is not a danger. Even if the government does its best

---

[29] See, for example, Schwartz, "Property, Privacy, and Personal Data."
[30] Solove, "Privacy and Power," 1426.

to keep it confidential, there is always the danger of its becoming known to those I don't want to know it. Nor do I want to concede the issue, as Scott McNealy (relatively) famously recommended when he said, "You have zero privacy anyway. Get over it."[31] Rather, it suggests that what we need is not to refrain from information gathering by the government, in what will be relatively few cases, but rather legal redress against a whole spectrum of misuses of information. For example, some have suggested that greater transparency should be mandated, so that transparency would help individuals figure out what exactly it is that they are getting into when, for example, they make an on-line purchase. We could have a society "in which everything is out in the open,"[32] where "public feedback regulation"[33] would allow the public itself to report on practices to inform other members of the public, causing, in theory, companies to change injurious practices so as to avoid losing clientele. Transparency would, in theory, put us in a better bargaining position, if nothing else. People could make a rational cost–benefit calculation as to whether the loss of privacy is worth the benefits of whatever business they are engaged in.

Indeed, transparency certainly seems like a good idea, at least in the context of the trade in personal information. As I have argued earlier, one of the ways in which others' access to our information could indeed be disrespectful of our worth is if there were a class society, those who are known and those who know. While the inequality brought about by corporate spying is perhaps more of a patchwork than is government spying – no one corporation would know everything about you, and no member of a corporation would be immune to having things known about them – it still puts each of us, as individuals, on the defensive against those who have access to our information without being accountable. So, transparency makes accountability much easier, and where there is accountability there is at least less inequality. While this seems like a good idea, it has also been argued that it won't be enough. Knowing what others know is helpful, but doesn't, in itself, provide complete protection against knowledge that may be used to hurt us. The literature on transparency abounds with suggestions as to what might successfully address the discrepancy in power between private individuals and those who want

---

[31] McNealy was quoted by Polly Springer in "Sun on Privacy: 'Get Over It,'" *Wired*, January 26, 1999, www.wired.com/politics/law/new/1999/17538. Some sources quote him as having said, alternatively, "You already have zero privacy. Get over it."

[32] David Brin, *The Transparent Society: Will Technology Force Us to Choose Between Privacy and Freedom?* (New York: Perseus, 1998), p. 8.

[33] Ibid., pp. 252 ff.

to manipulate them through the use of personal data. Other suggestions include regulations to make private companies adopt adequate security; decreasing the accessibility to records kept by the state; an improved legal understanding of what should be considered "private," and thereby subject to protection; and improvement in people's ability to opt out of data collection.[34] These, too, seem good ideas, as far as they go.

The problem, though, is that they do not in themselves address a large source of the problem – we ourselves, who continuously give up information that allows others to manage us. It is we who broadcast our birthdays, children's names, alma mater, interests, place of work, marital status, romantic inclinations, whereabouts, and of course, pictures, on Facebook, on the grounds that, for example, the chances of reaping some birthday greetings outweighs the dangers of identity theft; we who are willing to implant biological sensors in our bodies so that our entire health histories and current physical status, as well as other personal information, can be wirelessly uploaded to a "telemedical" system, just in case we're discovered unconscious.[35] Is this the result of a rational cost–benefit calculation that correctly estimates the rewards to be worth the risks? Very possibly not. In some cases it may be; for a few individuals there may be good reasons to share such intimate information. In other cases, though, and probably the majority, we make such information available because we don't sufficiently think through the ramifications. Even with full information as provided by the transparency requirement, and protection against hidden secondary uses of our information, we are likely to endanger our own status by foolish behavior. Knowing the costs, we are nonetheless frequently bad bargainers. This is familiar territory – we often are not good at bargaining because we suffer, here as elsewhere, from cognitive bias.

It has been persuasively argued, for example, that if those who want our information put their cards on the table and offer us a deal – so that we know they will place cookies in our computers, but offer compensation for that, for example, or, as has been suggested, pay us to accept telemarketing calls, and then keep records of what we agree to[36] – we are unlikely to come out ahead. We have a strong tendency, in situations where the outcome is uncertain, to accept the default option – to accept the deal as it

[34] Solove, "Privacy and Power," 1456 ff.
[35] See, for example, Aleksander Milenkovic, Chris Otto, and Emil Jaranov, "Wireless Sensor-Networks for Personal Health Monitoring: Issues and an Implantation," *Computer Communications* 29.13–14 (2006), 2521–2533.
[36] See discussion in Schwartz, "Property, Privacy, and Personal Data."

is given to us – even though it is not advantageous, and even when the costs of changing it are not great. Russell Korobkin calls this the "inertia theory" of contract bargaining: "The common conclusion of all the experimental results is that negotiators tend to favor terms that will take effect if the negotiators do nothing, as opposed to terms that become operational through affirmative actions of negotiators."[37]

One possible explanation is that this is a function of our general aversion to regret. We don't want to do something that we will later look back on as having been a mistake. Having "done something" to bring about a bad conclusion (bad relative to what might have been) may bother us more than the bad conclusion itself. Rationally, one has "done something" whether one accepts the default option or declines the default option and chooses something else, but it doesn't feel that way to us. We experience more regret (or guilt) when we deviated from the status quo.[38] This doesn't entail that inaction is always preferable; it depends on what the default was. If we always buy a lottery ticket with a certain number, and, in a fit of rationality, see that buying lottery tickets is completely irrational, we may nonetheless be so fearful of regret at deviating from our normal procedure that we go ahead and buy the ticket – because think how awful we would feel if on this occasion we didn't buy the ticket and then it won! Similarly, if we actively interfere in the terms of a contract, and that turns out to be worse for us than if we had accepted the terms as offered, we will feel more regret than if we had left the contract "as is" and suffered the same negative consequence. This is not rational: "The paradox in this behavior stems from the view that utility for final assets should not depend upon the decision maker's current asset position."[39] When both avenues are equally open to us, we are equally responsible whether we choose to stay with the status quo or introduce an alteration. Rationally, we know that; but irrationally, we don't act as if that is true when making our decision. We act as if (a) we are more causally responsible for consequences of an action, even when action and inaction are equally within our control, and (b) we will suffer more regret for the bad consequences of an action. As it happens, this second belief, like the first, is false: in the long run we actually regret inaction more than we regret action, and we furthermore are aware of that fact, when asked to

[37] Russell Korobkin, "Inertia and Preference in Contract Negotiation: The Psychological Power of Default Rules and Form Terms," *Vanderbilt Law Review* 51 (November 1998), 1587.

[38] Daniel Kahneman and Amos Tversky, "The Psychology of Preferences," *Scientific American* 246 (1972), 160–173.

[39] David Bell, "Regret in Decision-making Under Uncertainty," *Operations Research* 30 (1982), 961.

predict what, in reference to *other* people, will produce the most regret.[40] Despite this, we continue to err on the side of inaction when we decide before the fact what to do. We suffer, apparently, from an "omission bias," pushing us to embrace the status quo even though that is disadvantageous.[41]

So, leaving the control of information to the private sphere – "private" in this context meaning extragovernmental – doesn't seem likely to protect our information as much as it needs to be protected. The free market will put the individual at too much of a disadvantage. As Warren and Brandeis put it, the common law, in its eternal youth, needs to grow to meet the demands of society. And among these laws that clearly need to be created to protect privacy are laws that protect us from our own misjudgment in questions of privacy. If, of course, one does not accept the rationale for paternalistic laws, such protection becomes considerably more difficult. The acceptance of paternalism, however, opens the door to regulations that will prevent us from putting out dangerous information in ways that private interests are likely to capitalize on. Since ultimately it is we ourselves who are the best source of information about ourselves, controlling this source of information will provide much greater security than will measures that simply provide for transparency as to initial or secondary uses of our information.

The upshot of this psychological discourse is that the effect of paternalism on privacy is not univocal. On the one hand, it would doubtless put some information into the public realm (where "public" simply means known to more than the individual himself), information which otherwise might have stayed entirely private. On the other hand, it provides a justification for taking the mass of information that might otherwise have become public and making it stay private, in the sense of known only to you and those known personally to you. If posting your complete birth date on Facebook actually makes you significantly more vulnerable to identity theft, we can stop you from doing that. If wearing implantable chips that broadcast your health statistics and status actually hurts you more than it helps, we can make those unavailable. I don't know that it's true that it is dangerous to post your full birth date, nor that wearing implantable information chips will give access to unauthorized persons to see your entire medical history and other identifying facts.

[40] Thomas Gilovich and Victoria Husted Medvec, "The Experience of Regret: What, When, and Why," *Psychological Review* 102.2 (1995), 379–395.

[41] L. Ritov and J. Baron, "Status-quo and Omission Biases," *Journal of Risk and Uncertainty* 5 (1992), 49–61; and M. Spranca, E. Minsk, and J. Baron, "Omission and Commission in Judgment and Choice," *Journal of Experimental Social Psychology* 27 (1991), 76–105.

What is clear is that some people fear that they, and other activities like them, are dangerous, and yet fear that paternalism will exacerbate the problem by taking away our control over even more information. In fact, just the opposite is true. Paternalism justifies interference with "free" trade in information if we discover that some bargainers are, due to the peculiarities of their position, going to be systematically and significantly disadvantaged by being allowed complete liberty of action. When it comes to state information, it is true here, as always, that paternalism will operate on a cost–benefit basis; if the collection of information, whether it is about your medications, seat belt wearing or some as yet to be imagined paternalistic interest, is more harmful than helpful, this can be addressed, because paternalism is, if nothing else, pragmatic.

Thus, the argument that paternalistic laws, since they do typically involve the aggregation of information concerning individuals, will necessarily subject those individuals to harmful exposure, can be met by the countervailing consideration that paternalism also provides the justification for imposing restrictions on information sharing.

CONCLUSION

All government is dangerous. To have a government at all is to have given others power over us. There is no need to think, though, that paternalistic measures make a government any more dangerous than one that is not paternalistic. Legislation is always subject to misuse and abuse. We always need democracy; transparency, free and fair elections; the minimizing of the power of wealth. In the United States, we have most of these things to some degree, but none of them entirely. However, even when we consider the reality of our political system, rather than the ideal, we consider the benefits of law to be greater than the costs. There is no reason this should not be true of paternalistic laws, which, after all, are intended to benefit all.

CHAPTER 6

Applications

WHEN IS COERCIVE PATERNALISM JUSTIFIED?

Joel Feinberg, while admitting that in some few circumstances mild forms of paternalism might be acceptable, has said that "[t]he trick is stopping short once we undertake this path, unless we wish to ban whiskey, cigarettes, and fried foods, which tend to be bad for people, too, whether they know it or not."[1] He is quite right: the reasons that justify the instances of paternalism we accept, such as seat belt laws, do indeed justify other interventions. He is wrong, however, in thinking that this in itself is a reason for avoiding paternalism. It is one of the merits of good paternalistic arguments that they justify many sorts of interventions. Not all of those Feinberg mentions are likely, to be sure: I think that the benefits of alcohol outweigh its dangers, and furthermore, history has proven that drinking is so entrenched in our culture – in many of our cultures – that it is very difficult to stop people from drinking, even if we decide to do so. That cigarettes should be illegal seems likely, though, and while banning fried food per se seems both unnecessary and impractical, requiring restaurants to reduce portion sizes, and thus portions of the fried fats which do seem to be major causes of our national obesity, is probably a good idea. In the light of present information, we can see that coercive paternalistic intervention seems increasingly justified. Having, for example, spent a great deal of money on soft paternalistic methods for getting people to change their ways – educating them thoroughly on the dangers of smoking, for example, and disincentivizing the purchase of cigarettes by taxing them to the point where they might seem virtually unaffordable – we know that even with full information, and nudges amounting to pushes, people will continue to choose the wrong thing. This is not true of everyone, of course; some forms of noncoercive

---

[1] Feinberg, *Harm to Self*, p. 4.

persuasion work for some people, in some circumstances, for some particular choices. There are those of us who have been lucky enough to resist the lures of cigarettes or fatty foods (even though at the same time we may pursue mortgages that will break us – clear thinking in one case does not guarantee it in another). Others, though, continue to suffer the destructive consequences of their own poor choices in these areas. If we are not to abandon those who will do themselves irreparable harm when left to their own autonomous choices, then we need to help them, and in some cases the only way to help them is to stop them.

In what follows I will consider some situations that have been suggested as suitable for coercive paternalism, and some that have not but that seem to fall into the same category. Whether paternalistic solutions will work in these or in other situations is as yet an open question: these are empirical issues and thus require facts. Not all the relevant facts are yet available, and I am not a scientist capable of authoritatively assessing those facts we do have. It seems likely, though, that in many cases, coercive paternalism will prove to be the most plausible strategy for helping us do what we need and want to do. What we need, in order to conclude that coercive paternalism is the appropriate strategy, is for it to meet these four criteria:

1. The activity to be prevented on paternalistic grounds really is one that is opposed to our long-term ends. As discussed in Chapter 4, we don't want to allow a "paternalistic" intervention just because an action, or its result, is, say, vulgar, or aesthetically unpleasing, or immoral, or silly, as long as it helps a person reach his own goals. Interference is justified on paternalistic grounds only when it reflects individuals' actual values, not the values we might like them to have. (Naturally, in some cases there will be third-party considerations that can justify preventing behavior that is aesthetically unpleasing, immoral, and so on, but here we are discussing only paternalistic interventions.) It is incomprehensible to me that people should find it fulfilling to collect license plates, but some do, and if that is the way they want to spend their money, or time, or whatever exactly it takes to get "good" license plates, that is their option.

2. Coercive measures actually have to be effective. Sometimes they aren't. As we know, Prohibition did not end alcohol consumption. It is foolish to introduce a legal constraint on an activity if that won't actually work to end or reduce that activity. And, we need the measure to be effective in two ways. In most cases, there will be an immediate goal (to stop someone using a substance, for example) and an ultimate

goal to which that immediate goal is to lead (improving health). If a measure succeeds in the first, but not the second, then the measure is pointless. If, for example, we wanted to ban cupcakes to alleviate obesity, and succeeded in removing cupcakes from people's diets only to find that they had filled that gap with layer cake, then the cupcake ban would be foolish. We need efficacy throughout.

3. The benefits have to be greater than the costs. The benefits and costs are both material and psychological, with neither having absolute priority: a measure that greatly improves health, for example, could in fact be so psychological painful, over the long run, as not to be worth it.

4. The measure in question needs to be the most efficient way to prevent the activity. This criterion really implies criteria 2 and 3, but since many people dwell on the first three without noticing that a paternalist would also accept the fourth, I want to stress each individually. It is one thing to say that a policy achieves its goal. It is another to say that its benefits outweigh its costs. It is yet another to say that it is the most efficient way to achieve that goal. For a program to be justified, it needs to be the strategy that has the greatest margin of benefits over costs. As we know, hard paternalistic measures typically have some costs that soft paternalistic measures don't. They are more intrusive, which means they often feel worse to the person to whom they're applied. Given this, we don't want to introduce them unless they are the least costly way to achieve the goal for which we are striving. On the other hand, some soft paternalistic measures actually have costs that coercion doesn't. Gerald Dworkin once argued that hard paternalistic measures might indeed be justified in some circumstances, but that if "there is an alternative way of accomplishing the desired end without restricting liberty, even though it may involve great expense, inconvenience, etc., the society must adopt it."[2] This perhaps reflects Dworkin's belief that that we should aim to promote freedom and autonomy, not just happiness, but even so it doesn't follow – a coercive action might protect an individual's freedom in the long run just as effectively (or more) than the softer methods of education and persuasion, and without some of the costs. While we don't like being forced to do something, we might sometimes prefer it to being constantly hectored to choose the right thing. We cannot assume that soft paternalism is always preferable even in those cases

[2] Dworkin, "Paternalism," p. 34.

where it does achieve the desired goal. Given that, this proviso does not say that hard paternalism should only be introduced when soft paternalistic measures are ineffective. Rather, they should be introduced when they are the most efficient measure available.

CASES

The question is what measures fit these parameters. More and more interventions into personal decisions are being considered as we become increasingly informed as to the poor results that arise from individual decisions. We are increasingly, and frighteningly, obese; many of us still risk premature death through smoking; we consume artificial trans-fats and other food additives that seem to have no individual benefit (no one really has a taste for trans-fats), even while they endanger our hearts. Because these dangers are obvious, the field of public health has been one of the few to systematically suggest interventions in behavior. Some of these suggestions involve hard paternalistic methods, where the individual is given no choice about what to do, and others use soft methods, where education or disincentives are used as methods to produce change. I will first examine a few existing paternalist regulations with a view to their suitability, and then will go on to look at policies not yet enacted that seem like reasonable interventions.

The New York City trans-fats ban

I start with the trans-fats ban because it is straightforward. This appears to be one of the easiest cases of coercive paternalism to justify, with almost nothing reasonable to be said against it, and is consistent with other government actions, in which, for example, known carcinogens have been removed from the market. The only unusual thing about the trans-fats ban is that in the United States it has been undertaken by a municipality instead of by the federal government.

Starting on July 1, 2008, the use of added trans-fats in New York City restaurants and cafeterias has been made illegal.[3] The New York City Department of Health and Mental Hygiene inaugurated the law against trans-fats (more properly, trans-fatty acids) because trans-fats have been shown to greatly increase the risk of coronary heart disease. While they

---

[3] New York City Department of Health and Mental Hygiene, Press Release, September 26, 2006, www.nyc.gov/html/doh/htmlpr2006/pr093–06.shtml

typically constituted a fairly small percentage of our overall fat intake, they were (and remain) particularly dangerous —a 2 percent increase in the number of calories taken from trans-fats increases the incidence of heart disease by 23 percent in women.[4] The ban has received both praise for its intention and abuse for constituting an unwarranted intrusion into privacy by the "food police." However, whatever objections there may be, more and more areas are adopting trans-fats bans: Boston and Philadelphia have enacted similar regulations; California introduced a ban of all trans-fats from restaurants, beginning in 2010, with a ban on their use in bakeries starting in 2011. Denmark preceded New York in banning trans-fats, beginning in 2004; Austria and Switzerland have now adopted a national ban on the use of artificial trans-fats. What justifies this?

1. *Does it advance long-term goals?* It certainly seems it would. Heart disease causes premature death. Most of us would agree that health "is valued for its own sake, and it is a means to almost all ends . . . No matter how eccentric a person's values and tastes are, no matter what kind of activities are pleasurable, it is impossible to engage in them unless alive."[5] It "is necessary for much of the joy, creativity and productivity that each person derives from life."[6] Staying alive, and being able to function normally while we are alive, is something we want.

2. *Is it effective?* Compliance has been investigated, and the ban appears to be working. Overall use of trans-fats has clearly been reduced, even though in New York trans-fats are still available in packaged food (since these are controlled by the Food and Drug Authority, and not the city of New York.) In New York City, for example, the regulation cut the prevalence of use of trans-fats in restaurants from 50 percent to less than 2 percent.[7] While it was feared at one point that restaurants and bakeries might use other, equally or more dangerous saturated fats to substitutes for trans-fats, this has turned out not to be true. Having once embarked on the change, food purveyors apparently decided that they might as well concede the need for relatively healthy fats.[8] Has it been effective on

---

[4] Andy Tan, "A Case Study of the New York City Trans-Fat Story for International Application," *Journal of Public Health Policy* 30.1 (2009), 5.

[5] Wikler, "Persuasion and Coercion," p. 41.

[6] Lawrence Gostin, "Part I: Law as a Tool to Advance the Community's Health," *Journal of the American Medical Association* 283.21 (2000), 2838.

[7] Dariush Mozaffarian, "Removing Industrial Trans-Fats from Foods," *British Medical Journal*, 2010; see also Maria Newman, "With Grace Period Over, Compliance Seen with Trans-Fat Ban," *New York Times*, October 11, 2007.

[8] Dariush Mozaffarian, Michael F. Jacobson, and Julie S. Greenstein, "Food Reformulation Reduces Trans-Fatty Acids," *New England Journal of Medicine* 362 (May 27, 2010), 2031–2039.

achieving the overall end, an improvement in health? It is early times to tell this, but it would appear so; at least in Denmark, whose ban has been in place several years longer, coronary heart disease seems to have been reduced. It is hypothesized that the end result will produce a 50 percent decrease in deaths from the sort of heart disease that trans-fats contribute to.[9] Given this, it looks as if the reduction in restaurant trans-fats use will indeed result in better heart health. Meanwhile, taste, price, and availability have remained unaffected.[10]

3. *Are the benefits worth the costs?* That said, while the fact that something contributes to disability and early death strongly suggests it is incompatible with the overall attainment of our goals, that isn't in itself definitive of whether or not it's worth pursuing. After all, enjoyment during life is also a long-term goal, and in many cases we are perfectly willing to risk some damage to health for the sake of enjoyment: Dan Wikler notes that many unhealthy habits won't kill us, if they do, until relatively late in life, and it may be worth it for a young person to engage in a dangerous action that won't have serious consequences until fifty years later – he will still have twenty-five years worth of desirable activities left to him.[11] Even if death is an immediate risk, if the activity is sufficiently rewarding it may be worth it – we ski despite the danger of breaking our necks running into a tree, we drive, and so forth. It would be counterproductive to ban every dangerous activity. In this case, though, we have no reason to think the health risks of trans-fats could be offset by enjoyment. No one has a particular taste for trans-fats per se, and while they do have a taste for pastries, trans-fats can be substituted for by other fats without loss of flavor. Indeed, many cooks claim that things taste better when they use oils or fats that don't contain added trans-fats. So, in this case, there appears to be no trade-off at all of enjoyment for health.

4. *Is it the most efficient way of cutting back on trans-fats?* New York only introduced the ban after attempting to get restaurants to reduce trans-fats use voluntarily. Their trans-fats education campaign was deemed a failure, which is why the city moved to the ban. In the words of the city's press department: "While some restaurants reduced or stopped using artificial trans-fat, overall use did not decline at all. In restaurants where it could be

---

[9] Steen Stender and Jorn Dyerberg, "Influence of Trans-Fatty Acids on Health," *Annals of Nutrition and Metabolism* 48.2 (2004), 61–66.

[10] Steen Stender, Jorn Dyerberg, and Arne Astrup, "Consumer Protection through a Legislative Ban on Industrially Produced Trans-Fatty Acids in Foods in Denmark," *Scandinavian Journal of Food and Nutrition* 50.4 (2006), 155–160.

[11] Wikler, "Persuasion and Coercion," pp. 41–42.

determined whether trans-fat was used, half used it in oils or spreads both before and after the year-long campaign. A year after this voluntary effort, New Yorkers are still being exposed to high levels of dangerous trans-fat."[12]

Following the Danish ban, McDonalds reduced its use of trans-fats in Denmark so that a meal of French fries and chicken nuggets in Copenhagen contains less than 1 gram of trans-fats. Meanwhile, the same meal has 10 grams of trans-fats in most parts of the US, where reduction is not required.[13] So, outright prevention does seem to be needed to get restaurants to change their ways.

I write, again, provisionally, since new facts may yet be revealed. At present, though, the New York City ban seems justified from all perspectives. It is, of course, coercive, and thus presents a good case for coercive intervention. The only peculiar thing about this ban is that it is, so far, local: the United States government has not yet stepped in to ban trans-fats use nationally. If we do want to ban trans-fats, a national ban would be far more effective: first of all, it would obviously reach more people. Second, municipalities and states don't have the power to ban trans-fats use in all products – packaged goods are controlled by the Food and Drug Administration, which is why New York could not regulate their trans-fats use. Researchers point out that a national ban would not only be more effective in producing health, but would be simpler for the food industry than the present situation, where different municipalities and states adopt different standards. "For a company that is creating a product or exporting food or a restaurant trying to comply with different legislations this actually makes it more complicated for them."[14] The trans-fats ban is coercive, but appears to be justified. Its only flaw is that it is not more widespread.

The New York City food stamp soda ban

This is a complicated and interesting case. The City of New York in October 2010 asked the US Department of Agriculture, which issues food stamps, to allow the city to refuse the use of food stamps for the purchase

---

[12] City of New York, "Health department proposes two changes to city's health code for public comment," press release, September 26, 2006; www.nyc.gov/html/doh/html/pr2006/pr093–06.shtml.
[13] Stender, Dyerberg, and Astrup, "Consumer Protection."
[14] Dariush, et al., "Food Reformulation."

of sodas (or other sweetened drinks). Spokesmen stressed the existence of a causal connection between soda use and obesity. Soda consumption has doubled over the past thirty years, paralleling the rampant rise in obesity that is in turn causing a rampant rise in obesity-related illnesses. While correlation is not causation, this naturally leads some to suspect that soda is probably one of the major contributors to obesity. New York, like most of the United States, is suffering an obesity epidemic. We all know that Americans, and increasingly Europeans, are getting fatter and fatter.[15] (While the US is famous for being the most obese nation on earth, the prevalence of obesity has tripled in many European countries since the 1980s).[16] Obesity is defined medically as having a Body Mass Index of over 30. While in a few cases (like very muscular people) BMI doesn't reflect how fat someone is, the fact that close to 30 percent of people in the US have a BMI of over 30 means we are really, really big. (And that just considers obesity – more like 60 percent are merely "overweight.") Obesity, as we know, brings about a number of serious health risks, including heart disease, cancer, and diabetes. The rationale behind the food stamp soda ban is that if food stamp recipients can't use food stamps for soda, they will drink less of it; if they drink less of it, they will lose weight, or at least not increase their weight at the same rate; if they weigh less, they will be healthier. They will, furthermore, have more food stamps to use on foods that have less sugar and more nutritional value. Since New York City has 1.7 million users of food stamps, the hope is that this will constitute a not insignificant drop in soda consumption (if indeed the ban actually results in fewer purchases of soda by those who receive food stamps) and improvement in health (again, if the link between soda and obesity is correct).

   1. *Does it advance long-term goals?* Well, certainly good health is one of the most important long-term goals for most of us, for the reasons adduced above. Being found conventionally attractive, and social acceptance generally, are also pretty important to most of us. Obesity clearly contributes to ill health and to the psychological burden of being unattractive by conventional standards. If the use of soda, rather than the alternatives, contributes to obesity, reducing the amount of soda we drink, would, all things being equal, advance one or more of these goals. Questions arise, though, about both the efficacy and the net benefit of the

---

[15] "Crisis Looms in Obesity in Europe, Experts Say," *New York Times*, April 22, 2007.
[16] World Health Organization, www.euro.who.int/en/what-we-do/health-tiopics/noncommunicable diseases/obesity

policy. The soda ban aims at what are indeed two of our common long-term goals, but if it fails in efficacy or the cost–benefit analysis, it's not a good policy.

2. *Is it effective?* There is a lot of debate about whether the food stamp soda ban will accomplish what it sets out to do. For one thing, the role that soda drinking plays in obesity is not entirely obvious. While drinking orange juice instead of a Coke has clear nutritional advantages, any calorie counter can tell you that orange juice actually has more calories.[17] So does whole milk, along with significantly more fat. So, substituting juice for soda isn't necessarily a help, as far as obesity goes. If soda drinkers switched to water, that would cause weight loss, all things being equal, but to me, at least, this seems unlikely. This is part of the reason studies of the link between soda and obesity have had mixed results.[18] Second, even if it is desirable for people to stop drinking soda, it's not at all clear that denying food stamp users the power to buy it with stamps will stop them from using it. The problem is that soda is still available to food stamp users; they just can't use food stamps for it. Soda is pretty cheap (cheaper, in my market, than bottled water alone, something which always makes me wonder). It seems reasonable to think that if people want soda enough then they will get it, even without the use of food stamps. It is believable, too, that they will want it enough – people are very fond of their soda. This is a surmise: it will depend on the resources available to the buyer and the strength of the desire for soda. The circumstances for reducing its use are surely not propitious, then: having something readily accessible in grocery stores, convenience stores, gas stations, vending machines, and so on, that is also very cheap, and very popular, and that many people are used to consuming daily, does not bode well for a reduction in consumption.

3. *Are the benefits worth the costs?* If the policy is effective then there will be two costs involved in the program: loss of enjoyment and loss of status. Again, the evidence is that people are very fond of their soda. We certainly consume an enormous amount of it, and over time we spend a lot on it. We know, too, that people take some trouble to get soda: they certainly take active steps to get it, like going to the store and picking up liters of it, when drinking readily available tap water would be much easier and cheaper. Soda drinkers, too, are very sensitive to differences in taste

---

[17] According to the LoseIt program on my phone, 12 ounces of orange juice rings in at 165 and 12 ounces of Classic Coke at 140.

[18] Sigrid Gibson, "Sugar Sweetened Soft Drinks and Obesity: A Systematic Review of the Evidence for Observational Studies and Intervention," *Nutrition Research Review* 21.2 (2008), 134–147.

(why the new Coke was such a failure, and why waiters always take care to explain if they don't have Coke, only Pepsi, rather than assuming you'll be okay with either one), which suggests that they actually enjoy the particularities of sodas' flavors. Soda isn't addictive, either, so the drive to drink it isn't just the desire to extinguish an unpleasant feeling of craving. These are all behaviors we normally interpret as exhibiting a strong liking, to say the least. It seems most reasonable to assume, then, that a real loss of enjoyment will accrue insofar as people are denied access to soda. Many people say they simply "need" soda: to them, the calories are not empty, even though they may be nutritionally empty.

The second issue, that food stamp users will suffer a loss of status as a result of the ban, has received a good deal of discussion in New York, where some people argue that the ban "stigmatizes" those who are on food stamps. This, in itself, is not a terribly powerful argument: a stigma is not necessarily a bad thing. Sometimes it can serve as a motivator. If the activity that is stigmatized is sufficiently bad for the person, and being stigmatized would cause the person to stop doing whatever makes them merit the stigma, that might achieve a net good; furthermore, others might avoid taking up the activity in question, in order to avoid the fate of the stigmatized. However, if the stigma is not a motivator to change, it may be an unmitigated harm. This interdict in particular may send an unfortunate political message. Making something absolutely illegal sends a message about that product – that it is bad for you. If the government bans red dye number 2 on the grounds that it is carcinogenic, we pretty much take it for granted that they are right. Denying a substance only to *some* people, though, doesn't send this same message. Rather, it is liable to be interpreted as a message about the people to whom it is denied, since the substance itself continues to be offered to others. Of course, as said before, the food stamp soda ban doesn't literally prevent food stamp recipients from having soda – it just prevents them from using food stamps to pay for them. Still, the majority of the discussion in New York has been in terms of food stamp users themselves, not their means of currency: what makes people need food stamps, whether the poor have blameworthy buying habits, whether food stamp users create undue health care costs for others, and so forth. So, it is not surprising that some interpret the food stamp soda ban more as sending a message about the rights of those who live off public support, rather than about the merits of soda: to wit, that they shouldn't be allowed to spend public funds on mere frivolities.

This is more than just a stigmatizing judgment; it is one that raises serious questions about the standing of those who are on public support. Does the fact that some people depend on public support mean they should live as meagerly as possible, on the grounds that they are spending someone else's money? Should they be allowed to buy tickets to movies, if that is only possible because they are getting food stamps to cover other needs? Should they be allowed to get new clothes if their old ones aren't worn out yet? To waste money on make-up or hair products when those aren't required for working? Should people on public assistance be allowed to have fun, in other words, on (what is arguably) someone else's dime? For me, the answer is certainly yes – people are on public assistance because they need help in order to live a minimally decent life, and to my mind a bit of frivolity is necessary to living a minimally decent life. Frivolity in some form is something we all have an equal claim to. To many, though, measures like the soda ban suggest that those who use public funds should live as Spartan an existence as possible because they do not deserve some (very) small luxuries the rest of us enjoy. At the very least, this is a question that deserves open discussion, rather than a message that suggests that the issue is clear-cut, that products that aren't necessary for life itself should be denied to those who are dependent on others, because they don't have the right to amuse themselves.

The Bloomberg administration presumably did not intend to send this message. Rather, those who developed the program seem to have wanted to help the recipients of food stamps be healthier, both for their own sake and to keep down health care costs. Indeed, the Bloomberg administration would like everyone to drink less soda, as evidenced by their support for the failed attempt to get the state of New York to raise statewide taxes on soda.[19] It is too likely, however, that this is how the message will be read.

4. *Is it the most efficient way of cutting back soda use?* I am arguing that it doesn't seem likely to be terribly effective, but of course there are still questions as to what, if anything, would be better (putting aside the unresolved question as to whether cutting soda use will actually help in the fight against obesity). One possibility, popular in other contexts where we want to change behavior, is that we could disincentivize the purchase of soda by raising taxes on it.[20] At the time of writing, thirty-three states

---

[19] Maria Gay, "Proposed Food Stamp Soda Ban Leaves a Sour Taste," www. Aolnews.com/2010/10/07/; Sarah Gilbert, "Why NYC's Proposed Soda Ban is Good for Food Stamp Recipients," www.dailyfinance.com/2010/10/11/

[20] Travis A. Smith, Bing-Hwan Lin, and Yong-Ying Lee, "Taxing Caloric Sweetened Beverages: Potential Effects on Beverage, Consumption, Calorie Intake, and Obesity," Economic Research Report 100 (US Department of Agriculture, Economic Research Service, July 2010; www.ers.usda.gov/Publication/ERR100) argue that a tax-induced 20 percent price increase on "caloric sweetened beverages" could cause an average reduction of 37 calories per day, or 3.8 pounds over a year for adults, and 4.5 pounds for children.

have soda taxes. New York has twice debated taxes on soda, but legislation has so far been unsuccessful (due, in part, to heavy lobbying by the soda industry.)[21] A statewide increase in tax would at least avoid the equivocal message of the food stamp ban, since it would obviously apply to everyone equally. And, since we are used to paying taxes, and used to paying outsize taxes on potentially unhealthy items (cigarettes and alcohol, and to some extent snacks), it would avoid some of the resentment that novel methods of modifying behavior tend to generate – there was a fair amount of fuss over banning trans-fats, which no one is particularly fond of. However, financial disincentives have various disadvantages. First, they don't necessarily stop even the people to whom the tax is a real burden – people may just pour more and more of their income into the item in question, if they want it enough. Taxing the item has been tried with cigarettes, and, to be sure, has provided the state with a steady source of revenue. How much cigarette taxes have reduced smoking, however, rather than just driving people to spend a disproportionate amount of their income on cigarettes, is a question. Clearly it has not reduced smoking enough, since roughly 20 percent of Americans still smoke (see below). Granted, soda is not addictive in the way that cigarettes are, so the pull to spending on soda should be less. Still, people are very, very fond of their soda, and it may be they would continue to buy it at a significantly higher price. Second, financial disincentives only work for poorer people, those who don't have enough money to afford the item when it costs more. How many people would be able to afford soda with a higher tax depends, of course, on how highly the soda is taxed, so its efficacy in discouraging purchases can't be gauged until we know that. If the tax is small (the mean for present state soda taxes is 5.2%), most users will continue to drink a lot of soda, making it ineffective. If the tax is hefty (some recommend a tax that would increase soda costs by 15–20%),[22] we run into a third problem: using financial incentives can promote class distinctions. If the financial disincentive is actually great enough to stop a good number of people from drinking soda, or great enough at least to significantly reduce how much soda they drink, they will suffer from its loss. Meanwhile, the rich (and presumably middle class, again depending on how great the tax actually is) can get all the soda they want. Of course, in the US we are used to richer people being able to get things poorer ones can't, since it is the way

---

[21] Bao Ong, "New York's Soda Tax Plan Dies After Industry Ad Campaign," *New York Times*, July 2, 2010.
[22] See Kelly Brownell, et al., "The Public Health and Economic Benefits of Taxing Sugar-Sweetened Beverages," *New England Journal of Medicine* 361 (October 15, 2009), 1599–1605.

our country works. Still, when it comes to something that we are used to regarding as a staple, this will presumably induce more resentment than does the fact that only a few of us can afford our own private island.

Another option, of course, is simply education. Schools now incorporate discussions in health classes that relate specifically to diet choices, and talk of "empty calories" is popular. Education is an attractive strategy to many in that it doesn't seem to cost the individual anything to learn more about what he is eating, and in particular the knowledge that soda is high in sugar and makes you fat without making you any healthier might have some effect. (Speaking for myself, I expect I would drink soda sometimes, if it didn't make me fat and rot my teeth. As it happens, I only use it when I am sick to my stomach, when it seems worth the costs.) However, again, this doesn't seem to have had the desired effect so far, and it's a real question how increased information (as in having calorie and nutrient content posted in fast food restaurants, discussed below) will make a difference. Newer attempts that don't dwell on facts but go for emotional appeal may be more effective. New York has produced two ads both designed to disgust people – one of a man drinking a soda can's worth of globular, visually repellent fat, and one of a man eating the amount of sugar found in a can of soda (16 teaspoons.) Insofar as these bypass rational thinking altogether and go straight for the gross-out effect, they may motivate in a way mere facts do not. On the other hand, they may lose their shock value when they've been seen too often, so we'll see.

A third option would be the draconian approach, to make soda illegal. This has some appeal. It would presumably achieve the goal, a reduction in soda use, much more effectively than any other strategy. And without soda, people would be forced to drink things that are better for them, both in having fewer calories and having more nutritive advantages. I hesitate to recommend it, though, for the reasons given in sections 2 and 3 above – people really enjoy soda. If diet soda were a suitable replacement that would be one thing, since it would presumably supply some of the benefits of soda (a taste which, while to soda drinkers not as good as soda, presumably comes a lot closer than do milk, water, or juice) without the calories. Unfortunately, diet soda appears to have its own problems: recent studies suggest not only that it is tied to higher risk of strokes and heart attack,[23]

---

[23] A study headed by Hannah Gardener of the Miller School of Medicine at the University of Miami, presented to the American Stroke Association's International Stroke Conference in September 2011 found a correlation between the use of diet soda and cardiovascular events. See "Miller School Researchers Link Diet Soda and Salt to Cardiovascular Risk" at www.med/miami.edu/news/

but that it may encourage weight gain![24] This research is preliminary, however; it may still turn out that the best policy would be for soda to be banned and for diet soda to take its place. Well, the best policy might be for everyone to develop a love of unadulterated water (and from the tap, not from plastic bottles), but that is not going to happen. The best policy in the real world, one that attempts to accommodate our actual tastes, not ideal ones, is one that would trade off the loss to health against the love of sugar. Reducing the use of soda is, after all, a means towards an end, the end of better health, and there are other ways of attaining those ends, other ways, for example, of reducing obesity, as we will see below. A reasonable case can be made that soda is sufficiently important to people that in some form it should remain available.

Portion size regulation

As far as I can tell, no state or municipality has actually tried to mandate smaller portion sizes in restaurants, or tried to reduce the size of single serving packaged foods, like potato chips and cookies. It might, however, be a good idea. Obesity, the driving force behind the soda ban, is also the issue here. More and more researchers endorse the idea that an increase in the size of restaurant portions plays a significant role in this increasing obesity. Their reasoning includes various factors. For one thing, we eat out significantly more than we used to, so we consume more restaurant portions.[25] Portion sizes for all types of food, except pizza, increased markedly between 1978 and 1998,[26] and current portion sizes in fast food restaurants for French fries, hamburgers, and sodas are two to five times larger than the originals. Having larger sizes – larger than previously, and larger than the competitor's – is seen as making brands (like candy bars) and meals more desirable to the consumer. Fast food chains routinely tout the increased size of their offerings, and convenience stores push the size of their takeaway sodas ("Big Gulp") as a way to get people to stop in. Even Lean Cuisine and Weight Watchers advertise increased sizes in their meals.[27]

---

[24] Susan Swithers, and Terry L. Davidson, "A Role for Sweet Taste: Caloric Predictive Relations in Energy Regulation by Rats," *Behavioral Neuroscience* 122.1 (February 2008), 161–173.

[25] Lisa Young and Marion Nestle, "The Contribution of Expanding Portion Sizes to the US Obesity Epidemic," *American Journal of Clinical Nutrition* 92.2 (2002), 246–249.

[26] Samara J. Nielsen, and Barry M. Popkin, "Patterns and Trends in Food Portion Sizes, 1977–1998," *Journal of the American Medical Association* 289.4 (2003), 450–453.

[27] Young and Nestle, "Contribution of Expanding Portion Sizes"; see also B. J. Rolls, "The Supersizing of America: Portion Size and the Obesity Epidemic," *Nutrition Today* 38.2 (2000), 42–53.

And, as anyone who's ever eaten can testify, we eat more when we have a bigger serving. It doesn't matter whether it is a serving we ourselves dish up (which might perhaps correspond to hunger), or one we are given by someone else; numerous studies show that when portion sizes are larger, we eat more. This holds true of both restaurant servings and packaged foods – the bigger the bag of chips, the more we eat of them at one time.[28] Why this is something of a question: it may be that we've been trained to clean our plate, or it may have more biological roots. One factor is that as we eat bigger portions, we often don't feel more full than we do from smaller portions; signals that we are satiated are ignored.[29] So, we just keep eating until it's all gone. Lastly, these gargantuan portions at one meal aren't compensated for by Lilliputian ones at the next – despite the fact that we've consumed an entire day's worth of calories, we eat the next meal as if we'd previously had a salad and sparkling water.[30]

So, it seems plausible that increased portion size plays a significant role in our increased obesity. If this is so, then we may reasonably wonder whether there should be some sort of regulation of portion size. The federal government has its own system of "serving" sizes, but these bear little resemblance to portions actually served in restaurants. (Indeed, in packaged foods, federal serving sizes sometimes confuse us, rather than aiding us in making wise choices, since a package may state in large letters on the front that it contains only xxx calories per serving, and only mention in tiny letters on the back that that package, while clearly intended as a one-person portion, is actually three "servings.") Government "servings" could, though, be useful: they could be used as standards as to what portion sizes would be allowed in restaurants. This could, first and foremost, lessen how many calories people consume now. It could also stave off an even worse future, since it would eliminate the "size wars" between fast food chains that threaten to drive serving sizes up and up and up. Would the regulation of fast food portion sizes be a justified paternalistic policy?

---

[28] B. J. Rolls, L. S. Roe, J. S. Meengs, and D. E. Wall, "Increasing the Portion Size of a Sandwich Increases Energy Intake," *Journal of the American Dietetic Association* 104 (2004), 367–372; N. Diliberti, P. L. Bordi, M. T. Conklin, L. S. Roe, and B. J. Rolls, "Increased Portion Size Leads to Increased Energy Intake in a Restaurant Meal," *Obesity Research* 12 (2004), 562–568; B. J. Rolls, L. S. Roe, T. V. E. Kral, J. S. Meengs, and D. E. Wall, "Increasing the Portion Size of a Packaged Snack Increases Energy Intake in Men and Women," *Appetite* 42 (2004), 63–69.

[29] J. A. Elio-Martin, J. A. Ledikwe, and B. J. Rolls, "The Influence of Food Portion Size and Energy Density on Energy Intake: Implications of for Weight Management," *American Journal of Clinical Nutrition* 82.1 (2005), supplement 236S–241S.

[30] Ibid.

1. *Would it promote a long-term goal?* As with all measures that decrease the chances of serious illness and premature death, the answer certainly appears to be yes. We want longer lives and we want good health, both as ends in themselves and as means to doing everything else we want to do. Furthermore, despite its prevalence, obesity carries a social stigma. People who are fat are typically ashamed of it, presumably because they are indeed looked down upon by other people. Many people suffer acutely from the recognition of their failure to live up to the popular cultural standard of attractiveness. As if this loss of self-esteem and self-confidence were not bad enough, overweight women, at least, also suffer career setbacks stemming from their obesity, earning less and advancing more slowly than their thinner counterparts.[31] All things being equal, career advancement is considered desirable by most people, and failing to advance because of a feature irrelevant to job performance is painful to everyone.

2. *Is it effective?* Since there are as yet no regulations over portions, we cannot know this for certain. The facts adduced above, though, as to the overall effect on calorie intake of larger portion sizes, suggests that it would be, if restaurants were compliant, and the trans-fats experience here and abroad suggests that restaurants are willing to be compliant, at least where that costs them nothing.

3. *Are the benefits worth the costs?* The difficult question, of course, is what the costs to the individual would be if restaurant portion sizes were controlled. On the one hand, eating smaller portions can still satisfy our appetite, so losing supersizes wouldn't mean suffering hunger pangs. On the other hand, a lot of our eating has very little to do with satisfying hunger. We eat with others to enjoy a social occasion; we eat alone because we are bored; and first and foremost, we eat because we like the taste. We eat as much as we do out of the pure enjoyment of food. Fast food may not present a sophisticated, innovative, complex combination of flavors of the sort that entices restaurant reviewers, but that doesn't make it less appealing. Part of the reason public pleas to eat more salads and fruits fall on deaf ears is that to most people, they just don't taste as good. We love salt, we love sugar, we love fat.

Since we are not talking about eliminating fast food altogether, though, the question is how much more enjoyment people derive from eating

[31] Tinna Laufey Asgeirsdottir, "Do Body Weight and Gender Shape the Work Force? The Case of Iceland," *Economics and Human Biology* 9.2 (March 2011), 148–156; John Cawley, "The Impact of Obesity on Employment," *Journal of Human Resources* 39 (2004), 451–474; S. Morris, "The Impact of Obesity on Employment," *Labour Economics* 14 (2007), 413–433.

larger, rather than smaller, portions. The mere fact that we continue to eat doesn't entail that we are continuing to enjoy it – often we eat absent-mindedly, simply because there is food in front of us, particularly if it is salty.[32] If we had to do something active to get those fries – to put a penny in the table-side dispenser to get each fry rather than paying up front for the whole serving – how many would we buy? And even if we do continue to enjoy as we eat our way through the supersized portion of fries, it seems likely that there will be diminishing marginal returns – we enjoy the fifty-second French fry a lot less than the first. It becomes less and less worth the cost. My guess is that a lot of the eating associated with larger portion sizes is passive eating, the sort we do because it is in front of us. This is presumably augmented by the fact that eating salt makes us crave more salt, something which no amount of fries is going to satisfy, since the last fry, whatever its number in the series, will still leave that salty taste in our mouths. For those few who really are suffering at not having the "rest" of their portion once portion sizes are reduced, a second trip to the counter is always an option. My guess is that most people won't want it, even as now they don't make second trips after finishing whatever portion size is in front of them. As long as portion sizes are within reasonable limits, when you're done you feel you've had enough, just because you're done.

A second issue is the emotional pain we may feel at knowing that our portions are now controlled; and not only controlled, but smaller than they once were. Some people feel this is a significant issue, that consumers will see the move to require smaller portions as unacceptably restrictive. This strikes me as odd, however. I have no control over restaurant portion size as it is now, without there being paternalistic restrictions in place. Yes, I can choose, in a fast food restaurant, to order small, medium, or large, but no one asks me exactly how much I would like; and in other restaurants I am given no choice whatsoever. The waiter brings the food and I discover what exactly I've got. We've never experienced freedom when it comes to portion size, because portion sizes have always been entirely up to the restaurant, so the only thing that changes with portion size regulation is that someone else – an outside agency, not a private business – is making the decision, and furthermore, is making it in order to benefit us, rather than to make a profit. That doesn't seem so daunting. And for what it is worth, we can still exercise our much vaunted freedom;

---

[32] Aside from the fact that we can all attest to this, it has been studied and discussed extensively in Brian Wansink's *Mindless Eating: Why We Eat More Than We Think* (New York: Bantam Books, 2010).

we will be able to choose small, medium, or large orders, but what exactly we will get for that will be different. And if we really want more, we can always return to the counter and order a second portion. We're not so likely to want to, but we can if we want.

Not only does this not constitute a painful loss of control, it will also help us in those areas in which we have complete control – eating at home. Just as larger portion sizes have changed our perception of what constitutes a normal size for a serving, smaller portion sizes should do the same, eventually. This Aristotelian habituation means that portion size regulation in restaurants actually has a more far-reaching beneficial effect than it might at first seem, and we will end up choosing more rationally than before.

After the initial shock when our order of large fries turns out to have only 380 rather than 500 calories (the amounts in medium and large portions of McDonald's fries, respectively, according to the McDonald's website), it seems likely that we will adjust our expectations and won't feel disappointment at seeing a smaller small of fries, or a burger that is not too tall to fit into our mouth. We'll get at least very close to the same enjoyment, won't suffer from a lack of food portion freedom, and will be healthier and more conventionally attractive. Those who pine after the good old days, when you could eat more than your entire daily recommended dose of calories in one fast food meal, will eventually sound like any other set of old people who complain that things have gone down hill since their youth, when the matinee was 75 cents and a candy bar a nickel.

4. *Is it the most efficient way to get people to eat less fatty food?* This, of course, is a controversial question. The most popular approach to overcoming obesity now is education, and it is being pursued vigorously in especially one form, labeling. The basic idea is this: people don't want to be fat. They are fat because they eat more calories than they use in exercise, and they eat more than they should because they don't know how many calories they are consuming. Thus, there has been a lot of emphasis on letting people know how many calories fast foods contain. This is why the Obama health care reform measure includes a requirement that calorie information should be posted in fast food restaurants. The question is whether pointing out the relevant facts will be successful in getting people to change their ways.

It doesn't seem likely. Increasing numbers of researchers in obesity admit that irrationality plays a significant role in our failure to make healthy choices. One problem with fast food may be that weight gain is incremental: no single two-patty burger with cheese is going to endanger your life. Presumably, if we knew we were going to follow our burger and fries with an immediate heart attack, instead of with a deep-fried apple turnover, none of us would eat it, no matter how strong our cravings, just as we won't drink antifreeze, no matter how thirsty. When this meal is only one out of a very long series, though, no one of which strikes the fatal blow, we find it easier to dismiss. Whatever the specific mechanisms may be, there is a growing recognition that poor reasoning plays a role in those who consistently choose what is bad for them. Recent studies tie poor dietary choices to particular cognitive biases of various sorts.[33] Here, as elsewhere, our poor reasoning leads us astray.

Human food consumption and dietary behaviors seem to invalidate conventional economic theory that assumes we each make rational, calculated decisions based on an analysis of the information presented to us. Were we real rational, economic creatures, it would follow, for example, that we eat ice cream sundaes and candy bars only after assessing the utility (including pleasure) that we may gain from that food against the future health consequences. Food consumption, however, is also governed by cravings, emotions, and environmental conditions that create irrational and often unhealthy dietary behaviors.[34]

Indeed, we have experience of food labeling, and it suggests that this just isn't sufficient to change people's eating habits. Labeling on packaged foods, including both calories (typically listed first!) and nutrients, has been around a long time, but as we've seen, people still consume enormous amounts of soda, as well as chips and other forms of high-fat, low nutrition snacks. Some people, of course, don't read labels, and won't read caloric information in restaurants, either. But even when they do, there is some evidence that it doesn't affect what they eat. New York City has had a law requiring that fast food restaurants display calories per portion since 2008, but a recent study suggests this has had no effect: while 57 percent of the people in the study noticed the information, only 9 percent said it influenced their choices, and information from customer receipts shows no difference in purchases before and after labeling.[35]

---

[33] R. Calitri, E. M. Pothos, K. Tapper, J. M. Brunstrom, and P. J. Rogers, "Cognitive Biases to Healthy and Unhealthy Food Words Predict Change in BMI," *Obesity* 18 (2010), 2282–2287; and K. Tapper, E. M. Pothos, and A. D. Lawrence, "Feast your Eyes: Hunger and Trait Reward Drive Predict Attentional Bias for Food Cues," *Emotion* 10 (2010), 949–954.

[34] Cheryl L. Hayne, Patricia A. Moran, and Mary M. Ford, "Regulating Environments to Reduce Obesity," *Journal of Public Health Policy* 25.3–4 (2004), 391–407, at 392.

[35] Brian Elbel, Joyce Gyamfi, and Rogan Kersh, "Child and Adolescent Fast Food Choices and the Influence of Calorie Labeling: A Natural Experiment," *International Journal of Obesity* 35.4 (April 2011), 493–500.

These may be the same people who spend tens of billions of dollars per year on trying to lose weight through Nutrisystems, Weight Watchers, Jenny Craig, Herbalife, thousands of diet books, gym memberships, and machines that will magically jiggle the fat away. The individual eater obviously experiences some disconnect between the goal of losing weight and the choice to eat the 780-calorie Angus bacon and cheese burger with the 560-calorie order of fries and 1,100-calorie shake.

Yet, most people hesitate to try approaches that would actually address the effects of such irrationality. Most often we see recommendation for increased food labeling, and at most more regulation for children, both of advertising of unhealthy food geared to children and control of school food options – but this is a strange response to admitted irrationality. If we don't think clearly, giving us the facts on a food label will not produce a marked change. Perhaps reducing advertising geared towards children will reduce children's desire for unhealthy foods, and probably preventing their access to junk food at school will have some effect – but what about the rest of us? Given our failure to think well when it comes to choosing means to ends, it is not clear how additional education about calories will make us change our ways. Even if labeling has some effect, it seems likely that enforced portion sizes will have much more, without great cost. It's this that has prompted a number of obesity experts to doubt the efficacy of education alone in changing eating patterns.

As public health advocates, we know all too well that teaching the world's population about the dangers of obesity and the need to avoid obesogenic foods that are inexpensive, tasty, and convenient will never work if food corporations are permitted to continue to spend massively to encourage the public to eat more of their products. Efforts to control obesity will have to enlist the public to focus on *behavior*, with a shift from a sole focus on citizens to a new one on the *behavior* of food corporations ... We have come to believe that research studies concentrating on personal behavior and responsibility as causes of the obesity epidemic do little but offer cover to an industry seeking to downplay its own responsibility.[36]

Forcing corporations to downsize food servings is one reasonable approach to helping people who, left to their own autonomous choices, only make themselves worse off. Of course, we can imagine other options: enforced exercise classes, for example, or licenses to buy fattening food

[36] Anthony Robbins and Marion Nestle, "Call for Papers," *Journal of Public Health Policy* 32 (2011), 143–145.

available only to those whose BMI is under 25. These seem a lot more burdensome on the individuals who must undergo them, though, as well as having implementation costs for society as a whole that seem much greater. Of the various options that might actually reduce obesity, reducing portion sizes seems practical, humane, and effective.

Cigarettes

Cigarettes are legal, and there are no efforts being made to make them illegal. We may wonder, though, if that wouldn't be a good idea. It is obvious that we'd have been better off if cigarettes had never been made legal. Who thinks that if such a product were introduced today the FDA would approve it? Further, they seem to present a clear case where irrational thinking plays a role. That the choice to smoke involves a number of cognitive biases has been argued vigorously, and in great detail, by Robert Goodin.[37] Goodin writes that the choice to smoke typically involves the cognitive biases of "wishful thinking" – when we believe something is safe only because we are in fact already engaged in doing it; "anchoring" – falsely assuming that since smoking has not perceptibly hurt us in this one instance, it never will; and "time-discounting" – disproportionately discounting future pains when trading them off against present pleasures.[38] Without these, he argues, no one would choose to pursue an expensive, addictive (and with the expulsion of smokers from many public places, we might add, inconvenient) habit with profound negative effects on health. So, that cigarettes were ever legal was the result of an error – we didn't know the health consequences – compounded by an inability to take the factual knowledge we do have at present and use it effectively.

On the other hand, they were introduced, and so that some people do want to smoke, and depriving them of this will cause both pain and protest. So, should they be banned?

1. *Does the action promote long-term goals?* Smoking is incompatible with some of the most significant long-term ends of the majority of the population. It greatly increases the chances of debilitating illness and premature death. As in the case of trans-fats and obesity, smoking is at odds with the fulfillment of most of our most dearly held desires.

2. *Is it effective?* Many people argue that attempts to ban popular substances, however dangerous, are doomed to failure. They refer to

---

[37] Goodin, "Ethics of Smoking," 574–624.   [38] Ibid., 579.

Prohibition, where a constitutional amendment was not enough to prevent the sale and consumption of alcohol. This is a reasonable concern.
For many people, Prohibition seems to have been a consummate waste of
money, whose only achievement was making criminals rich. The last
thing we want is to provide the basis for cigarette gangs on a par with
drug gangs – not only do such fruitless prohibitions cost money without
eliminating the problem, and enrich people who break the law, but
countless people have been killed in drug violence. These are policies that
don't work.

Cigarettes, however, are different. For most people, alcohol and marijuana don't appear to be as harmful as cigarettes, and we know that. The
illegality of alcohol presumably struck many people during Prohibition as
unjustified, since they were accustomed to drinking without ill effects. On
the other hand, we do accept that smoking is dangerous. A wholesale
exclusion of cigarettes from the market would not strike us as a pointless
exercise, but as something genuinely protective.

This is not to say there would be no black market in cigarettes, at least
initially, or simply cigarettes smuggled in from countries where they are
legal for personal use. Some smokers will want them, because those cravings
are strong. There are markets for things more generally believed to be
harmful, like heroin. There may be also markets for things we all admit to
be harmful that, like cigarettes, are furthermore not initially enjoyable,
although how long such a market would survive after the present gener-
ation of legal smokers fades away is a real question. It seems likely that
illegality would significantly reduce the number of people who smoke.

3. *Do the benefits outweigh the costs?* The question is whether the
enjoyment derived from cigarettes is sufficiently great for that to outweigh
the losses we risk in our other ends.

Since this is a discussion of the paternalistic arguments for making
cigarettes illegal, I won't discuss the claims of third parties who are injured
by other people who smoke, whether it is through second-hand smoke,
higher health costs caused by others who smoke, or financial or emotional
loss from the illness or death of someone who smokes. The question here
is whether we can outlaw cigarettes for the sake of the smoker. Or,
alternatively, do smokers get sufficient benefit from smoking to make this
a rational choice, given their ends? It seems likely that it is not. Cigarettes
appear to be most enjoyable after a person is addicted to them – they are
enjoyable insofar as they satisfy a craving that doesn't exist until after a
person has become a smoker. For those who are not addicted, but
who try smoking anyway, the initial physical experience is usually not at

all pleasant – rather, it is one of nausea, leavened by the occasional coughing fit. After this passes, it is true that smoking is enjoyable for its own sake, or, presumably, people wouldn't continue to smoke, but the strongest pull to smoke seems to occur after people have become addicted to them: the physical pleasure eventually felt by practiced smokers appears to be largely negative, in that it is the elimination of something like a pain, rather than purely enjoyable in itself. This is not to say it isn't pleasant – it's been said that the greatest pleasure is the alleviation of pain. We don't normally think it is worth it to undergo pain just for such pleasures, though – while having someone step on your foot causes a great surge of relief when they get off, we don't seek out heavy people to stomp on us just so we can enjoy their departure. This is presumably why so many not long past the stage of learning how to smoke are trying to quit, going from initiation to satiation with lightning speed – they themselves don't think the pleasure of the cigarette is worth the costs in health and longevity. If future people fail to become addicted to cigarettes, then this pain of deprivation won't be felt, so we don't seem to be in danger of losing a net total of pleasure, given the losses to health (and the pocket) that smoking is likely to cause.

There is no doubt that those already addicted to smoking will suffer if there are no more cigarettes to smoke. For many such people, the gains to their health will be greater than the losses induced by not being able to satisfy the craving for cigarettes, especially since the craving for cigarettes becomes less severe and more infrequent as time passes. For others, it may not – the loss to their health may already be irreparable. This is a real cost. If cigarettes were illegal, though, over time fewer and fewer people would find themselves suffering from this unfulfilled craving. It seems plausible, however, that on the whole the gains of the policy will outweigh the costs for almost all individuals. On the whole, most arguments suggest that we will be better off, as a society, without cigarettes.

4. *Is coercion the most effective way to eliminate smoking?* Our present methods, educating people about the dangers of smoking, and disincentivizing smoking by making it very expensive and very inconvenient, haven't worked sufficiently. The facts about smoking are now drummed into us from an early age, so we can't not know it's dangerous: we learn it every year in school, and we see public service alerts featuring families mourning their departed smoker. And disincentives abound: people can pay $9 per pack, which, at a pack a day, is $3,285 a year. Individuals in many places can't smoke in bars, restaurants, work places, near the doorways of their office buildings, public transportation, campuses, and

now parks, but they still smoke. It's hard to imagine more "soft" paternalistic methods that we could use. And, they have not been without effect: the smoking rate has gone down. However, it is still all too high. In the US it remains at about 20 percent. Even if soft methods were to drive it down to 10 percent, something not even on the horizon, that seems too high: it's a dangerous, expensive habit that doesn't advance anyone's goals. So, why not just make it illegal? Soft paternalistic methods, persuasion, and incentivizing better behaviors have done what they can, but that is not enough. Coercion may be needed to achieve the rest. If this doesn't work, then we can change the laws once again. It seems reasonable to give a ban a try.

The policies discussed above are either ones already proposed or may be seen as extensions of existing practices. I have focused on health regulations, because this is an area in which we have generally recognized the need for coercive paternalism. A long history of banning carcinogens and other harmful substances has shown us that government interference in "choice" – preventing us from opting for foods or drugs that harm us – benefits us without undercutting any substantive sense of control. Indeed, we have come to see such controls as not only permissible but obligatory – a government would be remiss if it allowed toxic substances into our food or medications. Extensions of paternalistic regulations often evoke an emotional reaction, it is true: "[a] longstanding tension, often styled as that between paternalism and individual liberty, pits public health against American individualism."[39] However, reason, when we resort to it, shows that individualism and other such values are not advanced by ill health or early death, nor diminished by protection.

EXTENSIONS

These are just a few of the more obvious cases where paternalist policies either have been, or could be, proposed. Others are under contemplation. Elizabeth Anderson has argued for a nonpaternalistic justification for compulsory donations to retirement programs and health insurance,[40] but I am sympathetic to Peter de Marneffe's claim that it is easier to justify such compulsory actions through paternalistic considerations. The Obama health care program that would require that everyone buy health insurance (while also making it possible for people to do this) is similarly

---

[39] Rachel I. Weiss and Jason Smith, "Legislative Approaches to the Obesity Epidemic," *Journal of Public Health Policy* 25.3–4 (2004), 379.
[40] Elizabeth Anderson, "What is the Point of Equality?," *Ethics* 109 (1999), 287–337.

best justified through paternalistic considerations. It is certainly true that the uninsured present a cost to others who still must pay, indirectly, for emergency care for the uninsured, and who are hurt by the loss of productivity that follows from the lack of heath care for the uninsured. Still, while these costs provide some basis in third-party considerations to force the uninsured to buy insurance, the cost to the third party is certainly not so great as the cost to the individuals themselves. The uninsured are the primary losers from not having health insurance, and the requirement that they get insurance is best seen as a paternalistic plan to benefit them. This is why many critics of mandated insurance see it as an unwarranted intrusion into personal liberty: as US District Judge Henry Hudson said, in declaring the Obama bill unconstitutional, "At its core, this dispute is not simply about regulating the business of health or crafting a scheme of universal health care – it's about individuals' right to choose to participate."[41] Whether or not he's right about the constitutionality of the measure, Hudson has probably correctly described the moral nexus: whether we are allowed to override personal choice in order to benefit the chooser. As always, the suitability of paternalism depends on empirical factors, not all of which are yet known, but there's at least a good prima facie case for mandating insurance. We know that those who are uninsured end up with worse health; we know that good health is a really high priority for most of us; and it is reasonable to think that here, as is often the case in imprudent behavior, cognitive bias plays some role in people's failure to acquire health insurance. We may weigh the near cost (payment) disproportionately more than the far cost (penury, discomfort, death) because the second is farther away; the optimism bias may convince us that the need for health care is distant – old age – because it makes us think we are less likely than most to suffer accidents or other unforeseen events that can cause even the young to need expensive care; inertia can prevent us from changing the status quo, and so forth. Of course, some people are prevented from buying health insurance for straightforward financial reasons – they can't afford it – so it is important that any plan for mandated insurance also addresses this. For those for whom financial availability of insurance is not sufficient to get them to buy, requiring that they do so is very likely the most humane option. And again, forcing individuals to perform such actions for our own sake is less of an imposition than forcing them to act for other people's sake.

---

[41] Commonwealth *v.* Sebelius, 10-cv-00188, US District Court, Eastern District of Virginia (Richmond), p. 32.

Health care, though, is not the only area where government regulation can enhance the pursuit of goals. What constitutes good areas for paternalistic interference will depend on circumstances. For example, it has been suggested that the recent debt crisis and subsequent collapse of the American and European economies can be traced in large part to a deregulation of the credit industry that occurred in the US in the late 1970s. Prior to 1978, banks had been relatively constrained in how much interest they could charge their clients. Since this meant their profit margin was relatively low, they had a greater motivation to extend credit only to those people who were likely to pay back the principal they had borrowed. Following deregulation, banks were allowed to charge much higher interest rates, and thus were eager to extend high-interest, albeit riskier, loans.[42] Higher rates on credit cards were followed by similar deregulation in the mortgage industry.[43] Given their newfound ability to borrow, consumers did borrow, guided in their choices by the cognitive biases that make wishful thinking appear to be sound reasoning. Thus, those that were least likely to be able to pay back their loans were lent money at especially high interest rates, compounding the probability of their defaulting on their debts. Kevin Leicht has studied 2007 bankruptcies and has analyzed whether these families would have been able to run up the same amount of debt if pre-deregulation lending constraints still obtained; he concludes that "the debts of families in bankruptcy would have been dramatically reduced had they lived during the regulated credit market of the 1970s."[44] Thus, for many, bankruptcy might have been avoided.

As long ago as 2003 (that is, before the most recent collapse of the housing industry), Elizabeth Warren argued that we need to reintroduce regulations into the credit industry.

Congress could simply revive the usury laws that served this country since the American Revolution. Federal law could be amended to close the loopholes that let one state override the lending rules of another. Alternatively, Congress could impose a uniform rate to apply across the country. Such a provision would enable the states or the federal government to reimpose meaningful limits on interest rates.[45]

---

[42] This was the result of a Supreme Court decision, Marquette National Bank of Minneapolis *v.* First Omaha Service Corporation (439 US 299 [1978]) that allowed banks to export their credit rates to other states, thus bypassing local state caps on how much interest could be charged.

[43] See Cathy Lesser Mansfield, "The Road to Subprime 'HEL' was Paved with Good Intentions: Usury Deregulation and the Subprime Home Equity Market, *South Carolina Law Review* 51 (spring 2000).

[44] Kevin Leicht, "Borrowing to the Brink: Consumer Debt in America," in *Broke: How Debt Bankrupts the Middle Class*, ed. Katharine Porter (Stanford University Press, 2012), 195–217.

[45] Elizabeth Warren and Amelia Warren Tyagi, *The Two-Income Trap: Why Middle-Class Parents are Going Broke* (New York: Basic Books, 2004), p. 144.

Would requiring lower interest rates be a good idea? According to this reasoning, such legislation would help people avoid running up huge debts. On the other hand, higher interest rates would make it harder for people to buy houses, and to make other purchases that may be important to their living the lives they want to. For myself, I am not sure what the net effect would be in terms of benefit, although it seems plausible to me that such controls would do more good than harm. The point here is that we should be open to the idea that, for paternalistic reasons, we might need to interfere with people's borrowing potential, if that is what works best for them – in the long run. The experience of the last few years does not support the claim that, left to its own devices, the free market will work to the advantage of all concerned: in some cases, no doubt, it does, but in others our propensity to poor instrumental thinking results in everyone being the loser. The Consumer Financial Protection Bureau has recently been started to help consumers in some ways, making it easier to understand the risks they run in incurring certain kinds of debt, on the one hand, and enforcing federal consumer financial laws, on the other. This should be helpful, since it will, for example, make it easier for consumers to compare interest rates, by preventing banks and others from using mystifying language that obscures, rather than discloses, what risk the consumer is running. This may prove to be enough to save consumers from running into destructive debt; on the other hand, it may not, and if not, we may well need to use stronger measures. Here, as in many cases, paternalistic regulations designed to protect individuals from themselves will also have positive consequences for other people. In some cases, benefitting others – or perhaps more specifically, avoiding harms to others – may itself justify constraints on individual action, but in other cases that won't be sufficient, and interference is only justified by the degree of benefit to the individual whose actions are constrained.

Other situations suitable for paternalistic regulation will no doubt be discovered. The point is to remember that paternalistic practices should be considered as acceptable options where they are efficient. Even in the United States, generally greatly protective of individual liberty, there has been a willingness, at times, to adopt coercive measures to achieve obvious goods. Many carcinogens have been banned, even if cigarettes haven't; safety standards in automobiles have been adopted, even though that makes cars more expensive than people might be willing to pay if they had the choice to buy the cheaper, more dangerous car, and will prevent absolutely some people from buying the car they want. And of course there are motorcycle helmet and seat belt laws. We accept paternalism in some cases, but, at times, are uncomfortable in acknowledging that acceptance, and are very uncomfortable about extending it. As we become more familiar with the concept of coercive paternalism, and understand the rationale for it, we will come to welcome it when it is indeed the most effective method for getting what we in fact want. Such laws manifest, rather than deprecate, our regard for the value of human life.

REPRISE: BUT IS THIS HARD PATERNALISM?

In these circumstances, paternalistic intervention is plausible. However, some may argue that it is plausible here precisely because this isn't really hard paternalism; that is, this isn't paternalism of a sort that fails to respect people's autonomy. Indeed, in some cases – notably the New York trans-fats ban – one may ask whether it is paternalism at all. As was discussed in Chapter 1, the terms "hard" paternalism and "soft" paternalism are used in two ways. On the one hand, they are used, as I tend to use them here, to differentiate the *means* a paternalist may use, where hard paternalism forces people to behave in certain ways, and soft paternalism merely persuades or entices them. The terms are also used, we recall, to differentiate the *content* of the paternalistic measure: hard paternalism, in this sense, imposes actions that are not what the agent would voluntarily choose, whereas soft paternalistic methods simply make the agent act in a way that is in accordance with his real wishes, when, because of some significant impediment, he is able to do that. Using forceful methods to prevent someone from simply making a mistake – walking across the bridge he doesn't know is broken – for many people doesn't suggest any real interference with autonomy, since the person's choice to walk across the dangerous bridge isn't really voluntary.

One way of resolving this might be to say it depends on your definition of paternalism, and of hard paternalism, of which there are quite a few. This doesn't really capture the doctrinal issue, though. The question is what we can extrapolate from these examples as to when intervention is justified. It might be argued that these cases don't show much: in the case of the trans-fats ban, I've argued that one reason the ban is costless is that no one has a taste for trans-fats per se, and the pastries, crackers, etc. we do like are still available. So, eliminating it doesn't do anything that is contrary to what we want. In other cases (portion control, cigarettes) we do have a desire that is frustrated, in the sense that people want big stacks of French fries and cigarettes enough to seek them out and consume them, but even there I've argued that much of our jumbo eating is passive, and that while people want cigarettes, they generally want not to want them, and that they are not opposed to the idea of insurance per se. Thus, it may seem that we are not imposing upon people in any way contrary to their own expression of will. If that is true, then they don't provide evidence that it is acceptable to disrespect people's autonomy by preventing them from acting as their own decisions would direct them.

However, the fact that people don't derive a lot of satisfaction from their choices doesn't mean they aren't acting voluntarily when making those choices. Insofar as we are interfering with voluntary actions, we do impede people's autonomy. If we agree that it is rational to interfere with people's autonomous choices here, we may be able to extend that principle to other autonomous actions when the costs and benefits warrant. The question, then, is whether people's choices to smoke, and so forth, are voluntary, not whether it is one from which they will derive a lot of satisfaction, or even net satisfaction.

In Chapter 1 I used the reasoning of John Kleinig to argue that the fact that a choice is not entirely rational does not mean it isn't voluntary.[46] Richard Arneson makes the same point in discussing Joel Feinberg's categorization of acts involving any sort of deviation from pure rationality as involuntary – that this simply casts too wide a net.[47] Very few acts will qualify as voluntary if complete rationality is needed to make them voluntary. So, I will take it as a given here that an irrational choice may nonetheless be a voluntary one. On the other hand, some irrational choices surely aren't voluntary. If the choices of the smoker or the over-eater are so irrational as to qualify as involuntary, the fact that we can permissibly coerce them doesn't show that autonomy need not be respected. It depends on how much, and what kind, of irrationality is involved. Those who successfully claim the insanity defense, for example, have shown that they are too irrational for their actions to be considered voluntary, and thus don't bear responsibility for their actions; similarly, those who are declared incompetent lose the right to make their own decisions without this being considered an invasion of their rights. If smokers, or the obese, are acting involuntarily, our intrusion into their decision-making process is not an argument for the acceptability of intrusions into irrationality more generally.

One argument that such actions are involuntary is that those who do these imprudent things are ignorant, in which case their actions don't count as voluntary. Ignorance is indeed a good excuse: I didn't voluntarily

---

[46] Kleinig, *Paternalism.*   [47] Arneson, "Mill Versus Paternalism," 470–489.

kill someone if I was ignorant of the fact that he was deathly allergic to nuts when I handed him the walnut brownie. I am not a murderer. (Of course, in some cases my ignorance might be culpable, if I should have known about his allergy – in such cases, responsibility is still thought to be mine, even though I intended no harm.) Ignorance doesn't generally seem to be a factor in the cases discussed above, though. It is true that there are those who argue, for example, that we don't know just how many calories fast foods contain.[48] I find this unlikely, in the main: while we don't know the specifics of the calorie content, it's hard to find anyone who doesn't know that a burger and French fries has way, way more calories than a salad, that a salad is good to eat if you want to avoid gaining (or to lose) weight. In my experience women are more aware of calorie content than are men, given the culture, but it's hard to imagine that at this point there are many people who are actually clueless. The facts about cigarettes are now drummed through our heads all through school, and of course are printed on every pack. The one case where ignorance could play a role would be trans-fats. Some people presumably are not aware of the dangers of trans-fats, since this hasn't been the subject of quite as much education and publicity as have the other things discussed here. On the other hand, a good number of people are aware of it, which is why product makers think it is worthwhile to write "No Trans-Fats" in big letters on the front of packages. In this instance, the most likely thing is that for some people, eating trans-fats is truly not voluntary, because they are unaware of its presence in the food or unaware of the dangers attached to it. For others, though, it is voluntary, as we normally construe that – while they don't positively want the trans-fats per se, they are willing to have them in order to eat the packaged food they have a yen for. Trans-fats are not desired for their own sake, but chosen in an informed way – just as in the many common cases where we knowingly choose something we don't want because it is linked to something we do want, like paying a high price for a beautiful dress. While I regret the high price of the dress, my choice to buy it is still voluntary.

The second way these actions might be involuntary is that our thinking is simply so confused that we don't know what we are doing, despite our possession of the facts. Goodin, who argued for the presence of cognitive bias in the choice to smoke, argued that its presence meant the actions in question were involuntary.[49] Part of Goodin's motivation seems to

---

[48] See Alex Rajczi, "A Liberal Approach to the Obesity Epidemic," *Public Affairs Quarterly* 22.3 (July 2008), 269–287.

[49] Goodin, "Ethics of Smoking."

have been that he wanted to make cigarettes illegal, but not being a coercive paternalist, could only justify this by showing that the actions are involuntary. That is understandable, but it doesn't show that smoking is an involuntary act. As we saw in Chapter 1, the presence of irrationality in the form of cognitive bias doesn't make actions involuntary, as we understand that. It would take something greater than our accustomed poor thinking to say that an action is involuntary or that all our bad decisions could be categorized as involuntary ones. There is no evidence that there is more cognitive disfunction involved in smoking than in general, though. It is true that, aside from the involvement of cognitive bias, smoking is addictive, and while this is irrelevant to the voluntariness of the actions of those who choose to smoke in the first place, it clearly affects the motivational structure of those who are already hooked. It's hard to say the drive to smoke is so overwhelming as to make the act involuntary, though; smokers do, after all, have enough control to pick the time and place, exiting the building, bus, airport, and so on, when they need to. Goodin says that we usually regard a state as involuntary if the only way to avoid it is to undergo a pain, but surely that depends on the degree of the pain – the bank teller who gives the robber the money under the threat of a slight pinch is not regarded as having had no choice. We wouldn't forgive someone who broke into stores to steal cigarettes as having acted involuntarily – we don't even excuse drug addicts who do this, and their addiction may be less manageable. So while being a smoker certainly places us under pressure, it's not sufficient pressure for us to regard the person who acts under it as having acted involuntarily. There are actions that are so irrational as to be involuntary, but even smoking, the most likely candidate, doesn't meet the criteria of involuntary action. The other choices discussed here don't even come close.

It is true that when justifying a policy on a cost–benefit basis, it helps if the costs are relatively low. Paternalistic policies, in particular, must benefit the person, all things considered, so naturally it is easier to justify policies when the costs to the individual is not that great, or when the benefit to be gained is very high. This demonstrates the not too surprising fact that paternalism is a humane theory of what constitutes a justified action. It is nonetheless true that what we see in these cases is that coercing someone in order to prevent their performing a voluntary action is OK – permissible, or even obligatory. The reason for intervention is that we don't trust you to choose rightly. We are taking away freedom of choice in these cases because we don't think people will choose well themselves. We don't think preserving your autonomy, your freedom to act based on your own decision, is worth the costs, in part because your decision making is done so badly that your freedom is used very poorly.

So, there are times when hard paternalism – coercive interference – is called for. This is not to say that there is never a time for soft paternalism, for education and persuasion rather than coercion. In some cases, offering incentives may be the more effective method. In Mexico, authorities have decided to fight both childhood disease and truancy by adopting a program known as "Oportunidades," which consists entirely of straight-forward incentives: parents are paid to take their children for check-ups, and for seeing to it that they attend school. The program has been phenomenally successful, and is being copied in a number of other countries.[50] This is a case where incentivizing is more successful than coercion would be, such as prosecuting parents of truants, or those who don't provide sufficient clinic visits or nutrition to their children: law enforcement in Mexico is not terribly efficient for various reasons, and in any case the cost to poor families of fining or incarcerating parents is prohibitive, to say the least. In some situations, then, incentives can make a real difference: the incentive needs to be sufficiently great to the recipi-ent to motivate them (the Oportunidades program increases the income of rural families by about 25 percent; clearly a significant gain) and the alternatives relatively inefficient. Mark Bittman, food guru, has suggested a combination of hard and soft policies to improve American diets: ending government subsidies for processed food, and instead subsidizing both food grown for direct consumption, such as that in small farms, and home cooking; outlawing factory farming on the grounds that it produces tainted meat, eggs, and fish; and taxing the market and sale of unhealthful foods.[51] These programs, in tandem, might have the desired results of getting us to eat healthier food, as well as producing tastier foods we'd enjoy more.

Education, too, can play a positive role. While I have deprecated the ability of education alone to motivate a change in behavior, at least when it comes to merely revealing the likelihood of incremental damage by things we're already fond of and used to using, it can produce some sorts of positive psychological change. For example, education about the harm certain behaviors produce can help people understand just why

[50] "Reaching Mexico's Poorest," *Bulletin of the World Health Organization* 84.8 (2006); Gustavo Nigenda and Luz Maria Gonzales-Robledo, "Lessons Offered by Latin American Cash Transfer Programmes, Mexico's Oportunidades and Nicaragua's SPN: Implications for African Countries," Health Systems Resource Centre, Department for International Development (June 2005).

[51] Mark Bittman, "A Food Manifesto for the Future," *New York Times*, February 2, 2011.

coercive measures are in place, in a way that reduces, or eliminates, their resentment at finding that they've lost certain freedoms. We don't resent finding that our favorite hamburger has been recalled when we're also told there's been an E. coli outbreak at the plant, and we won't resent reduced portion sizes as much when we understand exactly why it's happening. Not only does this reduce one cost of coercion, the sense of infringement; it also makes it more likely such controls can continue: in a democracy, there needs to be general support for a program for it to be able to continue.

CONCLUSION

Finally, even where there is a good paternalistic motivation for interference, we do need to consider the costs to third persons of these interventions. In some cases, it may not be worth it to society to intervene to help people, if doing that is simply too expensive. Sadly, not every need for help can be met. In most of the cases discussed in this chapter, I think the costs to third parties are not so great as to make the paternalistic interventions too big a burden. On the contrary, they will make other people come out ahead. For example, while there will be the costs of enforcement – making sure there are no illegal cigarettes out there – which we will all be paying, there will not be the $96 billion in medical costs that we now pay for smoking-related diseases.[52] These questions, as to whether a paternalistic policy will impose a net cost on others, and if it does, whether it is worth pursuing, will need to be worked out. The point here is that at least we know that such restrictions on behavior are morally justified.

[52] www.cdc.gov/Features/TobaccoControlData

CHAPTER 7

Final justifications

To many, paternalism, no matter how genuinely benevolent, is a frightening prospect. Those who do accept the paternalistic interventions with which we are commonly familiar may do so only grudgingly, as the best of a set of poor alternatives, and reject the idea of adding to them. And then there are those, however rare, who continue to think that all paternalistic constraints are unjustified – who would prefer a world without prescriptions for medicines, seat belts, or limits on interest rates, whatever the human cost. For those who reject any paternalistic attempt to help people avoid the results of their own ignorance or poor choices, no argument may avail: they may have a fundamentally different, and by most lights unrealistic, picture of human ability, and a fundamentally different, and I would argue, morally unjustified, sense that people deserve to suffer for their own mistakes. For those who admit the occasional need for paternalistic intervention, but who are worried about its extension into unsuitable areas of life, there are several things we can keep in mind when we consider whether this is a permissible way to approach people's too frequent failures to get what they want from their lives. These discussions may provide some comfort to those who are worried about such a change in approaching regulation; to those who support paternalism, they simply serve as an elaboration of how paternalism can work and why it is a good idea.

LIMITS

First, we will discover some limits on the sorts of things paternalistic policies can be used for. I have argued that there should be no a priori restrictions on behaviors that can be subject to coercive paternalism, but in some areas it will not be practically feasible, in part because these are areas where we simply don't want it. Consider, for example, love and romance. I have been asked more than once whether paternalism would dictate that we have arranged marriages, rather than choosing our spouse on the basis of (so often ephemeral!) romantic motivations. This is a sensible question. After all, marriage as it proceeds now cannot be regarded as a success. No one who gets married wants the marriage to end in divorce, and yet as we know, half of them do. So, many of us are not getting the outcome we want. And divorce, most of the time, is excruciatingly painful for both parties, before, during, and (for at least a while) after it takes place. For women, it often contributes to a decided downturn in income, from which they may continue to suffer long after the initial pangs of heartbreak have faded. Furthermore, we often have the thought that such failures were predictable: we say, how could they ever have thought it would work, given their complete antimonies of character, values, and style? The pain of divorce and what strikes us as available foreknowledge make it look as if the paternalist would endorse arranged marriages, marriages whose partners would be chosen by reliable professionals after careful review of psychological and sociological factors. It looks as if the paternalist practitioner would make marriage licenses conditional on this sort of background check for both parties, and permission from an appropriate professional, preventing a doomed entry into such a precarious contract. And, of course, many people find this a *reductio* against paternalism, because interference in this most personal area of choice strikes many of us as absolutely repellent, the paradigm of what government ought not to do.

In fact, though, marriage is not an occasion for paternalist interference.[1] For one thing, we just don't know enough. While the couples who "obviously" shouldn't have got together and then proceed to go down in flames stick in our minds, there are probably just as many divorces between people who, from the external eye, looked ideal. And some of those very odd couples do stay together, and not only stay together but are happy. Even professionals don't have the data about long-term compatibility we would need in order to make successful predictions. And then, compatibility in terms of personalities, with all their complexities, is not the only factor relevant to divorce. The way you change over the years, both in character and in health, the patterns of your parents' marriages, the kind of community you are in, your religion, how your career is going,

---

[1] Perhaps we should say not an occasion for more interference than we already have: that there are licenses at all, and the common waiting period between the application for a license and an actual marriage, have some paternalistic justification.

the health and welfare of your kids, whether you're short of money, all these can affect whether you stay together. There is no way we can know all these things before the fact. Any prediction will be, at best, a very broad guess.

Second, and more important, though, is the fact that marriage is a particular kind of choice. I have argued that in many choices external interference won't bother us – we want to reach a certain end, and having someone else constrain the means we can choose is not felt as a burden. Thus, I want to be healthy, and having someone else decide whether eating trans-fats is compatible with that doesn't bother me. I don't particularly value making nutritional food choices per se; I want to enjoy eating and I want to have food that doesn't do me harm, and someone else can do the legwork as to how best to do that. Romance, though, is obviously different. There are cultures where arranged marriages are the norm, and in those situations marriage is presumably thought of differently. In those contemporary cultures that celebrate romance, though, finding, on your own, your true love – going through the early stages of attraction and flirtation, and getting together, suffering the vicissitudes of maturing relationships and break-ups before you end up with "the one" – all these are valued as ends in themselves, so much so that they are probably worth, to us, the possibility of eventual failure. We really enjoy the process, even if the outcome is a failure. Beyond enjoyment, it makes up a large part of the narrative of our lives, and while as I've argued above, it would be a mistake to think these narratives can be completely controlled by our own choices, this is one area where, in western culture, we like to think we are at least in control of our half of the romance. Since good paternalists want to respect your ends, rather than impose what they may think of as more sensible ones upon you, they will take seriously that an enormously significant end for us is to engage in the pursuit of love, with all the ramifications that entails.

It's similar for career choices. One vision of paternalistic societies is that you don't get to choose your own work, but are placed in the job for which you are most suited.[2] Again, the truth is that we don't have the information before the fact to know who will be good at what: we all remember that J. K. Rowling's first Harry Potter book was rejected by twelve publishers, and how Fred Astaire's initial screen test read: "can't

[2] Lois Lowry's *The Giver*, winner of the Newbery Award for the best children's book of 1993, portrays a dystopian paternalist society in which authorities place each individual in a suitable job upon adulthood.

sing, can't act, balding, can dance a little."[3] Even professionals with years of experience and a big investment in accurate judgments can make huge mistakes in predicting someone's success in a given field. And, even where someone does make a poor initial career choice, they can typically change that themselves: people can adjust career goals, going from the early wish to be a doctor to more feasible work as a health technician, from the desire to be prima ballerina at the Bolshoi to satisfaction in being a dance teacher. We don't need to be prevented from ever trying the unsuitable job. Indeed, it may be only trying and failing at their first goal that they are reconciled to pursuing something different, or discover that something different actually makes them happier: advice from others is often not a sufficient dissuasion. For such people, being prevented from trying the field they want to be in by benevolent paternalists isn't necessary, and is costly. Sometimes we need to find out for ourselves. Of course, not everyone is like this: some people have no particular career in mind, and are willing to be pushed in whatever direction works for them, pushed either by the availability of jobs or, indeed, by the advice of others. For those people, though, paternalistic intervention is again not necessary, since they are malleable enough to reconcile themselves to whatever circumstances arise without outside interference. Realistically, a board of paternalists who give the thumbs up to aspiring applicants *á la American Idol* isn't going to happen.

Thus, although no area is exempt from consideration as to whether paternalistic interventions in it might be feasible, we will discover that in the choices nearest and dearest to us, who to form a family with, and where and how to work, no such intervention will be forthcoming. This makes sense: as has been said, we have tended to resist the idea of interference here, and often our "intuitive" resistance to interference in a given area doesn't stem from some insightful judgment that paternalism is inherently wrong or degrading, but from the perception that in some area such interference wouldn't actually be effective. Where participation in the process is itself a large part of the end, interference tends not to be called for. It's this way for a number of endeavors, some insignificant, some extremely important: some people like to cook, and would rather engage in cooking than go to a restaurant and entrust their meal in the hands of expert chefs, even if they might get a better taste experience that

---

[3] According to Wikipedia, Fred Astaire himself reported the evaluation as "Can't sing. Balding. Also dances." In either case, the testers did not recognize that he would be one of RKO's greatest stars, still greatly enjoyable into the next century.

way. Some people like to paint, and they want to make decisions about form and color themselves; they don't want to be restricted to painting by numbers. At least in western culture, at this point in time the engagement in romance seems to be worth the many failures we experience when it comes to outcome. That could change, since the importance of romance has changed in the past. It has become incomparably more important in the past few hundred years than it typically was before that – or at least, it's become much more important as part of the process of acquiring a spouse than it previously was. When it comes to work, the possibilities open to us have always been constrained by personal ability and economic opportunity, but again, within those limitations we seem to prefer taking our chances on a career to having a paternalistic guidance counselor hold the reins. So at present, this emotional engagement takes priority over eventual success, and there isn't a foreseeable future in which paternalistic interventions based on compatibility assessments or talent evaluations will play a role.

COUNTERVAILING CONSIDERATIONS: PATERNALISTIC VIRTUES

There are other considerations that can assuage some of our concerns about the supposed harshness of a paternalistic system. It is true that we may suffer some irritation from the implementation of paternalistic policies, and the paternalist must concede that irritation is irritating, even when in the service of greater overall achievement. However, we should remember that there will be countervailing considerations that will soften the experience of paternalism. Generally, when we've accepted a moral standard, we encourage the development of virtues that make living up to those standards easier. That is, we try to develop attitudes, habits, and emotional orientations that will help us do what we need to do. There is a reasonable expectation that the acceptance of the justification for pater-nalism will encourage the development of some such concomitant virtues. These are virtues that will both help us in being good paternalists and make the experience of its restrictions more palatable.

The duty to aid: compassion

For one thing, our judgments of others, and of ourselves, will be softened. Many of those who argue against paternalism do this, as we know, on the grounds that it is disrespectful of the autonomy of those who are so restricted by paternalistic actions. There, is, though, another theme that is persistently sounded, which is that those who fail to do what is good for them deserve to suffer. If we assume that we are all rational choosers, who typically take the best means to our ends, then the conclusion is that those who end up sick and poor either wanted that (or, to put it more accurately, wanted cheap thrills more than they wanted physical or financial health) or were victims of some sort of vice of character that undercut their rationality: they were subject to untrammeled passions or weakness, or some sort of negligent inattention to possible outcomes. We are then free to blame people who do imprudent things, because they have got what they asked for, and their suffering is only fair. This, in turn, serves to excuse our failing to help them: we tell ourselves that those who have somehow injured themselves deserve to suffer for having made foolish decisions. There are some who think we positively should not help those who are, through their own actions, in bad shape, because to help them would violate some retributive principle of fair desert, and furthermore encourage others to live lives of similar short-sightedness (since there will be no salutary lesson [others' suffering] to frighten them into more prudent ways). Others think that we may help them if we choose, but that we have no duty to do so, since their plight is their own fault; if we believe this, as soon as helping is at all costly to ourselves we are likely to give up what we already regarded as supererogatory acts of charity.

At the same time, those who have taken such imprudent actions are encouraged to be ashamed of themselves. Since needing help is thought to be proof of bad character, those in need do correspondingly (often) lose self-esteem when they recognize that they have done something greatly imprudent. This is at the least painful, and worse, such a loss of confidence may lead to greater feelings of helplessness, and a corresponding failure to try to help themselves. Accepting their (putatively) culpable flaws makes them worse off.

The acceptance that we naturally suffer from frailty of judgment, however, changes the way we view people who make mistakes. It gives us less (or no) grounds to condemn those who err. People who end up in foreclosure, for example, may strike us less as wastrels than as victims of forces beyond their control, and when people have been hurt by forces beyond their control we sympathize rather than condemn – hence our immediate concern for people hit by tsunamis or earthquakes. And, it allows those who make mistakes to think differently about themselves. Rather than feeling we should be ashamed of our undue optimism, or whatever has spurred us to imprudent action, we realize that such errors are not a function of a culpable lack of willpower but rather of the way our brains typically work. Some of us, sometimes, have help in avoiding the pitfalls of bad choice, and some of us don't. Some of us are lucky, and some are not. When we move a tendency to failure from the category of vice – foolishness, laziness – to one of a cognitive deficit, we are much more prone to empathize with those who suffer from it. To take an example from a different cognitive area, there was a time students were simply dismissed as lazy or stupid if they had unusually great difficulty in learning to spell or read as well as their peers. Much more recently we have recognized the existence of learning disabilities, where through a trick of the brain some of us have a much harder time than others reading letters, or putting letters together, or remembering sequences. Now such students are identified and helped, because we recognize that they are not responsible for their particular difficulties, and feel bad for them, rather than contemptuous. Similarly, once we recognize that these are errors that have been visited upon us rather than chosen, our treatment of frailty in others should be governed not by disdain but by sympathy and a recognition that help is due. When we take poor instrumental reasoning as a reason for paternalistic intervention, it does allow for coercive interference; this would be accompanied by a more general recognition that compassion, rather than condemnation, is called for when we deal with natural human errors. Along with this comes a justification for a positive duty to aid those who have suffered the effects of such errors.

Recognition that we are all prone to mistakes: humility

It is, further, good for us to recognize our own frailty. It's good when we are deciding how other people should be treated, and it's good when we are deciding what we should do ourselves. When we contemplate constraining others, we need to recognize that our ability to take in the facts correctly, and to choose appropriate means in addressing a problem, is also open to error. My own certainty that I am right, clung to in the face of all countervailing evidence, is something that leads me astray, and it will help me to have a general recognition that my subjective feeling of conviction is not itself strong evidence that I am right. It is hard to take in evidence of our own frailty: for many of us, an initial feeling of certainty is enough to convince us that our choice is correct. This is something we seem only gradually to be coming to realize in the realm of criminal law, for example. It has taken a great deal to convince us that eyewitness testimony is not the most reliable: what could be more convincing than evidence of the person who actually saw what happened? We have learned, though, about the mistakes that often accompany such "first-hand" evidence, even though we are still waiting for the courts to react in the face of the extensive research attesting to this fact.[4] Confidence in our own ability to leap to the truth without reflection on suitable evidence has led to countless injustices: developing appropriate self-skepticism will help us be more discriminating in what we come to trust.

Learning to distrust ourselves; learning to undercut our pride in our infallibility; learning to be, in short, a bit more humble will be an improvement in the way we deal with ourselves and the way we deal with others. When humility is appropriate, it is a virtue. The more we recognize our weaknesses of reason, the more we can try to circumvent them. While the recognition that we fail frequently in reasoning justifies interfering in people's decisions for their own sake, it also entails that we approach this carefully, searching out errors of our own judgment when we are making paternalistic laws. We can learn to exercise more caution than we have hitherto done in the prosecution of all laws, whether these are laws to others from an individual's actions or to protect the individuals from themselves. Such humility will benefit us all.

AUTONOMY REVISITED

We need to reflect, finally, on what reasons led us to value unconstrained freedom of action – autonomy – in the first place. From Kant to the present, people have justified deference to individual choice by reference to rational agency. That we are rational agents, and that the choice of rational agents must be respected, has been something of a litany. Much of the discussion has centered on the rationality of ends – on whether some goals are inherently more rational than others, or whether what end it is rational to pursue is simply a function of our individual desires. This issue about the rationality of ends has differentiated the vastly influential traditions of Immanuel Kant and David Hume; and with that, their different notions of morality. Proponents of both positions seem to have taken it for granted, though, that once we have discovered the appropriate ends, using our reason to choose the appropriate means to those ends is unproblematic: we can be assumed to be rational enough when it comes to taking in relevant facts, assessing relevant strategies, and choosing what

---

[4] See, for example, Gary L. Wells and Elizabeth A. Olson, "Eyewitness Testimony," *Annual Review of Psychology* 54 (2003), 277–295; and Patricia Williams, "Our Dangerous Devotion to Eyewitness Testimony," *Nation*, January 18, 2012 (print edition, February 6, 2012), www.thenation.com/article 1165725l/

best will get us where we have decided to go. Our instrumental rationality is taken for granted. Just what defenders of rationality mean when they talk about the ability to reason is not always clear, of course – there is a tendency to avoid acknowledgement of actual psychological evidence as to how we in fact think, as if mere empirical evidence is irrelevant to our conception of what rational agency would consist in, or how we measure up to that. Whatever defenders of rational agency may have in mind, though, when they think of rational agency, they need to acknowledge that actual humans reason badly in some very significant circumstances. Not always, of course: we are rational at many times, and in many ways. We are often good at figuring out means to ends; we are often good at assessing value. Sometimes, though, we are really bad at this; not just because we are not trying, but because our abilities are limited. Insofar as the argument for autonomy is based on respect for a supposed ability to make almost infallible decisions as to means, it should be amended.

That the major argument for respecting autonomous choice is that we are rational agents does not entail that if we are not so rational, there is no reason to value autonomy, to be sure – there may be other reasons to value it. There is usually some significant instrumental value in allowing people to direct their own actions: often, it will be the most efficient way of their pursuing their long-term ends; sometimes it gives people a sense of satisfaction; sometimes it gives them a sense of self-respect. All these are important. But sometimes it is disastrous, and leads people away from the satisfaction of their desires. The fact that we can reason well in some circumstances does not undercut the need for help. It's as if someone were trying to swim the English Channel, but failing: the fact that she is a really good swimmer under many circumstances doesn't mean that when we look at her and see that here she is floundering we should say "she can often swim well, so let's not help her out here just because she is sinking." Freedom to act can lead to long-term disasters. So, while there indeed may be reasons to value people's being able to act on their own decisions, at other times any positive value is outweighed by other considerations.

Self-conception

It is sometimes said, too, that even if we are not entirely rational, we need to think of ourselves that way: it is part of our very self-conception that we are rational agents. Again, how true this is depends on exactly what we mean by "rational." We obviously can't help but think of ourselves as people who think and choose, because we can't help but think and choose. (And since we can't help but think of ourselves this way, it's not endangered by any recognition of ourselves as occasionally fallible.) It is also trivially true that we believe what we believe: at any given moment when we've come to a decision about what is right, we think our decision is right. None of this means that our self-conception requires that we are always right, nor that our self-conception means we should never be interfered with. Indeed, I doubt that for most people their self-conception is based primarily on an idea of themselves as rational agents. It's more complicated than that. People identify with many traits that have nothing to do with reasoning: what town they live in (and how its sports team does), how they look, talents they've inherited, characteristics of person-ality that demarcate them from others, peculiarities of taste. Some people feel pride and self-worth in having an unusual disease (at least, if it isn't too severe) or an especially problematic digestion, or a weird allergy. Of course, our self-conception involves being *conscious*, but this doesn't entail that we exclusively identify with our reasoning: for most people, reasoning in the sense of decision making is part of a package, along with our likes and dislikes, interpersonal attachments, and so forth. And we can gener-ally stand some degree of emendation in any of these aspects of self-conception. What we value about ourselves is much more varied than the proponents of rationality (possibly a subset of people who do pride themselves especially on their mental acuity) would acknowledge.

And then there may be proponents of rationality who really think, not so much that our self-conception is grounded in a picture of ourselves as rational agents, but that our self-conception *ought* to be grounded in our rational agency. They may feel that it is our rationality, and only ration-ality, that gives us worth. This, though, is a highly problematic assertion, and as I've argued, the claim doesn't hold up well if it entails that we take pride in a kind of, or degree of, rationality that we don't actually possess.

Control

It is also suggested that my self-conception is that of a chooser, someone who has a life plan that she makes up for herself, and who takes actions to that end herself, thus constructing her own life. It is this self-control, it is suggested, that gives me a sense of myself as a distinctive and valuable being. Some, of course, identify the possibility of self-control with an internal rationality that subjugates nonrational parts of the self. This picture of agency is perhaps dated, but even if we don't buy into this old-fashioned picture of the internal power dynamic of a bipartite soul, it may seem essential to my living my own life that I am in control of my actions. After all, we may feel that if someone else controls me, it is no longer really my life, but the life of whoever controls me. I will be doing what someone else wants me to do, and there will thereby be a disconnect between my life as it is lived and my life as I envision it.

As I have discussed in Chapters 2 and 3, though, this picture is too simple. What matters is not so much that external forces restrict my actions as the way they restrict them. There are choices I don't much care about, and where indeed I may welcome someone else's being in control: it is not up to me to determine what constitutes sufficient purity in the water I drink from the tap, and that is fine with me, as long as someone competent makes that determination and the water district does what it should. Every medication I put into my body has been controlled by someone else – I am forcibly prevented from buying stuff that hasn't been checked out by the federal government, and thank God for that. Medication can be quite intimate, but I want someone else involved. It is neither possible nor desirable that we should live in ways that are free of other people's decisions. None of this undercuts my sense of self. At the same time, freedom can sometimes undercut that sense. When I choose badly, the freedom to act autonomously can give me a sense of failure, and can lead me to despise myself for the hash I have made of my life. And the results of such decisions can make me feel conspicuously out of control: who, in the grip of a serious illness, feels in control of their life, even if it was their decision to smoke that brought them to this pass? Who, in financial foreclosure due to amassing too much debt, feels that they can now create a future in line with their own values? Freedom of choice can undercut the sense of control, for the simple fact that it can result in our actually losing control. To see oneself as in charge of one's own future at this point would be delusional.

When it comes to respect for autonomy, we can see that our belief that autonomous actions should not be interfered with was based on a mistake. We have been used to thinking of such actions as the expression of our true selves, bringing our desires to fruition in a way no outside agency could duplicate. It turns out this often isn't so. We are not as smart as we thought we were; or, at least, not as smart in every area. We have scientific proof of this, and indeed, upon reflection such actions may cohere more with personal experience than the alternative explanation for certain behaviors, that those who choose poorly are, all of them, morally remiss. We need to move on with a more realistic psychological conception if we are to create the world we want.

INTUITIONS, AND WHAT THEY ARE WORTH

Paternalism will be limited in its use by some of our underlying commitments to the process of choice in some areas. It will also be accompanied by the development of virtues that will make us both more kind and more accurate in our assessment of the need for help. It rests on a realistic picture of human decision making. It is true, though, that many people will react to this with a strong intuition that interference in the choices of competent adults just must be wrong. What should we do when we have recalcitrant intuitions? There will be many. We (often) just don't like the idea of interference. Furthermore, even as we will have to yield some control over ourselves, paternalism, as suggested above, is likely to generate greater duties towards others. While I have generally argued for the permissibility of paternalistic interference, in some cases the same argument will justify at least a prima facie obligation to help others. Only the most misanthropic would deny an obligation to inform Mill's walker that crossing the bridge before him end in his injury or death; now, it is argued, we probably have to take some more robust steps to save him. Here, as in all duties to others, there will be a complicated calculus of costs and benefits in individual cases as well as the overall feasibility of aid to others as a policy. All of these are changes in our way of thinking, both about what is permissible and what is obligatory, and we don't like change. We tend to think, naturally, that our present beliefs are correct, and that our present ways of doing things are the right ones. Psychologists tell us that even in the face of pretty obvious failure, we will try to come up with explanations as to why our present institutions are good.[5] At the same time, while, as said, it is trivially true that of any given belief, we believe it to be true, it is also true that if we think of the set of our beliefs as a whole, we recognize that some of them are likely to be false. This is a case where we need to assess our beliefs; more specifically, those non-empirical beliefs about morality that we often call intuitions.

Not all intuitions are equal. While in the long run we need to rely on intuition at some point, this is not to say that it is always legitimate to use an intuition to refute an argument. In gauging whether an intuition is to be held to or not, there is a difference in those that are more justified and those that are less. The key is not how strongly you feel a given intuition,

[5] John T. Jost, Mahzarin R. Banaji, and Brian A. Nosek, "A Decade of System Justification Theory: Accumulated Evidence of Conscious and Unconscious Bolstering of the Status Quo," *Political Psychology* 25.6 (December 2004), 881–919.

but how it coheres with other intuitions. So, intuitions should be analyzed, and held to be justified or not, in the way that we generally weigh beliefs. Some of my beliefs are harder to give up than others – I hold to some more strongly, for various sorts of reasons. But a rational person will see how that strongly held belief fits in with other beliefs. If I look up from my desk in the night and catch a swift glimpse of white disappearing into a wall, I may feel really strongly that I've seen a ghost. But I should check that initial conviction to see if that coheres with my other beliefs – the other person in the room with me is rational, and honest, and he says they didn't see it; I've been exhausted and without sleep, and I've read Gary Paulsen's description of hallucinating after days racing in the Iditarod;[6] I have always been a materialist, and have many beliefs that cohere with materialism, and so forth. Even the vivid first-person experience may not justify my believing I saw a ghost, no matter how real it looked to me at the time. Insofar as I am rational, I can see that the vividness of my experience, and the immediate degree of certainty I feel about its verisimilitude, doesn't stand up to examination. "Intuition" is just a word we use for a certain kind of belief, and insofar as we are rational we know that it is prudent to subject our beliefs to scrutiny when there are good arguments against them.

CONCLUSION

I think that on reflection, even recalcitrant intuitions about autonomy will yield to the conclusion that coercive paternalism is justified in many cases we might previously have rejected. We can leave people to suffer the effects of their errors, errors that can ruin their lives, or we can intervene. Coercive paternalism is humanitarian, engages us in the social interaction of mutual aid, and, finally, reflects the value of human choice, since it helps individual to reach the goals they have set for themselves. It's a policy whose value we need, finally, to acknowledge.

---

[6] Gary Paulsen, *Winterdance: The Fine Madness of Running the Iditarod* (New York: Harcourt Brace, 1994).

Select bibliography

Anderson, Elizabeth, "What is Equality For?," *Ethics* 109 (1999), 287–337.

Arpaly, Nomy, *Unprincipled Virtue: An Inquiry into Moral Agency* (Oxford University Press, 2003).

Ariely, Dan, *Predictably Irrational: The Hidden Forces that Shape our Decisions* (New York: Harper Perennial, 2010).

Arneson, Richard, "Mill Versus Paternalism," *Ethics* 90 (July 1980), 470–489.

Asch, S. E., "Opinions and Social Pressure," *Scientific American* 193 (1955), 31–35.

"Studies of Independence and Conformity," *Psychological Monographs* 79.9 (1956), 1–70.

Banaji, Mahzarin R., and R. Bhasker, "Implicit Stereotypes and Memory: The Bounded Rationality of Social Beliefs," in *Memory, Brain, and Belief*, ed. Daniel Schacter and Elaine Scarry (Cambridge Mass.: Harvard University Press, 2000), pp. 139–175.

Banaji, Mahzarin R., and Nilanjana Dasgupta, "The Consciousness of Social Beliefs: A Program of Research on Stereotyping and Prejudice," in *Metacognition: Cognitive and Social Dimensions*, ed. V.Y. Yzerbyt, G. Lories, and B. Dardenne (London: Sage, 1998), pp. 157–170.

Bell, David, "Regret in Decision-Making Under Uncertainty," *Operations Research* 30 (1982), 961.

Benn, S.I., "Freedom, Autonomy, and the Concept of a Person," *Proceedings of the Aristotelian Society* 76 (1976), 109–130.

"Privacy, Freedom, and Respect for Persons," in *Philosophical Dimensions of Privacy*, ed. Frederick Schoeman (Cambridge University Press, 1984), pp. 223–244.

Berlin, Isaiah, "John Stuart Mill and the Ends of Life," in *Four Essays on Liberty* (Oxford University Press, 1969), pp. 173–206.

Berns, Gregory S., Jonathan Chappelow, Caroline F. Zink, Giuseppe Pagnoni, Megan E. Martin-Skurski, and Jim Richards, "Neurobiological Correlates of Social Conformity and Independence during Mental Rotation," *Biological Psychiatry* 58.3 (2005), 245–253.

Bittman, Mark, "A Food Manifesto for the Future," *New York Times*, February 2, 2011; http//opinionator.blogs.nytimes.com/2011/02/01/a-food-manifesto-for-the-future

Bloustein, Edward J., "Privacy as an Aspect of Human Dignity," *New York University Law Review* 39 (1964), 962–1007.

Brafman, Ori and Rom, *Sway: The Irresistible Pull of Irrational Behavior* (New York: Doubleday, 2008).

Brennen, Samantha, "Paternalism and Rights," *Canadian Journal of Philosophy* 24.3 (1994), 419–439.

Brin, David, *The Transparent Society: Will Technology Force Us to Choose Between Privacy and Freedom?* (New York: Perseus, 1998).

Brock, Dan, "Paternalism and Autonomy," *Ethics* 98 (1988), 550–565.

"Paternalism and Promoting the Good," in *Paternalism*, ed. Rolf Sartorius (Minneapolis: University of Minnesota Press, 1983), pp. 239–260.

Brownell, Kelly, T. Farley, W. Willett, B. Popkin, F. Chaloupka, J. Thompson, and L. David, "The Public Health and Economic Benefits of Taxing Sugar-Sweetened Beverages," *New England Journal of Medicine* 361 (October 15, 2009), 1599–1605.

Buckley, F.H., *Fair Governance* (Oxford University Press, 2009).

Burton, Robert A., *On Being Certain: Believing You are Right Even When You're Not* (New York: St. Martin's Griffin, 2008).

Calitri, R., E. M. Pothos, K. Tapper, J. M. Brunstrom, and P. J. Rogers, "Cognitive Biases to Healthy and Unhealthy Food Words Predict Change in BMI," *Obesity* 18 (2010), 2282–2287.

Camerer, Colin, and Dan Llavallo, "Overconfidence and Excess Entry: An Experimental Approach," *American Economic Review* 89 (1999), 306–318.

Christman, John, "Autonomy and Personal History," *Canadian Journal of Philosophy* 21 (1991), 1–24.

Cialdini, Robert B., "Crafting Normative Messages to Protect the Environment," *Current Directions in Psychological Science* (August 2003), 105–109.

Dahl, Norman O., "Paternalism and Rational Desire," in *Paternalism*, ed. Rolf Sartorius, (Minneapolis: University of Minnesota Press, 1983), pp. 261–271.

Darwall, Stephen, "The Value of Autonomy and Autonomy of the Will," *Ethics* 116.2 (January 2006), 263–284.

Dasgupta, Nilanjana, Mahzarin R. Banaji, and Robert P. Abelson, "Group Entativity and Group Perception: Associations Between Physical Features and Psychological Judgment," *Journal of Personality and Psychology* 77 (1999), 991–1003.

Daynard, Richard A., Tom P. Howard, and Cara L. Wilking, "Private Enforcement: Litigation as a Tool to Prevent Obesity," *Journal of Public Health Policy* 25.3–4 (2004), 408–417.

DeJoy, David M., "The Optimism Bias and Traffic Accident Risk Perception," *Accident Analysis and Prevention* 21.4 (1989), 333–340.

De Marneffe, Peter, "Avoiding Paternalism," *Philosophy and Public Affairs* 34.1 (2006), 68–94.

Donner, Wendy, *The Liberal Self: John Stuart Mill's Moral and Political Philosophy* (Ithaca, NY: Cornell University Press, 1991).

Dworkin, Gerald, "Moral Paternalism," *Law and Philosophy* 24.3 (May 2005), 305–319.

"Paternalism," in *Paternalism*, ed. Rolf Sartorius (Minneapolis: University of Minnesota Press, 1983), pp. 19–34.

"Paternalism, Some Second Thoughts," in *Paternalism*, ed. Rolf Sartorius (Minneapolis: University of Minnesota Press, 1983), pp. 105–123.

The Theory and Practice of Autonomy (Cambridge University Press, 1988).

" What is a Good Life?," *New York Review of Books* (February 10, 2011), 41–43.

Elbel, Brian, Joyce Gyamfi, and Rogan Kersh, "Child and Adolescent Fast Food Choices and the Influence of Calorie Labeling: A Natural Experiment," *International Journal of Obesity* 35.4 (April 2011), 493–500.

Elbel, Brian, Rogan Kersh, Victoria Briscoll, and L. Beth Dixon, "Calorie Labeling and Food Choices: A First Look at the Effects on Low-Income People in New York City," *Health Affairs* 28.6 (November–December 2009), 1110–1121.

Elster, Jan, *Rational Choice* (New York University Press, 1986).

Solomonic Judgments (Cambridge University Press, 1989).

Sour Grapes (Cambridge University Press, 1985).

Etzioni, Amitai, *The Limits of Privacy* (New York: Basic Books, 1999).

Feinberg, Joel, "The Child's Right to an Open Future," in *Whose Child? Children's Rights, Parental Authority, and State Power*, ed. William Aiken and Hugh Lafollette (Totowa, N. J.: Littlefield, Adams & Co., 1980).

Harm to Self: The Moral Limits of the Criminal Law (Oxford University Press, 1986).

"Legal Paternalism," in *Paternalism*, ed. Rolf Sartorius (Minneapolis: University of Minnesota Press, 1983), pp. 3–18.

Fine, Cordelia, *A Mind of its Own: How Your Brain Distorts and Deceives* (New York: W. W. Norton, 2008).

Fried, Charles, "Privacy," *Yale Law Journal* 77 (1968), 475–493; reprinted in Frederick Schoeman, ed., *Philosophical Dimensions of Privacy* (Cambridge University Press, 1984), pp. 203–222.

Gaylin, Willard, and Bruce Jennings, *The Perversion of Autonomy* (Washington, D.C.: Georgetown University Press, 2003).

Greening, Leilani, and Carla C. Chandler, "Why it Can't Happen to Me: The Best Rate Matters, But Overestimating Skill Leads to Underestimating Risk," *Journal of Applied Social Psychology* 27 (1997), 760–780.

Gilovich, T., and V.H. Medvec, "The Experience of Regret," *Psychological Review* 102 (1995), 379–395.

Glaeser, Edward L., "Paternalism and Psychology," *University of Chicago Law Review* 73.1 (winter 2006), 133–156.

Goodin, Robert, "Ethics of Smoking," *Ethics* 99.3 (April 1989), 574–624.

Gostin, Lawrence, "Part I: Law as a Tool to Advance the Community's Health," *Journal of the American Medical Association* 283 (2000), 2837–2841.

"Part II: Public Health Powers and Duties," *Journal of the American Medical Association* 283 (2000), 2979–2984.

"Part III: Public Health Regulation: A Systemic Evaluation," *Journal of the American Medical Association* 283 (2000), 3118–3122.

Gray, John, "Mill's Conception of Happiness," in *J. S. Mill, "On Liberty": In Focus*, ed. John Gray and G. W. Smith (London and New York: Routledge, 1991).

Griffin, Dale, and Amos Tversky, "The Weighing of Evidence and the Determinants of Confidence," in *Heuristics and Biases: The Psychology of Intuitive Judgment*, ed. Thomas Gilovich, Dale Griffin, and Daniel Kahneman (Cambridge University Press, 2002).

Griffin, James, *Well-Being: Its Meaning, Measurement, and Moral Importance* (Oxford University Press, 1986).

Hall, C. A., "Anti-Anti-Anti-Paternalism," *New York University Journal of Law and Liberty* 2 (2007), 444–457.

Hallinan, Joseph T., *Why We Make Mistakes* (New York: Broadway, 2010).

Hart, H. L. A., *Law, Liberty, and Morality* (Oxford University Press, 1963).

Hayne, Cheryl L., Patricia A. Moran, and Mary M. Ford, "Regulating Environments to Reduce Obesity," *Journal of Public Health Policy* 25.3/4 (2004), 391–407.

Holland, Stephen, "Public Health Paternalism: A Response to Nys," *Public Health Ethics* 2.3 (2009), 294–298.

Jolls, Christine, Cass R. Sunstein, and Richard Thaler, "A Behavioral Approach to Law and Economics," *Stanford Law Review* 50.5 (May 1998), 1471–1550.

Jost, John T., Mahzarin R. Banaji, and Brian A. Nosek, "A Decade of System Justification Theory: Accumulated Evidence of Conscious and Unconscious Bolstering of the Status Quo," *Political Psychology* 25.6 (December 2004), 881–919.

Kahneman, Daniel, and Amos Tversky, eds., *Choices, Values, and Frames* (Cambridge University Press, 2000).

  "Intuitive Prediction: Biases and Corrective Procedures," in *Judgment Under Uncertainty: Heuristics and Biases*, ed. D. Kahneman, A. Tversky, and P. Slovic (Cambridge University Press, 1979), pp. 414–421.

  "The Psychology of Preferences," *Scientific American* 246 (1972), 160–173.

Kahneman, Daniel, J. L. Knetsch, and Richard Thaler, "Experimental Tests of the Endowment Effect and the Coase Theorem," *Journal of Political Economy* 98 (1990), 1325–1348.

Kalish, Charles, "Reasons and Causes: Children's Understanding of Conformity to Social Rules and Physical Laws," *Child Development* 69.15 (1998), 706–720.

Kleinig, John, *Paternalism* (Totowa, N. J.: Rowman & Allanheld, 1984).

Klucharev, Vasily, "Reinforcement Learning Signal Predicts Social Conformity," *Neuron* (January 15, 2009), 140–151.

Korobkin, Russell, "Inertia and Preference in Contract Negotiation: The Psychological Power of Default Rules and Form Terms," *Vanderbilt Law Review* 51 (November 1998), 1587.

Kraut, Richard, *What is Good and Why: The Ethics of Well-Being* (Cambridge, Mass.: Harvard University Press, 2007).

Leth, T., H. G. Jensen, A. A. Mikkelson, and A. Bysted, "The Effect of Regulation on Trans-Fatty Acids Content in Danish Food," *Atherosclerosis Supplements* 7.2 (2006), 53–56.

Lively, Jack, "Paternalism," in *Royal Institute of Philosophy Lecture Series* 15, *Of Liberty*, ed. A. Phillips Griffiths (Cambridge University Press, 1983), pp. 147–165.

Madrian, Brigitte, and Dennis Shea, "The Power of Suggestion: Inertia in 401(k) Participation and Savings Behavior," *Quarterly Journal of Economics* 116.4 (2001), 1149–1187.

Mehta, Ravi, Joandrea Hoegg, and Amitav Chakravarti, "Knowing Too Much: Expertise Induced False Recall Effects in Product Comparison," *Journal of Consumer Research* (October 2011), 535–554.

Meyers, Diana T., *Self, Society, and Personal Choice* (New York: Columbia University Press, 1989).

Mill, John Stuart, *On Liberty* (1859); reprinted in *Utilitarianism and On Liberty*, Meridian British Philosophers Series, ed. Mary Warnock (New York: World Publishing, 1971).

  Utilitarianism (1863); reprinted in *Utilitarianism and On Liberty*, Meridian British Philosophers Series, ed. Mary Warnock (New York: World Publishing, 1971).

  Collected Works of John Stuart Mill, ed. J. M. Robson (University of Toronto Press and London: Routledge & Kegan Paul, 1977).

Morrill, Allison C., and Christopher D. Chinn, "The Obesity Epidemic in the United States," *Journal of Public Health Policy* 25.3–4 (2004), 353–366.

Mozaffarian, Dariush, Michael F. Jacobson, and Julie S. Greenstein, "Food Reformulation Reduces Trans-Fatty Acids," *New England Journal of Medicine* 362 (May 27, 2010), 2031–2039.

Nagel, Thomas, *Concealment and Exposure* (Oxford University Press, 2002).

Nielson, S. J., and B. M. Popkin, "Patterns and Trends in Food Portion Sizes, 1977–1998," *Journal of the American Medical Association* 289.4 (2003), 450–453.

Nussbaum, Martha, *Women and Human Development: The Capabilities Approach* (Cambridge University Press, 2000).

Nys, Thomas, "Paternalism in Public Health Care," *Public Health Ethics* 1 (2008), 64–72.

O'Donoghue, Ted, and Matthew Rabin, "Procrastination in Preparing for Retirement," in *Behavioral Dimensions of Retirement Economics*, ed. Henry Aaron (Washington, DC: Brookings Institute, 1999).

Oshana, Marina, "Autonomy and the Question of Authority," *Social Theory and Practice* 33.3 (July 2007), 411–429.

  "Autonomy and Self-Identity," in *Autonomy and the Challenges to Liberalism*, ed. John Christman and Joel Anderson (Cambridge University Press, 2005), pp. 77–97.

  "How Much Should We Value Autonomy?," *Social Philosophy and Policy* (2003), 99–126.

"Personal Autonomy and Society," *Journal of Social Philosophy* 29.1 (spring 1998), 81–102.

Pelham, Brett W., and William B. Swann, Jr., "From Self-Conception to Self-Worth: On the Sources and Structures of Global Self-Esteem," *Journal of Personality and Social Psychology* 57.4 (1989), 672–680.

Powell, Connie Davis, "'You already have zero privacy. Get over it.' Would Warren and Brandeis Argue for Privacy for Social Networking?," *Pace Law Review* 31.1 (winter 2011), 146–180.

Priest, Graham, "Contradiction, Belief, and Rationality," *Proceedings of the Aristotelian Society* 86 (1985/6), 99–116.

Rachlinski, Jeffrey J., "Cognitive Errors, Individual Differences, and Paternalism," *University of Chicago Law Review* 73 (2006), 207.

Rainbolt, George W., "Prescription Drug Laws: Justified Hard Paternalism," *Bioethics* 3 (1989), 45–58.

Rajczi, Alex, "A Liberal Approach to the Obesity Epidemic," *Public Affairs Quarterly* 22.3 (July 2008), 269–287.

Raz, Joseph, *The Morality of Freedom* (Oxford University Press, 1986).

Regan, Donald H., "Paternalism, Freedom, Identity, and Commitment," in *Paternalism*, ed. Rolf Sartorius (Minneapolis: University of Minnesota Press, 1983), pp. 113–138.

Ritov, L., and Baron, J., "Status-quo and Omission Biases," *Journal of Risk and Uncertainty* 5 (1992), 49–61.

Rolls, B.J., "The Supersizing of America: Portion Size and the Obesity Epidemic," *Nutrition Today* 38.2 (2000), 42–53.

Rolls, B. J., and E. L. Morris, "Portion Size Affects Food Energy Intake in Normal Weight and Overweight Men and Women," *American Journal of Clinical Nutrition* 76 (2002), 1207–1213.

Ryan, Alan, "Mill in a Liberal Landscape," in *The Cambridge Companion to Mill*, ed. John Skorupski (Cambridge University Press, 1998), pp. 497–540.

Sartorius, Rolf, *Individual Conduct and Social Norms* (Belmont, Calif.: Dickenson Publishing, 1975).

Schapiro, Tamar, "What is a Child?," *Ethics* 109.4 (1999), 715–738.

Schauer, Frederick, *Profiles, Probabilities, and Stereotypes* (Cambridge, Mass.: Belknap–Harvard University Press, 2003).

Schwartz, Paul M., "Property, Privacy, and Personal Data," *Harvard Law Review* 17.7 (May 2004), 2056–2128.

Scoccia, Danny, "In Defense of Hard Paternalism," *Law and Philosophy* 27 (2008), 351–381.

  "Paternalism and Respect for Autonomy," *Ethics* 100.2 (January 1990), 318–334.

Sherif, Muzafer, *The Psychology of Social Norms* (New York: Harper, 1936).

Shiffrin, Seana, "Paternalism, Unconscionability Doctrine, and Accommodation," *Philosophy and Public Affairs* 29 (2000), 205–250.

Slovic, Paul, "The Construction of Preference," *American Psychologist* 50.5 (May 1995), 364–371.

Smith, Travis A., Bing-Hwan Lin, and Yong-Ying Lee, "Taxing Caloric Sweetened Beverages: Potential Effects on Beverage, Consumption, Calorie Intake, and Obesity," *Economic Research Report* 100 (July 2010).

Solove, Daniel H., "Conceptualizing Privacy," *California Law Review* 90.4 (2002), 1087–1155.

"Privacy and Power: Computer Databases and Metaphors for Information Privacy," *Stanford Law Review* 53.6 (2001), 1393–1462.

Understanding Privacy (Cambridge, Mass.: Harvard University Press, 2008).

Spiegel, Jerry M., and Annalee Yassi, "Lessons from the Margins of Globalization: Appreciating the Cuban Health Paradox," *Journal of Public Health Policy* 25.1 (2004), 85–110.

Sroufe, L. Alan, "Attachment and the Roots of Competence," *Human Nature* 31 (1978), 50–59.

Stender, Steen, and Jorn Dyerberg, "Influence of Trans-Fatty Acids on Health," *Annals of Nutrition and Metabolism* 48.2 (2004), 61–66.

Stender, Steen, Jorn Dyerberg, and Arne Arstrup, "Consumer Protection through Legislative Ban on Industrially Produced Trans-Fatty Acids in Foods in Denmark," *Scandinavian Journal of Food and Nutrition* 50.4 (2006), 155–160.

Stender, Steen, Jorn Dyerberg, Ahette Bysted, Torben Leth, and Arne Astrup, "A Trans World Journey," *Atherosclerosis Supplements* 7.2 (2006), 47–52.

Sugden, Paul, "Why Incoherent Preferences do not Justify Paternalism," *Constitutional Political Economy* 19 (2008), 226–248.

Sumner, L. W., "The Subjectivity of Welfare," *Ethics* 105.4 (1995), 764–790.

Sunstein, Cass R., and Richard H. Thaler, "Libertarian Paternalism is not an Oxymoron," *University of Chicago Law Review* 70 (2003), 1159–1202.

Swithers, Susan, and Terry L. Davidson, "A Role for Sweet Taste: Caloric Predictive Relations in Energy Regulation by Rats," *Behavioral Neuroscience* 122.1 (February 2008), 161–173.

Tan, Andy S. L., "A Case Study of the New York City Trans-Fat Story for International Application," *Journal of Public Health Policy* 30.1 (2009), 3–16.

Tapper, K., E. M. Pothos, and A. D. Lawrence, "Feast your Eyes: Hunger and Trait Reward Drive Predict Attentional Bias for Food Cues," *Emotion* 10 (2010), 949–954.

Ten, C. L., *Mill On Liberty* (Oxford: Clarendon Press, 1980).

ed., *Mill's On Liberty: A Critical Guide* (Cambridge University Press, 2008).

Thaler, Richard H., and Shlomo Benartzi, "Save More Tomorrow: Using Behavioral Economics to Increase Employee Savings," *Journal of Political Economy* 112 (February 2004), S124–S187.

Thaler, Richard H., and Cass R. Sunstein, *Nudge: Improving Decisions About Health, Wealth, and Happiness* (New Haven, Conn.: Yale University Press, 2008).

Thomas, Matthew, and Luke Buckmaster, "Paternalism in Social Policy – When is it Justifiable?," *Parliamentary Library* (Australia), Research Paper 8 (15 December 2010).

Thomson, Judith, *The Realm of Rights* (Cambridge, Mass.: Harvard University Press, 1990).

Trout, J. D., "Paternalism and Cognitive Biases," *Law and Philosophy* 24 (2005), 393–434.

Why Empathy Matters (Harmondsworth: Penguin, 2010).

Ubel, Peter, *Free Market Madness: Why Human Nature is at Odds with Economics: And Why it Matters* (Cambridge, Mass.: Harvard Business Press, 2009).

Van Hecke, Madeline L., *Blind Spots. Why People do Dumb Things* (New York: Prometheus Books, 2007).

Van Rooij Martin, and Federica Teppa, "Choice or No Choice: What Explains the Attractiveness of Default Options," *DNB Working Paper* 165 (De Nederlandsche Bank; January 2008).

Van de Veer Donald, *Paternalistic Intervention: The Moral Bounds of Benevolence* (Princeton University Press, 1986).

Wansink, Brian, and Pierre Chandon, "Meal Size, not Body Size, Explains Errors in Estimating the Calorie Content of Meals," *Annals of Internal Medicine* (September 2006), 326–333.

Wansink, Brian, Collin R. Payne, and Pierre Chandon, "Internal and External Cues of Meal Cessation," *Obesity* 15.12 (2007), 2920–2924.

Mindless Eating: Why We Eat More Than We Think (New York: Bantam Books/Random House, 2010).

Warren, Samuel, and Louis Brandeis, "The Right to Privacy," *Harvard Law Review* 4.5 (1890), 193–220.

Watson, David, and Lee A. Clark, "Negative Affectivity: The Disposition to Experience Aversive Emotional States," *Psychological Bulletin* 96.3 (1984), 465–490.

Weinstein, Neil D., "Optimistic Biases About Personal Risks," *Science* 246.4935 (December 8, 1989), 1232–1233.

Weiss, Rachel I., and Jason A. Smith, "Legislative Approaches to the Obesity Epidemic," *Journal of Public Health Policy* 25.3–4 (2004), 379–390.

Wertheimer, Alan, *Coercion* (Princeton University Press, 1987).

Whiten, Andrew, "Conformity to Cultural Norms of Tool Use in Chimpanzees," *Nature* 437 (September 29, 2005), 737–740.

Whitman, Douglas Glen, and Mario J. Rizzo, "Paternalist Slopes," *New York University Journal of Law and Liberty* 2.3 (2007), 411–443.

Wikler, Dan, "Coercive Measures in Health Promotion: Can They be Justified?," *Health Education Monographs* 6 (July 1978), 223–241.

"Paternalism and the Mildly Retarded," in *Paternalism*, ed. Rolf Sartorius (Minneapolis: University of Minnesota Press, 1983), pp. 83–94.

"Persuasion and Coercion in Health: Ethical Issues in Government Efforts to Change Life Styles," in *Paternalism*, ed. Rolf Sartorius (Minneapolis: University of Minnesota Press, 1983), pp. 35–59; previously published in *Millbank Memorial Fund Quarterly/Health and Society* 56.3 (1978), 303–338.

"Who Should be Blamed for Being Sick," *Health Education Quarterly* 14.1 (spring 1987), 11–25.

Wilson, Fred, "Mill on Psychology and the Moral Sciences," in *The Cambridge Companion to Mill*, ed. John Skorupski (Cambridge University Press, 1998), pp, 35–59.

Young, L. R., and M. Nestle, "The Contribution of Expanding Portion Sizes to the U.S. Obesity Epidemic," *American Journal of Public Health* 92.2 (2002), 246–249.

Young, Robert, "The Value of Autonomy," *Philosophical Quarterly* 32.126 (1982), 35–44.

Zeelenberg, M., K. Van den Bos, E. Van Dijk, and R. Pieters, "The Inaction Effect in the Psychology of Regret," *Journal of Personality and Social Psychology* 82 (2002), 314–327.

Index

Printed in Great Britain
by Amazon